ENERGY POLICIES, POLITICS AND PRICES

ENERGY POLICIES AND ISSUES

ENERGY POLICIES, POLITICS AND PRICES

Additional books in this series can be found on Nova's website
under the Series tab.

Additional E-books in this series can be found on Nova's website
under the E-books tab.

ENERGY POLICIES, POLITICS AND PRICES

ENERGY POLICIES AND ISSUES

EDGAR R. THOMPSON
EDITOR

Nova Science Publishers, Inc.
New York

Copyright © 2011 by Nova Science Publishers, Inc.

All rights reserved. No part of this book may be reproduced, stored in a retrieval system or transmitted in any form or by any means: electronic, electrostatic, magnetic, tape, mechanical photocopying, recording or otherwise without the written permission of the Publisher.

For permission to use material from this book please contact us:
Telephone 631-231-7269; Fax 631-231-8175
Web Site: http://www.novapublishers.com

NOTICE TO THE READER

The Publisher has taken reasonable care in the preparation of this book, but makes no expressed or implied warranty of any kind and assumes no responsibility for any errors or omissions. No liability is assumed for incidental or consequential damages in connection with or arising out of information contained in this book. The Publisher shall not be liable for any special, consequential, or exemplary damages resulting, in whole or in part, from the readers' use of, or reliance upon, this material. Any parts of this book based on government reports are so indicated and copyright is claimed for those parts to the extent applicable to compilations of such works.

Independent verification should be sought for any data, advice or recommendations contained in this book. In addition, no responsibility is assumed by the publisher for any injury and/or damage to persons or property arising from any methods, products, instructions, ideas or otherwise contained in this publication.

This publication is designed to provide accurate and authoritative information with regard to the subject matter covered herein. It is sold with the clear understanding that the Publisher is not engaged in rendering legal or any other professional services. If legal or any other expert assistance is required, the services of a competent person should be sought. FROM A DECLARATION OF PARTICIPANTS JOINTLY ADOPTED BY A COMMITTEE OF THE AMERICAN BAR ASSOCIATION AND A COMMITTEE OF PUBLISHERS.

Additional color graphics may be available in the e-book version of this book.

LIBRARY OF CONGRESS CATALOGING-IN-PUBLICATION DATA
Energy policies and issues / editor, Edgar R. Thompson.
p. cm.
Includes index.
ISBN 978-1-61122-685-0 (hardcover)
1. Energy policy--United States. 2. Renewable energy sources--United States. I. Thompson, Edgar R.
HD9502.U52E51735 2010
333.790973--dc22
2010041359

Published by Nova Science Publishers, Inc. † New York

CONTENTS

Preface		**vii**
Chapter 1	Renewable Energy Programs in the 2008 Farm Bill *Megan Stubbs*	**1**
Chapter 2	Estimating Offset Supply in a Cap-and-Trade Program *Jonathan L. Ramseur*	**25**
Chapter 3	Biochar: Examination of an Emerging Concept to Mitigate Climate Change *Kelsi S. Bracmort*	**41**
Chapter 4	Forest Carbon Markets: Potential and Drawbacks *Ross Gorte and Jonathan L. Ramseur*	**53**
Chapter 5	Anaerobic Digestion: Greenhouse Gas Emission Reduction and Energy Generation *Kelsi S. Bracmort*	**79**
Chapter 6	Gas Hydrates: Resource and Hazard *Peter Folger*	**97**
Chapter 7	Offshore Oil and Gas Development: Legal Framework *Adam Vann*	**107**
Chapter 8	Outer Continental Shelf Moratoria on Oil and Gas Development *Curry L. Haggerty*	**135**

Chapter 9	Accelerated Vehicle Retirement for Fuel Economy: "Cash for Clunkers" *Brent D. Yacobucci and Bill Canis*	**161**
Chapter 10	CRS Issue Statement on Agriculture-Based Biofuels *Randy Schnepf*	**181**

Chapter Sources   **187**

Index   **189**

PREFACE

Energy policy is the manner in which a given entity has decided to address issues of energy development including energy production, distribution and consumption. This book examines a number of energy policies put in place by the government, as well as the issues which continue to offset substantial improvements. Topics discussed herein include anaerobic digestion; forest carbon markets; gas hydrates; concepts designed to mitigate climate change; and offshore oil and gas development.

Chapter 1- The Food, Conservation, and Energy Act of 2008 (P.L. 110-246, the 2008 farm bill) extends and expands many of the renewable energy programs originally authorized in the Farm Security and Rural Investment Act of 2002 (P.L. 107-171, 2002 farm bill). The bill also continues the emphasis on the research and development of advanced and cellulosic bioenergy authorized in the 2007 Energy Independence and Security Act (P.L. 110-140).

Chapter 2- If allowed as a compliance option in a greenhouse gas (GHG) emission reduction program (e.g., a cap-and-trade system), offsets have the potential to provide considerable cost savings and other benefits. However, offsets have generated considerable controversy, primarily over the concern that illegitimate offsets could undermine the ultimate objective of a cap-and-trade program: emission reduction.

Chapter 3- Biochar is a charcoal produced under high temperatures using crop residues, animal manure, or any type of organic waste material. Depending on the feedstock, biochar may look similar to potting soil or to a charred substance. The combined production and use of biochar is considered a carbon-negative process, meaning that it removes carbon from the atmosphere.

Biochar has multiple potential environmental benefits, foremost the potential to sequester carbon in the soil for hundreds to thousands of years at an estimate. Studies suggest that crop yields can increase as a result of applying biochar as a soil amendment. Some contend that biochar has value as an immediate climate change mitigation strategy. Scientific experiments suggest that greenhouse gas emissions are reduced significantly with biochar application to crop fields.

Chapter 4- Forests are major carbon sinks (storehouses), and activities that alter forests can release or sequester carbon dioxide (CO_2), the most common greenhouse gas (GHG). Some carbon markets have been formed under mandatory GHG reduction regimes, such as the Kyoto Protocol and various regional and state initiatives in the United States. Other markets have formed for voluntary efforts to reduce GHG emissions. Offsets, or credits for sequestering carbon or reducing emissions in unregulated sectors, are typically allowed in both mandatory and voluntary markets. Forestry activities are among the largest-volume and lowest-cost opportunities for generating offsets

Chapter 5- Anaerobic digestion technology may help to address two congressional concerns that have some measure of interdependence: development of clean energy sources and reduction of greenhouse gas emissions. Anaerobic digestion technology breaks down a feedstock—usually manure from livestock operations—to produce a variety of outputs including methane. An anaerobic digestion system may reduce greenhouse gas emissions because it captures the methane from manure that might otherwise be released into the atmosphere as a potent greenhouse gas. The technology may contribute to the development of clean energy because the captured methane can be used as an energy source to produce heat or generate electricity.

Chapter 6- Solid gas hydrates are a potentially huge resource of natural gas for the United States. The U.S. Geological Survey estimated that there are about 85 trillion cubic feet (TCF) of technically recoverable gas hydrates in northern Alaska. The Minerals Management Service estimated a mean value of 21,000 TCF of in-place gas hydrates in the Gulf of Mexico. By comparison, total U.S. natural gas consumption is about 23 TCF annually. The in-place estimate disregards technical or economical recoverability, and likely overestimates the amount of commercially viable gas hydrates. Even if a fraction of the U.S. gas hydrates can be economically produced, however, it could add substantially to the 1,300 TCF of technically recoverable U.S. conventional natural gas reserves. To date, however, gas hydrates have no confirmed commercial production.

Chapter 7- The development of offshore oil, gas, and other mineral resources in the United States is impacted by a number of interrelated legal regimes, including international, federal, and state laws. International law provides a framework for establishing national ownership or control of offshore areas, and domestic federal law mirrors and supplements these standards.

Chapter 8- Moratoria provisions for the outer continental shelf (OCS), enacted as part of the Department of the Interior appropriations over 26 years, prohibited federal spending on oil and gas development in certain locations and for certain activities. These annual congressional moratoria expired on September 30, 2008. While the expiration of the restrictions does not make leasing and drilling permissible in all offshore areas, it is a significant development in conjunction with other changes in offshore leasing activity. The ending of the moratoria signals a shift in policy that may affect other OCS policies as well.

Chapter 9- In an attempt to boost sagging U.S. auto sales and to promote higher vehicle fuel economy, the President signed legislation on June 24, 2009, P.L. 111-32, establishing a program to provide rebates to prospective purchasers toward the purchase of new, fuel-efficient vehicles, provided the trade-in vehicles are scrapped. The program was known as Consumer Assistance to Recycle and Save (CARS), or, informally, as "cash for clunkers." It provided rebates of $3,500 or $4,500, depending on fuel economy and vehicle type of both the new vehicle and the vehicle to be disposed of. Congress appropriated $3 billion for the program in two separate installments. CARS ran for a month, from July 24, 2009, until August 25, 2009.

Chapter 10- Since the 1970s, federal incentives have played a major role in encouraging agriculture-based renewable energy production. Policy goals include the stimulation of alternative uses of domestic grain and oilseeds, the promotion of national security through greater energy independence, and the encouragement of rural economic development. Federal incentives, notably tax credits, a minimum renewable fuel use requirement, and research and development funding, have helped biofuels output (ethanol and biodiesel) to surge in recent years, growing from 1.4 billion gallons in 1998 to over 11 billion in 2009. Nearly all of the growth has been in corn-starch ethanol.

In: Energy Policies and Issues
Editors: Edgar R. Thompson

ISBN: 978-1-61122-685-0
© 2011 Nova Science Publishers, Inc.

Chapter 1

RENEWABLE ENERGY PROGRAMS IN THE 2008 FARM BILL

Megan Stubbs

SUMMARY

The Food, Conservation, and Energy Act of 2008 (P.L. 110-246, the 2008 farm bill) extends and expands many of the renewable energy programs originally authorized in the Farm Security and Rural Investment Act of 2002 (P.L. 107-171, 2002 farm bill). The bill also continues the emphasis on the research and development of advanced and cellulosic bioenergy authorized in the 2007 Energy Independence and Security Act (P.L. 110-140).

Farm bill debate over U.S. biomass-based renewable energy production policy focused mainly on the continuation of subsidies for ethanol blenders, continuation of the import tariff for ethanol, and the impact of corn-based ethanol on agriculture. The enacted bill requires reports on the economic impacts of ethanol production, reflecting concerns that the increasing share of corn production being used for ethanol had contributed to high commodity prices and food price inflation.

Title VII, the research title of the 2008 farm bill, contains numerous renewable energy related provisions that promote research, development, and demonstration of biomass-based renewable energy and biofuels. The Sun Grant Initiative coordinates and funds research at land grant institutions on biobased energy technologies. The Agricultural Bioenergy Feedstock and Energy Efficiency Research and Extension Initiative provides support for on-farm biomass energy crop production research and demonstration.

Title IX, the energy title of the farm bill, authorizes mandatory funds (not subject to appropriations) of $1.1 billion, and discretionary funds (subject to appropriations) totaling $1.0 billion, for the FY2008-FY2012 period. Energy grants and loans provided through initiatives such as the Bioenergy Program for Advanced Biofuels promote the development of cellulosic biorefinery capacity. The Repowering Assistance Program supports increasing efficiencies in existing refineries. Programs such as the Rural Energy for America Program (REAP) assist rural communities and businesses in becoming more energy-efficient and self-sufficient, with an emphasis on small operations. The Biomass Crop Assistance Program, the Biorefinery Assistance Program, and the Forest Biomass for Energy Program provide support to develop alternative feedstock resources and the infrastructure to support the production, harvest, storage, and processing of cellulosic biomass feedstocks. Cellulosic feedstocks—for example, switchgrass and woody biomass—are given high priority both in research and funding.

Title XV of the 2008 farm bill contains tax and trade provisions. It continues current biofuels tax incentives, reducing those for corn-based ethanol but expanding tax credits for cellulosic ethanol. The tariff on ethanol imports is extended.

Implementation of the farm bill's energy provisions is underway. President Obama, in May 2009, directed the U.S. Department of Agriculture (USDA) and the Department of Energy (DOE) to accelerate implementation of renewable energy programs. Notices and proposed rules have appeared in the *Federal Register* soliciting applications for the Biorefinery Program, the Rural Energy for America Program, and the Biomass Crop Assistance Program.

BACKGROUND

Renewable energy policy in the Food, Conservation, and Energy Act of 2008 (P.L. 110-246, 2008 farm bill) builds on earlier programs, many of which were established in the Farm Security and Rural Investment Act of 2002 (P.L. 107-171, 2002 farm bill). The 2002 farm bill was the first omnibus farm bill to explicitly include an energy title (Title IX). The energy title authorized grants, loans, and loan guarantees to foster research on agriculture-based renewable energy, to share development risk, and to promote the adoption of renewable energy systems. Since enactment of the 2002 farm bill, interest in renewable energy has grown rapidly, due in large part to a strong rise in domestic and international petroleum prices and a dramatic acceleration in domestic biofuels production (primarily corn-based ethanol).[1] Many policymakers view agriculture-based biofuels as both a catalyst for rural economic development and a response to growing energy import dependence. Ethanol and biodiesel, the two most widely used biofuels, receive significant federal support in the form of tax incentives, loans and grants, and regulatory programs.[2]

The 2008 farm bill became law six months after the enactment of the Energy Independence and Security Act of 2007 (EISA, P.L. 110-140), and many of its provisions also build on the goals of EISA.[3] The emphasis on facilitating production of biofuels derived from cellulosic feedstocks reflects the goals of the renewable fuels standard (RFS) in EISA. EISA includes a significant expansion of the RFS to 36 billion gallons by 2022, with carve-outs for biodiesel (1 billion gallons by 2012) and cellulosic ethanol (16 billion gallons by 2022) and an implicit cap on corn starch ethanol (15 billion gallons by 2015). Provisions in the 2008 farm bill reflect the increased role for biofuels mandated by the expansion of the RFS and its likely impact on the U.S. agriculture sector.[4]

The emphasis on cellulosic ethanol also reflects increasing concerns about the economic and environmental issues associated with corn starch-based ethanol.[5] Record high commodity prices in 2007 and mid-2008, combined with high energy costs, resulted in sharp increases in livestock feed costs, export prices, and domestic food price inflation. For the first time, an agricultural commodity is directly competing with petroleum in the marketplace. Ethanol production, the profitability of which depends directly on both petroleum and corn prices, accounts for about a third of U.S. corn production. The increase in corn used for U.S. ethanol production exceeds the increase in corn produced during the three years. When petroleum prices rise, so does demand for ethanol as a substitute, which in turn increases both the demand for and price of corn. The "food versus fuel" debate intensified during the 2008 farm bill debate as food price inflation accelerated both in the U.S. and globally—highlighting some of the potential problems associated with replacing even a small share of the nation's gasoline consumption with corn-based ethanol.

Competition for limited corn supplies between livestock producers, ethanol refiners, exporters, and other domestic users resulted in calls for at least a partial waiver of the RFS in 2009.[6]

Several of the federal programs that currently support renewable energy production in general, and agriculture-based energy production in particular, are outside the purview of the U.S. Department of Agriculture (USDA) and have legislative origins outside of the farm bill. For example, the RFS mandates the inclusion of an increasing volume of biofuels in the national fuel supply. This originated with the Energy Policy Act of 2005 (P.L. 109-58) and was more recently expanded in EISA. Similarly, the federal tax credits available to biofuel blenders were initially contained in the American Jobs Creation Act of 2004 (P.L. 108-357), although they have been incorporated in the farm bill.

MAJOR ENERGY PROVISIONS IN THE 2008 FARM BILL

The 2008 farm bill (P.L. 110-246) significantly expands existing programs to promote biofuels. Like the 2002 farm bill (P.L. 107-171), it contains a distinct energy title (Title IX) that covers a wide range of energy and agricultural topics with extensive attention to biofuels, including corn starch-based ethanol, cellulosic ethanol, and biodiesel. Research provisions relating to renewable energy are found in Title VII and tax and trade provisions are found in Title XV.

The enacted 2008 farm bill keeps the structure of Title IX as it was in the Senate-passed version of the farm bill. Title IX serves as a substitute amendment to the 2002 farm bill Title IX and consists of 3 sections. The first section, 9001, contains 13 new provisions which effectively replace the provisions of the 2002 bill. Sections 9002 and 9003 direct studies and reports on biofuels infrastructure and renewable fertilizer, respectively. See **Appendix A** for a side-by-side comparison of previous law with the energy provisions of the 2008 farm bill.

Key biofuels-related provisions in the enacted 2008 farm bill include:

- emphasis on cellulosic ethanol production through new blender tax credits, promotion of cellulosic feedstocks production, feedstocks infrastructure and refinery development;
- grants and loan guarantees for biofuels (especially cellulosic) research, development, deployment, and production;
- studies of the market and environmental impacts of increased biofuel use;

- expansion of biofuel feedstock availability;
- expansion of the existing biobased marketing program to encourage federal procurement of biobased products;
- support for rural energy efficiency and self-sufficiency;
- reauthorization of biofuels research programs within the USDA and Environmental Protection Agency (EPA);
- an education program to promote the use and understanding of biodiesel;
- reduction of the blender tax credit for corn-based ethanol;
- continuation and expansion of the federal bio-products certification program;
- environmental safeguards through greenhouse gas emission requirements on new biofuel production; and
- continuation of the import duty on ethanol.

ENERGY POLICY ISSUES IN THE 2008 FARM BILL

Cellulosic Biofuels

The 2008 farm bill energy title provides $1 billion in financial incentives and support to encourage the production of advanced (mainly cellulosic) biofuels.[7] Grants and loan guarantees leverage industry investments in new technologies and the production of cellulosic feedstocks. For instance, the Biomass Crop Assistance Program (BCAP, Section 9001) supports the production of dedicated crop and forest cellulosic feedstocks and provides incentives for harvest and post-production storage and transport. Advanced biofuels refinery capacity construction is assisted under the Biorefinery Assistance program (Section 9001) through grants and loans for the development, construction, and retrofitting of commercial-scale refineries to produce advanced biofuels. These programs are supported by increased funding for advanced biofuels research under the Agricultural Bioenergy Feedstock and Energy Efficiency Research and Extension Initiative (Section 7207), and the Sun Grant Program (Section 7526) which support and coordinate advanced biofuels research, extension, and development between government agencies, universities, and research institutions.

Cellulosic ethanol is produced from cellulose, hemicellulose, or lignin derived from the structural material that provides much of the mass of plants.

Besides corn, several other agricultural products are viable feedstock and appear to offer attractive long-term supply potential—particularly cellulose-based feedstock such as prairie grasses and fast-growing woody crops such as hybrid poplar and willow trees, as well as waste biomass materials (logging residues, wood processing mill residues, urban wood wastes, and selected agricultural residues such as sugar cane bagasse and rice straw). Some cellulosic feedstock, such as native prairie grasses (e.g., switchgrass), appear to offer environmental benefits over corn-based ethanol because they thrive on marginal lands (as well as on prime cropland) and need little water and no fertilizer.

Currently, cellulosic ethanol is not produced on a commercial scale. Only a few small refineries are scheduled to begin production in 2010, with an additional nine expected to commence production by 2013 for a total output of 389 million gallons per year (mgpy). In January 2009, USDA announced funding for a cellulosic biofuels plant under the Biorefinery Assistance program (Section 9001) with projected output of 20 mgpy, beginning in 2010. The RFS mandates cellulosic ethanol production of 100 mgpy in 2010, and 500 mgpy in 2012 (a year earlier than the projected output of 389 mgpy). For more information on cellulosic ethanol, see CRS Report RL34738, *Cellulosic Biofuels: Analysis of Policy Issues for Congress*.

Tax Credits and Tariffs

Title XV of the 2008 farm bill contains provisions which extend and modify tax credits and tariffs on ethanol. In keeping with the promotion of cellulosic ethanol, a blender credit of $1.01 per gallon applies to ethanol produced from qualifying cellulosic feedstocks. This tax credit is intended to spur investment in cellulosic ethanol production. The ethanol blender tax credit of $0.51 per gallon (which applies to all ethanol blended, including imports) was reduced to $0.45 per gallon in January 2009. Section 15331 of the farm bill requires the reduction starting the first year following that year in which U.S. ethanol production and imports exceed 7.5 billion gallons. Production and imports in 2008 were estimated to have exceeded 9 billion gallons.

Table 1. 2008 Farm Bill Energy Funding by Provision, FY2009 to FY2011 ($ in Millions)

Section[a]	Program	Funding Type	FY2009			FY2010			FY2011		
			Pres Req[b]	FB Auth[c]	Budget Auth	Pres Req[b]	FB Auth[c]	Budget Auth	Pres Req[b]	FB Auth[c]	Budget Auth
Sec. 7205	Nutrient Management Research and Extension Initiative	Discretionary	0	SSAN	0	0	SSAN	0	0	SSAN	NA
Sec. 7207	Bioenergy Feedstock and Energy Efficiency Research and Extension Initiative	Discretionary	0	50	0	0	50	0	0	50	NA
Sec. 7526	Sun Grant Program	Discretionary	0	75	0	0	75	0	0	75	NA
Sec. 9002	Federal Biobased Markets Program	Mandatory	—	2	2	—	2	2	—	2	NA
Sec. 9002	Federal Biobased Markets Program	Discretionary	0	2	0	0	2	0	0	2	NA
Sec. 9003	Biorefinery Assistance	Mandatory	—	75 TRAUE	75 TRAUE	—	245 TRAUE	245 TRAUE	—	TRAUE	NA

Table 1. (Continued)

Section[a]	Program	Funding Type	FY2009			FY2010			FY2011		
			Pres Req[b]	FB Auth[c]	Budget Auth	Pres Req[b]	FB Auth[c]	Budget Auth	Pres Req[b]	FB Auth[c]	Budget Auth
Sec. 9003	Biorefinery Assistance	Discretionary	0	150	0	17	150	0	17	150	NA
Sec. 9004	Repowering Assistance	Mandatory	—	35 TRAUE	35 TRAUE	—	TRAUE	TRAUE	—	TRAUE	NA
Sec. 9004	Repowering Assistance	Discretionary	0	15	0	0	15	15	0	15	NA
Sec. 9005	Bioenergy Program for Advanced Biofuels	Mandatory	—	55 TRAUE	55 TRAUE	—	55 TRAUE	55 TRAUE	—	85 TRAUE	NA
Sec. 9005	Bioenergy Program for Advanced Biofuels	Discretionary	0	25	0	0	25	0	0	25	NA
Sec. 9006	Biodiesel Education Program	Mandatory	—	1	1	—	1	1	—	1	NA
Sec. 9007	Rural Energy for America Program (REAP)	Mandatory	—	55 TRAUE	55 TRAUE	—	60 TRAUE	60 TRAUE	—	70 TRAUE	NA
Sec. 9007	Rural Energy for America Program (REAP)	Discretionary	0	25	5	68	25	40	40	25	NA

Table 1. (Continued)

Section[a]	Program	Funding Type	FY2009			FY2010			FY2011		
			Pres Req[b]	FB Auth[c]	Budget Auth	Pres Req[b]	FB Auth[c]	Budget Auth	Pres Req[b]	FB Auth[c]	Budget Auth
Sec. 9008	Biomass Research and Development	Mandatory	0	20 TRAUE	20 TRAUE	—	28 TRAUE	28 TRAUE	—	30 TRAUE	NA
Sec. 9008	Biomass Research and Development	Discretionary	0	35	0	0	35	0	0	35	NA
Sec. 9009	Rural Energy Self-Sufficiency Initiative	Discretionary	0	5	0	0	5	0	0	50	NA
Sec. 9010	Feedstock Flexibility Program for Bioenergy Producers	Mandatory	—	SSAN	0[d]	—	SSAN	0[d]	—	SSAN	NA
Sec. 9011	Biomass Crop Assistance Program (BCAP)	Mandatory	—	SSAN	SSAN	—	SSAN	SSAN	—	SSAN	NA
Sec. 9012	Forest Biomass for Energy	Discretionary	0	15	0	0	15	0	15	15[e]	NA

Table 1. (Continued)

Section[a]	Program	Funding Type	FY2009			FY2010			FY2011		
			Pres Req[b]	FB Auth[c]	Budget Auth	Pres Req[b]	FB Auth[c]	Budget Auth	Pres Req[b]	FB Auth[c]	Budget Auth
Sec. 9013	Community Wood Energy Program	Discretionary	0	5	0	0	5	0	5	5[e]	NA

Source: Compiled by CRS using the Food, Conservation, and Energy Act of 2008 (P.L. 110-246) and annual appropriation acts.

Notes: "Pres. Req." = Presidential budget request; "FB Auth." = 2008 farm bill authorized level; Budget Auth = Budget authority; "SSAN" = Such sums as necessary; "TRAUE" = to remain available until expended; and "NA" = not available.

a. Section 9001 of the 2008 farm bill (P.L. 110-246) amends title IX of the 2002 farm bill (P.L. 107-171). Sections 9001 through 9013 of the table are the amended section numbers.

b. The President's budget request typically does not include mandatory programs unless a reduction is requested. A "—" indicates that neither a reduction or increase was requested by the Administration for the mandatory program.

c. Many Title IX programs include funding that is authorized "to remain available until expended" (TRAUE), therefore carryover could exist from previous years if funds are unobligated.

d. This program is "triggered" when a sugar surplus exists. According to USDA, the Commodity Credit Corporation (CCC) does not have a surplus inventory of sugar, therefore this program has not been implemented.

e. The President's budget proposes to fund both the Forest Biomass for Energy Program (section 9012) and the Community Wood Energy Program (section 9013) using funds from the Hazardous Fuels program within the Forest Service.

The $0.54 per gallon import tariff for ethanol benefits the U.S. ethanol industry by protecting U.S. ethanol from lower-cost imports and also keeps imported ethanol from benefitting from the blender tax credit when it is blended into gasoline in the United States. The tariff was set to expire at the end of 2008 but has been extended to the end of 2010 by the farm bill (P.L. 110-246, Section 15333). With the decrease in the blender tax credit to $0.45, the tariff now exceeds the blender tax credit by nine cents, and so more than offsets the benefit of the blender tax credit.

Economic Impacts of Ethanol Production

The impact of increased ethanol production on agricultural and rural economies was a subject of debate during the farm bill process. As a result, the farm bill includes provisions requiring a series of reports assessing how ethanol production may be impacting the farm economy, the environment, and consumer food prices. Among these are the Comprehensive Study of Biofuels (to be conducted by the USDA, the EPA, the Department of Energy (DOE), and the National Academy of Sciences) and the Biofuels Infrastructure Study by USDA, DOE, EPA, and the Department of Transportation (DOT). The Biomass Crop Assistance Program (BCAP, Section 9001) requires an assessment of the economic impacts of expanded cellulosic biomass production on local economies and infrastructures. Likewise, the Biomass Research and Development Program (Section 9001) requires a report on the economic impacts of rural economies of biorefinery expansion and conversion by USDA.

FUNDING FOR ENERGY PROGRAMS

Appendix B illustrates mandatory and discretionary spending levels for renewable energy programs authorized in the 2008 farm bill. Mandatory funding is through USDA's Commodity Credit Corporation (CCC).[8] Programs identified as receiving mandatory funds are funded at these levels unless Congress limits funding to a lower amount through the appropriations or legislative process. Discretionary programs are funded each year through the annual appropriations process.

Title IX authorizes $1.1 billion in mandatory funding for FY2008 through FY2012, compared with $800 million in the 2002 farm bill (FY2002-FY2007). Mandatory authorization in the 2008 farm bill includes $320 million to the Biorefinery Assistance Program, $300 million to the Bioenergy Program for Advanced Biofuels, and $255 million to the Rural Energy for America Program (REAP). Authorizations for appropriations in the 2008 farm bill total $1 billion, four times the $245 million in the 2002 farm bill. Most of the increase is for the Biorefinery Assistance Program, which has an authorization $600 million higher than in the 2002 farm bill. **Table 1** provides a list of provisions in the 2008 farm bill's energy title, and selected energy programs in the research title, for FY2009 through FY2011, along with their funding levels (as requested by the President, authorized levels in the 2008 farm bill, and budget authority provided by Congress) where available.

APPENDIX A. COMPARISON OF THE ENACTED 2008 FARM BILL (P.L. 110-246) WITH PREVIOUS LAW

2002 Farm Bill (FSRIA, P.L. 107-171) or Other Law (as indicated)	Enacted Farm Bill (P.L. 110-246)
Title VII: Agriculture Research and Extension	
Nutrient Management Research and Extension Initiative	
Section 1673(h) of the Food, Agriculture, Conservation, and Trade Act of 1990 (P.L. 101-624) authorizes matching grants under the farm bill nutrient management research and extension initiative for finding innovative methods and technologies for economic use or disposal of animal waste. Extendes through 2007 in section 7120 of the 2002 farm bill. Such sums as necessary are appropriated annually for FY1999-FY2007. [7 U.S.C. 5925a]	Extends the nutrient Management research and extension initiative through FY2012 and adds dairy cattle waste as a type of waste to be studied. Also adds an amend-ment to include the production of renewable energy from animal waste as an eligible activity to receive grants under this section. Authorizes such sums as necess-ary annually for FY2007-FY2012. [Sec. 7205]
Agricultural Bioenergy Feedstock and Energy Efficiency Research and Extension Initiative	
No provision.	Establishes the Agricultural Bioenergy Feedstock and Energy Efficiency Research and Extension Initiative, a program to award competitive

Renewable Energy Programs in the 2008 Farm Bill

Table. (Continued)

2002 Farm Bill (FSRIA, P.L. 107-171) or Other Law (as indicated)	Enacted Farm Bill (P.L. 110-246)
	matching (up to 50%) grants for projects with a focus on supporting on-farm biomass crop research and the dissemination of results to enhance the production of biomass energy crops and the integration of such production with the production of bioenergy. Discretionary appropriations of $50 million annually are author-ized for FY2008-FY2012. [Sec. 7207]
Sun Grant Program	
Section 9011. This provision was added subsequent to the 2002 farm bill under the Sun Grant Research Initiative Act of 2003. Establishes 5 national Sun Grant research centers based at land-grant universities, each covering a different national region, to enhance coordination and collaboration between USDA, DOE, and land-grant univer-sities in the development, distribution, and implementation of biobased energy technologies. Competitive grants are available to land-grant schools within each region. Authorized appropriations of $25 million in FY2005, $50 million in FY2006, and $75 million for each of FY2007 through FY2010 for total discretionary funding of $375 million during FY2005-FY2010. [7 U.S.C. 8109]	Reauthorizes the Sun Grant Program through FY2012 and establishes a 6th regional center—Western Insular Pacific Sub-Center—at the University of Hawaii. Authorizes discretionary funding of $75 million annually for FY2008-FY2012. [Sec. 7526]
Title IX: Energy	
Definitions	
Sec. 9001. Defines Administrator, Biomass, Biobased Product, Procuring Agency, Renewable Energy, Rural Small Business, and Secretary. [7 U.S.C. 8101]	New section 9001 of FSRIA. Adds several definitions including "Advanced Biofuels," which excludes any fuel derived from corn starch, but includes ethanol derived from other plant starches (e.g., sorghum), sugar, as well as cellulosic biomass or organic waste; it also includes organically-

Table. (Continued)

2002 Farm Bill (FSRIA, P.L. 107-171) or Other Law (as indicated)	Enacted Farm Bill (P.L. 110-246)
	derived biogas, butanol or other alcohols; and, notably, biodiesel. Other definitions are biobased product; biomass conversion facility; biorefinery; intermediate ingredient or feedstock; renewable biomass; and renewable energy. Adopts the Senate definitions with amendments. Advanced biofuels include aviation, jet, and heating fuels made from cellulosic biomass. [Sec. 9001]
Biobased Markets Program	
Sec. 9002. Requires federal agencies to purchase biobased products under certain conditions and authorize a voluntary biobased labeling program. USDA regulations define biobased products, identify biobased product categories, and specify the criteria for qualifying those products for preferred procurement. Mandatory Commodity Credit Corporation (CCC) funding of $1 million is authorized for each of FY2002 through FY2007 for testing biobased products. [7 U.S.C. 8101]	New section 9002 of FSRIA. Renames program as the Biobased Markets Program. Requires procuring agencies to establish a program and specifications for procuring biobased products (excluding motor vehicle fuels, heating oil, or electricity). Establishes the volun-tary labeling program: "USDA Certified Biobased Product." Requires USDA to establish a national registry of biobased testing centers and a report on implementation. Mandatory CCC funding of $1 million in 2008, and $2 million annually for FY2009-FY2012. Discretionary funding of $2 million annually is authorized for FY2009-FY2012. [Sec. 9001]
Biorefinery Assistance	
No provision.	New section 9003 of FSRIA. Biore-finery Assistance Program. Assists in the development of new and emerging technologies for the development of advanced biofuels. Provides compete-tive grants and loan guarantees for construction and retrofitting of biore-fineries for the production of advanced biofuels. Biorefinery grants provided for up to 30% of total cost. Each loan guarantee is limited to $250 million or 80% of project cost. Mandatory funding

Renewable Energy Programs in the 2008 Farm Bill 15

Table. (Continued)

2002 Farm Bill (FSRIA, P.L. 107-171) or Other Law (as indicated)	Enacted Farm Bill (P.L. 110-246)
	of $75 million in FY2009 and $245 million in FY2010, available until expended for loan guarantees. Discretionary funding of $150 million annually is authorized for FY2009-FY2012. [Sec. 9001]
Repowering Assistance	
Section 9003. Establishes a grant program to help finance the cost of developing and constructing biorefineries and biofuel production plants to carry out projects to demonstrate the commercial viability of converting biomass to fuels or chemicals. Mandatory funding is not authorized and discretionary funding has not been appropriated for the program. Therefore, no implementation regulations have been developed. [7 U.S.C. 8103]	New section 9004 of FSRIA. Pro-vides payments to encourage biorefineries in existence on the date of enactment to convert from fossil fuel to renewable energy power sources. Encourages new production of energy for refineries from renewable biomass. Mandatory funding of $35 million for FY2009, to remain available until expended. Discretionary funding of $15 million annually for FY2009-FY2012 is authorized. [Sec. 9001]
Energy Program for Advanced Biofuels	
Section 9010. Originally created by a 1999 Executive Order during the Clinton Administration, the bioenergy program provides mandatory CCC incentive payments to biofuels producers based on year-to-year increases in the quantity of biofuel produced. Mandatory CCC funding of $150 million is available for each of FY2002 through FY2006. No funding is authorized for FY2007. [7 U.S.C. 8108]	New section 9005 of FSRIA. Establishes the Bioenergy Program for Advanced Biofuels to encourage production of advanced biofuels. Not more than 5% of the funds can go to facilities with total refining capacity exceeding 150 million gallons per year. Producers of advanced biofuels contracts with USDA to receive payments based on the quantity and duration of production of advanced biofuels, the net renewable energy content of the biofuel, and other factors. Payments limited to ensure equitable distribution. Mandatory funding of $55 million for 2009, $55 million for FY2010, $85 million for FY2011, and $105 million for FY2012. Discretionary funding of $25 million annually is authorized for FY2009-FY2012. [Sec. 9001]

Table. (Continued)

2002 Farm Bill (FSRIA, P.L. 107-171) or Other Law (as indicated)	Enacted Farm Bill (P.L. 110-246)
Biodiesel Fuel Education Program	
Section 9004. Administered by USDA's Cooperative State Research, Education, and Extension Service, the program awards competitive grants to nonprofit organizations that educate governmental and private entities operating vehicle fleets, and educates the public about the benefits of biodiesel fuel use. Mandatory CCC funding of $1 million is authorized for each of FY2003 through FY2007. [7 U.S.C. 8104]	New section 9006 of FSRIA. Extends the Biodiesel Fuel Education Program through 2012. Mandatory CCC funds of $1 million are provided annually for FY2008-FY2012. [Sec. 9001]
Energy Audit and Renewable Energy Development Program	
Section 9005. A competitive grant program for eligible entities to provide energy audits and technical assistance to agricultural producers and rural small businesses to assist them in becoming more energy efficient and in using renewable energy technology and resources. Authorized appropriations of such sums as are necessary to carry out the program for each of FY2002 through FY2007. [7 U.S.C. 8105]	See new section 9007 of FSRIA below.
Rural Energy for America Program	
The Renewable Energy Systems and Energy Efficiency Program (Section 9006), administered by USDA's Rural Development Agency, authorizes direct loans, loan guarantees, and grants to farmers, ranchers, and rural small businesses to purchase and install renewable energy systems and to make energy efficiency improvements. Grant funds may be used to pay up to 25% of project costs; combined grants and loans or loan guarantees may fund up to 50% of project cost. Eligible projects include those that derive energy from wind, solar, biomass, or geothermal sources. Projects using energy from	New section 9007 of FSRIA. Ren-amed as the Rural Energy for America Program. Provides grants and loan guarantees to state governments, tribal, or local governments, land-grant insti-tutions, rural electric cooperatives or utilities to provide energy audits and renewable energy assistance, and finan-cial assistance for energy efficiency improvements and renewable energy systems. Grants up to 25% of cost are provided. Loan guarantees up to $25 million. Combined amount of grant and guaranteed loans limited to 75% of cost. 20% of funds made available in this section to be reserved for grants of

Renewable Energy Programs in the 2008 Farm Bill

Table. (Continued)

2002 Farm Bill (FSRIA, P.L. 107-171) or Other Law (as indicated)	Enacted Farm Bill (P.L. 110-246)
those sources to produce hydrogen from biomass or water are also eligible. Mandatory CCC funding of $23 million is available for each of FY2003 through FY2007. Unspent money lapses at the end of each year. [7 U.S.C. 8106]	$20,000 or less until the end of the fiscal year. Mandatory CCC funds of $55 million in FY2009, $60 million in FY2010, $70 million in FY2011, and $70 million in FY2012. Discretionary funding of $25 million annually is authorized to be appropriated for FY2009-FY2012. [Sec. 9001]
Biomass Research and Development Program	
This program—created originally under the Biomass Research and Development Act of 2000 (BRDA, P.L. 106-224)—provides competitive funding for research, development, and demonstration projects on biofuels and bio-based chemicals and products, under the Biomass Research and Development Initiative, administered jointly by USDA and DOE. Creates Biomass research and Development Board to coordinate government activities in biomass research, and the Biomass Research and Development Technical Advisory Committee to advise on proposal direction and evaluation. Authorizes mandatory CCC funding of $5 million in FY2002 and $14 million for each of FY2003 through FY2007 (available until expended). Additional appropriation authority of $200 million for each of FY2006 through FY2015. [7 U.S.C. 8101]	New section 9008 of FSRIA. Moves the Biomass Research and Development Act of 2000 in statute to Title IX of FSRIA of 2002. Defines biobased product. Expands advisory committee. New technical areas for grants include feedstock development, biofuels and biobased products development, and biofuels development analysis with a minimum of 15% of funding going to each area. Minimum cost-share requirement for demonstration projects increased to 50% and research projects to 20%. Provides for coordination of biomass research and development, including life cycle analysis of biofuels, between USDA and DOE. Authorizes mandatory funding of $20 million for FY2009, $28 million for FY2010, $30 million for FY2011, and $40 million for FY2012. Discretionary funding of $35 million is authorized to be appropriated annually for FY2009-FY2012. [Sec. 9001]
Rural Energy Self-Sufficiency Initiative	
No provision.	New section 9009 of FSRIA. Establishes the Rural Energy Self-Sufficiency Initiative to assist rural communities with community-wide energy systems that reduce conventional energy use and increase the use of energy from renewable sources. Grants are made available to assess energy use in a rural

Table. (Continued)

2002 Farm Bill (FSRIA, P.L. 107-171) or Other Law (as indicated)	Enacted Farm Bill (P.L. 110-246)
	community, evaluate ideas for reducing energy use, and develop and install integrated renewable energy systems. Grants are not to exceed 50% of the total cost of the activity. Appropriations of $5 million annually are authorized for FY2009-FY2012. [Sec. 9001]
Feedstock Flexibility Program	
No provision.	New section 9010 of FSRIA. Requires that USDA establish (in FY2008) and administer a sugar-for-ethanol program using sugar intended for food use but deemed to be in surplus. USDA would implement the program only in those years where purchases are determined to be necessary to ensure that the sugar program operates at no cost. The use of such sums as necessary is authorized to carry out the program. [Sec. 9001]
Biomass Crop Assistance Program	
No provision.	New section 9011 of FSRIA. Establishes the Biomass Crop Assistance Program (BCAP) to provide producers committing to biomass production or a biomass conversion facility with contracts, which will enable producers in a BCAP project area to receive financial assistance for crop establish-ment costs and annual payments for biomass production. Producers must be within an economically practical distance from a biomass facility and adhere to resource conservation requirements. Cost-share payments cover costs of establishing crops and for collection, harvest, storage, and transportation to a biomass conversion facility. Annual payments authorized to producers to support biomass produc-tion. A report is required no later than 4 years after enactment. Mandatory CCC funds of such sums as necessary are made available for each

Renewable Energy Programs in the 2008 Farm Bill

Table. (Continued)

2002 Farm Bill (FSRIA, P.L. 107-171) or Other Law (as indicated)	Enacted Farm Bill (P.L. 110-246)
	of FY2008-F2012. [Sec. 9001]
Forest Biomass for Energy Program	
No provision.	New section 9012 of FSRIA. Forest Service competitive research and development program to encourage use of forest biomass for energy. Priority is given to projects that use low-value forest byproduct biomass for the production of energy; develop processes to integrate bioenergy from forest biomass into existing manufacturing streams; and develop new transportation fuels and improve the production of trees for renewable energy. Authorized appropriations of $15 annually for FY2009-FY2012. [Sec. 9001]
Community Wood Energy Program	
No provision.	New section 9013 of FSRIA. Establishes Community Wood Energy Program to provide matching grants to state and local governments to acquire community wood energy systems for public buildings. Participants must also implement a community wood energy plan to meet energy needs with reduced carbon intensity through conservation, reduced costs, utilizing low-value wood sources, and increased awareness of energy consumption. Authorizes discretionary funding of $5 million annually for FY2009-2012. [Sec. 9001]
Biofuels Infrastructure Study	
No provision.	Requests USDA, DOE, EPA, and DOT to jointly report on the infrastructure needs, requirements, and development approaches for expanding the domestic production, transport, and distribution of biofuels. Mandatory funding of $1 million for FY2008, and $2 million annually for each of FY2009-FY2012. Discretionary appropriations of $2

Table. (Continued)

2002 Farm Bill (FSRIA, P.L. 107-171) or Other Law (as indicated)	Enacted Farm Bill (P.L. 110-246)
	million annually are authorized for FY2009-FY2012. [Sec. 9002]
Renewable Fertilizer Study	
No provision.	Requires a report within 1 year of appropriations on the production of fertilizer from renewable energy sources in rural areas. Report must identify challenges to commercializetion of rural fertilizer production, processes and techno-logies and the potential impacts of renewable fertilizer on fossil fuel use and the environment. Appropriation of $1 million is authorized for FY2009. [Sec. 9003]
Title XI: Livestock	
Study on Bioenergy Operations	
No provision.	Requires a USDA study on the use of animal manure as a fertilizer; the impact of limitations placed on the use of animal manure on consumers and agricultural operations; and the effects of increased competition for manure due to biofuel uses. [Sec. 11014]
Title XV: Trade and Tax Provisions; Subtitle C Part II—Energy Provisions	
Credit for Production of Cellulosic Biofuel	
Under the American Jobs Creation Act (AJCA) of 2004, (P.L. 108-357), cellulosic ethanol, once developed, would receive the current tax credit of $0.51 per gallon available to any ethanol blended into gasoline as provided through Dec. 31, 2010. [26 U.S.C. 40]	Provides a fourth tax credit under 26 U.S.C. 40, the Cellulosic Biofuel Producer Credit. The credit is $1.01 per gallon less the amount of small-producer ethanol credit claimed and the alcohol mixture credit claimed for ethanol. [Sec. 15321]
Comprehensive Study of Biofuels	
No provision.	The Secretary of Treasury, with USDA, DOE, and EPA shall commission the National Academy of Sciences to produce a report on biofuels, including current and projected production, economic and environmental impacts, government program impacts, and the relative impacts of different types of biofuels. [Sec. 15322]

Table. (Continued)

2002 Farm Bill (FSRIA, P.L. 107-171) or Other Law (as indicated)	Enacted Farm Bill (P.L. 110-246)
Alcohol Fuel: Modification of Alcohol Credit	
Any ethanol blended into gasoline is eligible for a tax credit of $0.51 per gallon as provided under current law (AJCA of 2004, P.L. 108-357) through Dec. 31, 2010. [26 U.S.C. 40]	Reduces the ethanol tax credit of $0.51 per gallon to $0.45 per gallon beginning in the first calendar year after the year in which 7.5 billion gallons of ethanol is produced. [Sec 15331]
Alcohol Fuel: Calculation of Volume of Alcohol for Fuel Credits	
Under current law (AJCA of 2004, P.L. 108-357) the volume of bio-alcohol counted as fuel eligible for the tax credit may include up to 5% of the volume as denaturant. [26 U.S.C. 40]	Reduces the permissible volume of denaturant to 2% for purposes of calculating the volume of alcohol eligible for the tax credit. [Sec. 15332]
Alcohol Fuel: Ethanol Tariff Extension	
Under current law (Heading 9901.00.50 of the Harmonized Tariff Schedule (HTS)), imports of ethyl alcohol are subject to a duty of 14.27¢ per liter ($0.54 per gallon) and a duty of 5.99¢ per liter (Heading 9901.00.52; HTS) on imports of ethyl tertiary-butyl ether through Dec. 31, 2008. [19 U.S.C. Chapter 18]	Extends the tariff of $0.54 per gallon for imported ethanol or mixtures of ethanol (headings 9901.00.50 and 9901.00.52 of the HTS) through Dec. 31, 2010. [Sec 15333]
Alcohol Fuel: Limitations on, and Reductions of, Duty Drawback on Certain Imported Ethanol	
Section 1313 of the Tariff Act of 1930, as amended, permits the refund of duty if the duty-paid good is re-exported or used to make a good that is exported. A person who manufactures gasoline with ethanol subject to the duty imposed under HTS 9901.00.50 (see previous description), can export jet fuel (does not contain ethanol) and still obtain a refund of the duty paid. [19 U.S.C. Chapter 18]	Eliminates the ability to obtain a refund of duty imposed under HTS 9901.00.50, when imported ethanol is re-exported by substituting either ethanol not subject to the duty, or another petroleum product (e.g., jet fuel) that is exported to obtain the refund. [Sec. 15334]

APPENDIX B. AUTHORIZED FUNDING FOR ENERGY PROVISIONS

Table B-1. 2008 Farm Bill (P.L. 110-246): Authorized Funding for Energy Provisions, FY2008-FY2012 ($ Millions)

2008 Farm Bill Section	Provision Name	Funding Type	FY2008	FY2009	FY2010	FY2011	FY2012	Total: FY2008-FY2012
Title VII Research								
Sec. 7205	Nutrient Management Research and Extension Initiative	Discretionary	SSAN	SSAN	SSAN	SSAN	SSAN	SSAN
Sec. 7207	Bioenergy Feedstock and Energy Efficiency Research and Extension Initiative	Discretionary	50	50	50	50	50	250
Sec. 7526	Sun Grant Program	Discretionary	75	75	75	75	75	375
Title IX Energy								
Sec. 9002[a]	Biobased Markets Program	Mandatory	1	2	2	2	2	9
		Discretionary	0	2	2	2	2	8
Sec. 9003[a]	Biorefinery Assistance	Mandatory	0	75	245	0	0	320
		Discretionary	0	150	150	150	150	600
Sec. 9004[a]	Repowering Assistance	Mandatory	0	35	0	0	0	35
		Discretionary	0	15	15	15	15	60
Sec. 9005[a]	Bioenergy Program for Advanced Biofuels	Mandatory	0	55	55	85	105	300
		Discretionary	0	25	25	25	25	100

Table B-1. (Continued)

2008 Farm Bill Section	Provision Name	Funding Type	FY2008	FY2009	FY2010	FY2011	FY2012	Total: FY2008-FY2012
Sec. 9006[a]	Biodiesel Fuel Education Program	Mandatory	1	1	1	1	1	5
Sec. 9007[a]	Rural Energy for America Program	Mandatory	0	55	60	70	70	255
		Discretionary	0	25	25	25	25	100
Sec. 9008[a]	Biomass Research and Development Act	Mandatory	0	20	28	30	40	118
		Discretionary	0	35	35	35	35	140
Sec. 9009[a]	Rural Energy Self-Sufficiency Initiative	Discretionary	0	5	5	5	5	20
Sec. 9010[a]	Feedstock Flexibility Program for Bioenergy Producers	Mandatory	SSAN	SSAN	SSAN	SSAN	SSAN	SSAN
Sec. 9011[a]	Biomass Crop Assistance Program	Mandatory	SSAN	SSAN	SSAN	SSAN	SSAN	SSAN
Sec. 9012[a]	Forest Biomass for Energy	Discretionary	0	15	15	15	15	60
Sec. 9013[a]	Community Wood Energy Program	Discretionary	0	5	5	5	5	20
Sec. 9003	Renewable Fertilizer Study	Discretionary	0	1	0	0	0	1
	Total Discretionary Funding	**Discretionary**	**$125**	**$403**	**$402**	**$402**	**$402**	**$1,734**
	Total Mandatory Funding	**Mandatory**	**$2**	**$243**	**$391**	**$188**	**$218**	**$1,042**

Source: P.L. 110-246 (Food, Conservation, and Energy Act of 2008).

Notes: "SSAN" = Such sums as necessary.

a. Section 9001 of the 2008 farm bill (P.L. 110-246) amends title IX of the 2002 farm bill (P.L. 107-171). Sections 9001 through 9013 of the table are the amended section numbers.

End Notes

[1] For more information, see CRS Report R40488, *Ethanol: Economic and Policy Issues*.

[2] For a listing of federal incentives in support of biofuels production, see CRS Report R40110, *Biofuels Incentives: A Summary of Federal Programs*.

[3] For more information, see CRS Report RL34239, *Biofuels Provisions in the 2007 Energy Bill and the 2008 Farm Bill: A Side-by-Side Comparison*.

[4] For more information, see CRS Report R40155, *Selected Issues Related to an Expansion of the Renewable Fuel Standard (RFS)* and CRS Report R41106, *Meeting the Renewable Fuel Standard (RFS) Mandate for Cellulosic Biofuels: Questions and Answers*.

[5] For more information, see CRS Report RL34738, *Cellulosic Biofuels: Analysis of Policy Issues for Congress*.

[6] In April 2008, Texas Gov. Rick Perry wrote the Environmental Protection Agency seeking a waiver from the federal ethanol mandate, noting its contribution to higher food prices and dire impact on the cattle industry. The waiver request was denied. Also, see CRS Report RS22870, *Waiver Authority Under the Renewable Fuel Standard (RFS)*.

[7] Advanced biofuels include biofuels derived from cellulosic feedstocks; sugar and starch other than corn kernel-starch; waste material including crop residue, animal, plant, or food waste; diesel fuel produced from renewable biomass including vegetable oil and animal fat; butanol or other alcohols produced through the conversion of organic matter; and other fuels derived from cellulosic biomass. For more information, see CRS Report RL34738, *Cellulosic Biofuels: Analysis of Policy Issues for Congress*.

[8] The CCC is the funding mechanism for the mandatory payments that are administered by various agencies of USDA, including all of the farm commodity price and income support programs and selected conservation programs.

In: Energy Policies and Issues
Editors: Edgar R. Thompson

ISBN: 978-1-61122-685-0
© 2011 Nova Science Publishers, Inc.

Chapter 2

ESTIMATING OFFSET SUPPLY IN A CAP-AND-TRADE PROGRAM

Jonathan L. Ramseur

SUMMARY

If allowed as a compliance option in a greenhouse gas (GHG) emission reduction program (e.g., a cap-and-trade system), offsets have the potential to provide considerable cost savings and other benefits. However, offsets have generated considerable controversy, primarily over the concern that illegitimate offsets could undermine the ultimate objective of a cap-and-trade program: emission reduction.

An offset is a measurable reduction, avoidance, or sequestration of GHG emissions from a source *not covered* by an emission reduction program. An estimate of the quantity and type of offset projects that might be available as a compliance option would provide for a more informed debate over the design elements of a cap-and-trade program. It is difficult to estimate the supply of offsets that might be available in a cap-and-trade system, because the supply is determined by many variables, including:

Mitigation potential. Mitigation potential estimates are the raw data that feed into models estimating offset use in a cap-and-trade program. Recent estimates contain considerable uncertainty.

Policy choices. The design of the cap-and-trade system would be critical to offset supply. Particularly relevant design choices include which sources are covered; which types of offset projects are allowed; whether or not offset use is limited; and the degree to which set-aside allowances are allotted to activities that may otherwise qualify as offsets. Policymakers' treatment of international offsets would play a major role.

Economic factors. The development and market penetration of low- and/or zero-carbon technologies would likely have substantial effects. These technologies could lower the costs of the cap-and-trade program, making fewer offset projects cost effective.

Emission allowance price. The allowance price would determine the supply and type of offsets that would be economically competitive in a cap-and-trade system. As the price increases, more (and different types of) projects would become cost effective. Allowance price estimates are difficult to predict, as they are dependent on numerous variables, including offset treatment.

Other factors. Non-market factors, such as social acceptance, may influence offset use. In addition, information dissemination would likely be an issue, because some of the offset opportunities exist at smaller operations, such as family farms.

Although economic models have generated estimates of offsets that would be developed and used in a cap-and-trade system, the estimates are rife with uncertainty. This chapter examines the multiple variables that would help shape offset supply.

INTRODUCTION

An estimate of the quantity and type of offset projects that might be available in a cap-and-trade system would provide for a more informed debate over the design elements of a cap-and-trade system. (See text box below, "What is a Cap-and-Trade System?") An offset is a measurable reduction, avoidance, or sequestration of GHG emissions from a source *not covered* by an emission reduction program. From a climate change perspective, the location of the reduction, avoidance, or sequestration does not matter: a ton of

CO_2 (or its equivalent in another GHG) reduced in the United States and a ton sequestered in another nation would have the same result on the atmospheric concentration of GHGs. If a cap-and-trade program includes offsets, covered sources would have to submit offsets (in lieu of emission allowances) to meet compliance obligations.[1]

Offset projects vary by the quantity of emission credits they could generate and the implementation complexity they present. In general, agriculture and forestry activities offer the most potential, but these projects often pose multiple implementation challenges. These contrasting attributes may create a tension for policymakers, who might want to include the offset projects that provide the most emission reduction opportunities, while minimizing the use of offset projects that pose more implementation complications, or have the potential to be invalid.

If Congress enacts a greenhouse gas (GHG) emission reduction program, such as a cap-and-trade system, the treatment of offsets would be a critical design element. Economic models of cap-and-trade legislation have generally demonstrated that different offset scenarios—for example, unlimited offsets versus no offsets allowed—lead to significant variances in program costs.[2] However, offsets have fueled considerable debate, primarily for the concern that illegitimate offsets could undermine the ultimate objective of a cap-and-trade program: emission reduction.[3]

How many offsets would be available as a compliance option if Congress enacted a cap-and-trade program? Although economic models have generated estimates of offsets developed and used in a cap-and-trade system, the estimates are rife with uncertainty. This chapter examines the multiple variables that help shape offset supply.

WHAT IS A CAP-AND-TRADE SYSTEM?

A cap-and-trade system would create an overall limit (i.e., a cap) on GHG emissions from the emission sources covered by the program. Cap-and-trade programs can vary by the sources covered. The covered sources, also referred to as covered entities, are likely to include major emitting sectors (e.g., power plants and carbon-intensive industries), fuel producers/processors (e.g., coal mines or petroleum refineries), or some combination of both.

The emissions cap is partitioned into emission allowances. Typically, one emission allowance represents the authority to emit one (metric) ton of carbon dioxide-equivalent (tCO2-e). This term of measure is used because

GHGs vary by global warming potential (GWP). GWP is an index of how much a GHG may contribute to global warming over a period of time, typically 100 years. GWPs are used to compare gases to carbon dioxide, which has a GWP of 1. For example, methane's GWP is 25, and thus a ton of methane is 25 times more potent a GHG than a ton of carbon dioxide.

In general, policymakers may decide to distribute the emission allowances to covered entities at no cost (based on, for example, previous years' emissions), sell the allowances through an auction, or use some combination of these strategies. These decisions are typically a source of intense debate.

Covered entities that face relatively low emission-reduction costs would have an incentive to make reductions beyond what is required, because these further reductions could be sold (i.e., traded) as emission credits to entities that face higher emission-reduction costs. Likewise, entities who face higher reduction costs could purchase allowances on the market. At the end of each established compliance period (e.g., a calendar year), covered sources would be required to surrender emission allowances to cover the number of tons emitted. If a source did not have enough allowances to cover its emissions, the source would be subject to penalties.

Mechanisms, such as banking or offsets, may be included to increase the flexibility of the program.

For more information, see U.S. Environmental Protection Agency (EPA), Office of Air and Radiation, *Tools of the Trade: A Guide To Designing and Operating a Cap and Trade Program For Pollution Control* (2003); CRS Report RL33799, *Climate Change: Design Approaches for a Greenhouse Gas Reduction Program*, by Larry Parker; and CRS Report RL34502, *Emission Allowance Allocation in a Cap-and-Trade Program: Options and Considerations*, by Jonathan L. Ramseur.

FACTORS AFFECTING OFFSET SUPPLY

It is difficult to estimate the supply of offsets that might be available in a cap-and-trade system, because the supply is determined by many variables, including policy choices. **Figure 1** illustrates the various inputs and variables that would affect the potential supply of offsets in a cap-and-trade program. These factors—mitigation potential, policy choices, economic factors, emission allowance price, and other factors—are each discussed below. As

Figure 1 indicates, the factors do not act in isolation, but interact in a complex manner.

Mitigation Potential

Mitigation potential is not synonymous with offset supply potential (**Figure 1**). Some of the activities included in mitigation potential estimates would likely not qualify as offsets in a cap-and-trade system. A striking example is biofuel production, which has been projected by some studies to play a substantial role in GHG mitigation in later years. By placing a price on carbon, a cap-and-trade program is expected to increase biofuel and biomass production. If a power plant substitutes a carbon-intensive fuel (e.g., coal) with a less carbon-intensive fuel (e.g., biomass, such as switchgrass), the plant's GHG emissions would decrease. These emission reductions would be counted directly by the power plant. The increased biofuel use would mitigate GHG emissions, but would not count as an offset in a cap-and-trade program, because the reductions (from the fuel substitution) would be made directly by covered sources.

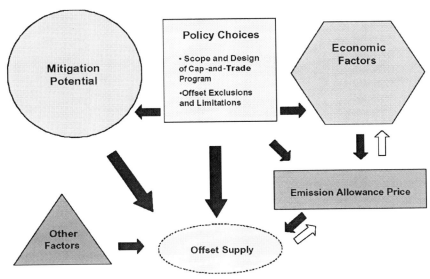

Source: Prepared by CRS.

Figure 1. Illustration of Inputs and Variables That Affect Potential Offset Supply

Mitigation potential estimates are often used as inputs for economic models of cap-and-trade legislation. For example, EPA's 2009 mitigation potential estimates were used in the EPA and Energy Information Administration's (EIA) analyses of H.R. 2454.[4] Both of these analyses generated estimates of the number and type of offsets that would be used by covered sources for compliance purposes. However, these offset supply estimates are imperfect, because the underlying data—mitigation potential estimates—contain considerable uncertainty.

Elements of Uncertainty

Modelers derive estimates of mitigation potential by assigning a price for GHG emissions and sequestration. Under the widely used Forest and Agriculture Sector Optimization Model (FASOM), for example, "landowners would receive annual payments for increasing sequestration and reducing emissions relative to their base case (additionality), but face the cost of having to make payments for increasing emissions or reducing sequestration."[5] As with all models, the mitigation potential simulations include numerous assumptions, including behavioral responses to economic incentives and disincentives. For example, actors (e.g., farmers) are assumed to have "perfect foresight." Perfect foresight assumes that "agents, when making decisions that allocate resources over time (e.g., investments), know with certainty the consequences of those actions in present and future time periods."[6] EPA recognizes that this assumption, which the agency states is used by most of the climate economic modeling community, does not reflect reality. The use of this assumption likely yields an overestimation of mitigation potential: in reality, market participants make imperfect judgments and leave some financial opportunities on the table.

Mitigation potential models must necessarily include certain technical assumptions, such as sequestration rates of various activities. Different models often use different underlying assumptions to generate results. Indeed, there is often disagreement within the modeling community, particularly for forestry sequestration simulations, over the use of various modeling inputs.[7]

In addition to the above limitations—which are generally inherent to some degree with all economic modeling—a critical factor for agriculture and forestry mitigation opportunities is land availability. More projects would become economically competitive as the emission allowance price rises. At certain price levels, one mitigation activity may replace another. For example, agricultural soil sequestration projects (e.g., conservation tillage practices) are expected to present cost-effective opportunities at relatively low prices. As the allowance price rises, afforestation projects are expected to become (1) cost effective in more places and (2) more cost effective than ongoing soil sequestration activities.[8] Thus, lands that once generated soil sequestration, while growing traditional commodities, may be replaced with afforestation projects (tree farms).

Other activities—preservation, recreation, fuel production—may compete for limited land resources. Some activities may preclude options for resource use, such as traditional crop production or afforestation. In other cases, more than one practice that reduces or sequesters CO_2 may be possible. For example, conservation tillage may be conducted in concert with biofuel production.

It is very difficult for most modeling tools to keep track of these competing or compatible activities, although some models may have the capability to account for some of these interactions. Thus, different analyses will produce varying results.

MITIGATION POTENTIAL ESTIMATES IN CONTEXT

It may be instructive to compare the mitigation potential estimates with current sequestration levels, emissions caps, and offset quantity limits from recent legislative proposals.

—The agriculture and forestry sectors sequestered (net of emissions) approximately 940 mtCO2-e in 2008 (EPA, *Draft Inventory of U.S. Greenhouse Gas Emissions and Sinks: 1990-2008* (March 2010)).

—In 2016, the emissions cap in H.R. 2454 would be 5,482 million emission allowances: each allowance equals 1 $mtCO_2$-e.

Recent cap-and-trade proposals would limit the use of domestic offsets in some fashion. For example, H.R. 2454 would allow covered entities, in aggregate, to annually submit 1 billion metric tons of *domestic* offset credits in lieu of emission allowances. However, each covered entity's compliance obligation would be limited: in 2016, 13.5% of the compliance obligation could be satisfied with domestic offsets; 18% in 2030; 33% in 2050. Based on EPA estimates of covered entity emissions under H.R. 2454, these percentages would allow (if used to the fullest extent) for approximately 615 $mtCO_2$-e of domestic offsets in 2016, 850 $mtCO_2$-e in 2030, and 1,275 $mtCO_2$-e in 2050.

Estimates from Agriculture and Forestry Activities

Over the past decade, several studies, including reports from EPA (2005 and 2009) and USDA (2004),[9] have produced estimates of *mitigation potential* from agriculture and forestry activities. The estimates from these studies vary, in some cases considerably. For example, **Table 1** lists the different results between EPA's 2005 and 2009 models. As the table indicates, the estimates of mitigation potential from the agriculture and forestry sectors decreased substantially in the 2009 model. In particular, estimates of agricultural soil sequestration activities decreased by 100% (or almost 100%) at several price scenarios. The explanation for these varied estimates is complex and beyond the scope of this chapter: for a comprehensive discussion of these estimates, see CRS Report R40236, *Estimates of Carbon Mitigation Potential from Agricultural and Forestry Activities*, by Renée Johnson, Jonathan L. Ramseur, and Ross W. Gorte. In short, the different estimates reflect different modeling assumptions, such as emission/sequestration baselines (or business-as-usual scenarios).

The dramatic differences between the 2005 and 2009 estimates (**Table 1**) highlight the uncertainty that pervades mitigation estimates. Regardless, both models demonstrate the influence of price. And both models indicate *relative* differences between the project types, with forestry projects providing much of the potential, particularly at higher price scenarios.

Estimates from Other Activities

Other potential mitigation activities—for example, methane abatement from landfills or the natural gas sector—are generally considered less complicated in terms of measurement than agriculture and forestry projects. In addition, these types of mitigation projects are typically not subject to competition for land resources. However, these estimates are only mitigation potential, not potential offset supply. Other factors, identified in **Figure 1** and discussed below, would likely constrain or exclude their development as offsets. For instance, some of the activities identified below would be covered under the cap of some legislative proposals.

Several of the mitigation activities in **Table 2** are projected to occur at $0/mtCO_2$-e. EPA states that these figures "represent mitigation options that are already cost-effective given the costs and benefits considered (and are sometimes referred to as "no-regret" options) yet have not been implemented because of the existence of nonmonetary barriers."[10] These are discussed below in "Other Factors."

Estimating Offset Supply in a Cap-and-Trade Program

The fact that parties are not acting in the most economically efficient manner at $0/mtCO_2$-e, calls into question the estimates for higher prices and further demonstrates the uncertainty contained in mitigation potential estimates.

Table 1. Mitigation Estimates from EPA's 2005 and 2009 Models Constant Price Scenarios (2025 Timeframe)

Mitigation Activity	Prices ($/mtCO_2$-e)					
	$5		$15		$30	
	EPA-2005	EPA-2009	EPA-2005	EPA-2009	EPA-2005	EPA-2009
Afforestation	12	21	228	81	806	221
Forest management	89	114	156	243	250	313
Agriculture soil sequestration	149	17	204	2	187	0
Agriculture CH_4 and N_2O mitigation	17	4	36	12	76	27
Total	267	156	624	338	1,319	561

Source: Prepared by CRS; EPA 2005 data from EPA, *Greenhouse Gas Mitigation Potential in U.S. Forestry and Agriculture* (2005), Table 4-10; EPA 2009 data from EPA, Updated Forestry and Agriculture Marginal Abatement Cost Curves, March 2009, available with data annex to EPA's analysis of H.R. 2454.

Notes: The prices in the table are in constant dollars, adjusted for inflation (per EPA (2005), p. 4-2). The 2005 figures represent estimates for the year 2025; the 2009 figures represent the net annual average mitigation for the decade 2020-2029. For further discussion of these estimates, see CRS Report R40236, *Estimates of Carbon Mitigation Potential from Agricultural and Forestry Activities*, by Renée Johnson, Jonathan L. Ramseur, and Ross W. Gorte.

Table 2. EPA Estimates of Mitigation Potential from Other Select Activities Constant Price Scenarios in 2020

Mitigation Activity	Prices ($/mtCO_2$-e) in $2007		
	$4	$17	$32
CH_4 from Landfills	54	73	91
CH_4 from Natural Gas Sector	16	16	31
CH_4 from Coal Mines	40	40	40
N_2O from Adipic Acid Production	9	9	9
N_2O from Nitric Acid Production	16	16	16
Total	$139.00	$171.00	$219.00

Source: EPA, *EPA Analysis of the American Clean Energy and Security Act of 2009 H.R. 2454 in the 111th Congress*, Data Annex, at *http://epa.gov/climatechange/economics/economicanalyses.html#hr2452*.

Note: The price scenarios in this table differ from the previous table, because the underlying data come from a different source.

Policy Choices

Policy decisions from Congress, U.S. states, and foreign governments would directly and indirectly affect the supply of offsets in a cap-and-trade program. The primary factor would be the design of the cap-and-trade system. Other policies would also help shape the pool of offsets that could be used for compliance purposes. These policy choices are discussed below.

Design of the Cap-and-Trade Program

Programmatic design elements could affect offset supply in several ways, from the overall structure of the cap (e.g., which sources are covered) to specific logistical details (e.g., monitoring and measuring protocols), including which agency or agencies would be responsible for developing the logistical details. Another critical element would be the program's use of set-aside allowances.

Scope of the Cap

The wider the scope of the cap, the smaller the offset universe. In other words, as more source categories are subject to the cap, the fewer the number of uncapped sources, thus the number of eligible offset project types decreases. Similarly, H.R. 2454 would set emission performance standards for CH_4 emissions from landfills and coal mines, reducing the opportunities for offsets from these categories.[11]

Eligible Offset Types

Policymakers may choose to restrict the types and locations (domestic versus international) of offsets eligible for use by a regulated entity. Biological sequestration generally offers the most potential, but these projects present substantial challenges. In some legislative proposals, the project types allowed are not specified in the text, but would be subsequently determined by an implementing agency.[12] In addition, the degree to which international offsets are allowed would have considerable impact on domestic offsets.

Offset Protocols

The protocol established for measuring and verifying offsets would affect supply. A more stringent protocol would likely reduce supply. Offsets that are questionable—for instance, in terms of their additionality—would likely be excluded or discounted (also reducing supply). Additionality determinations

Estimating Offset Supply in a Cap-and-Trade Program 35

(i.e., would the project have happened anyway) typically require some subjectivity in the decision process. A protocol with more constraints could remove some of the subjectivity, which, if left in place, could lead to an influx of questionable offsets.

Some protocols may include more conservative parameters for measuring tons of CO_2 sequestered for a particular project type. For example, one protocol may stipulate that carbon saturation for a given plant or tree species occurs in a shorter time frame, thus fewer offsets would be produced through the project.

Moreover, the stringency of the protocols would likely affect the costs of developing, implementing, and verifying an offset project. These costs might be described as transaction costs. For example, a protocol that required independent, third-party verification would entail higher costs for offset projects. If transaction costs increase, the number of cost-effective offset projects would decrease.

The proposed (and enacted) systems of measurement and verification vary. In many cases, legislative proposals direct various agencies to develop the protocols. In these cases, the level of protocol stringency would be uncertain at the bill's passage.

Set-Asides

If a cap-and-trade program provides set-aside allowances for specific activities,[13] these activities would impact the potential supply of offsets. Recent cap-and-trade proposals would give emission allowances (set-asides) to non-covered entities to promote various objectives, including biological sequestration. Set-aside allowances are taken from within the cap, so if the set-aside allowances do not lead to further emission reductions, abatement, or sequestration, the cap remains intact. Indeed, one strategy for policymakers is to allot set-asides for activities whose emission reductions, abatement, or sequestration may carry more uncertainty than other potential offset activities. However, a project that receives a set-aside cannot also qualify as an offset. Thus, set-aside allowances would reduce the pool of offsets available for compliance with the cap.

Actions in Other Nations or U.S. States

As other nations or U.S. states establish emission controls or climate-related policies, the pool of offsets would shrink. International offsets, particularly in the developing nations, are projected in models to provide numerous opportunities for compliance. However, these projections assume that these nations are decades away from requiring GHG emission reductions or other regulations (e.g., technology standards) that would exclude these projects as offsets.

Climate-related policies in U.S. states may also affect offset supply. A number of states have taken actions that directly address GHG emissions.[14] For example, 23 states have joined 1 of the 3 regional partnerships that would require GHG (or just CO_2) emission reductions. A state or regional emissions cap might cover more sources than a federal program, thus disqualifying emissions from these sources as potential offset opportunities. However, it is uncertain how these state actions would interact—for example, whether or not they would be pre-empted—with a federal cap-and-trade program.

Regardless of whether state and regional emission caps are subsumed into a federal cap-and-trade program, other state policies could play a role. For example, California recently developed methane emission performance standards for landfills.[15] Methane captured from California landfills in response to this standard would not be available to qualify as offsets in a federal program.

Other Policy Influences

Policies not directly related to a cap-and-trade program could also affect the potential supply of offsets. A comprehensive review of policies that could affect offset supply is beyond the scope of this chapter. However, several federal policy options stand out. As mentioned above, Congress has enacted energy legislation requiring certain levels of biofuel use in transportation sector. This policy affects the amount of land potentially available for agriculture and forestry offset projects.

If enacted by Congress, a federal renewable portfolio standard (RPS) or a renewable electricity standard (RES) would affect offset supply. Such a federal standard would stimulate the production of biomass for electricity generation. As discussed above, biomass for electricity generation would not qualify as an offset, but would instead compete with other offset projects for land resources.

Economic Factors

The potential supply of offsets would ultimately be affected by how the economy responds to a federal cap-and-trade program. Such a complex analysis is beyond the scope of this chapter. A critical factor is the

Estimating Offset Supply in a Cap-and-Trade Program   37

development and market penetration of low- and/or zero-carbon technologies. These technologies could lower the costs of the cap-and-trade program. Federal policies—for example, funding or tax incentives—could stimulate these technologies. If these technologies are available earlier than predicted (by models), the "Emission Allowance Price" (discussed below) would likely decrease, making fewer offset projects cost effective.

Emission Allowance Price

The supply and type of offsets available would largely depend on the emission allowance price in a cap-and-trade system. The market price—sometimes referred to as the price of carbon—of a tradeable emission allowance would be influenced by several factors, discussed above. The central factor would be the structure of the emission reduction program, particularly the program's scope (which sources are covered) and stringency (the amount and timing of required emission reductions).

In addition to the core structural design of the cap-and-trade program, the allowance price would be dependent on the program's treatment of offsets: which types would be allowed; whether international offsets could be used; whether covered sources would be limited (e.g., as a percentage of their allowance submission) in their use of offsets. As mentioned above, multiple analyses indicate that different offset treatments yield a substantial range in emission allowance prices.

The supply of offsets would fluctuate as the allowance price changes. If the allowance price is relatively low—that is, $1 to $5/mtCO$_2$-e—only the "low-hanging fruit" projects would be financially viable. If the allowance price is higher, more offset projects would become economically competitive.

It is impossible to predict with confidence what an allowance price would be in a cap-and-trade system. Although multiple studies have provided—through economic modeling—estimates of allowance prices under cap-and-trade proposals, the results vary considerably among studies. For more information on these issues, see CRS Report R40809, *Climate Change: Costs and Benefits of the Cap-and-Trade Provisions of H.R. 2454*, by Larry Parker and Brent D. Yacobucci.

Other Factors

An EPA study stated that "other non-price factors, such as social acceptance, tend to inhibit mitigation option installation in many sectors."[16] For example, farmers engaged in dairy operations for many generations may be hesitant to convert their land to forests, even if this would be the most profitable use of the land. In addition, institutional factors have been observed in the forestry sector, which was initially expected to play a much larger role in the CDM. A report from the Intergovernmental Panel on Climate Change (IPCC) stated that although the forestry sector can make a "very significant contribution to a low-cost mitigation portfolio ... this opportunity is being lost in the current institutional context and lack of political will to implement and has resulted in only a small portion of this potential being realized at present."[17]

Information dissemination may play a role. Many of the emission abatement and sequestration opportunities, particularly in the agricultural sectors, may be widely dispersed and under the control of relatively small operations (e.g., family farms). Similarly, many of the agriculture and forestry offset projects may present technical challenges, depending on requirements to measure emissions and verify projects. To generate offsets at these locations, parties would need to know that opportunities exist and are financially viable (based on the carbon price). In addition, the smaller operations may need technical support in order to initiate, measure, and verify the projects.

In addition, transaction costs may impact offset development. The definition of transaction costs can vary widely, but in general transaction costs would likely include (1) administrative costs, such as project registration or document preparation (e.g., project petitions) needed for compliance; and (2) measuring, monitoring, and verifying costs. Transaction costs would likely involve upfront, one-time costs to get the project up and running as well as annual or periodic costs to assure the project is performing as intended.

Different offset project types could have radically different transaction costs. These differences could affect the types and quantity of offsets developed in a cap-and-trade system. For example, agricultural soil sequestration projects would likely require annual monitoring, possibly at several sites, depending on the size of the project. In contrast, afforestation might need only periodic monitoring, perhaps every five years, to assure that carbon sequestration is occurring. In addition, afforestation carbon is above ground and can be estimated rather simply, with measurements of tree height and diameter. Soil carbon would likely require soil samples to be taken and analyzed, with the number of samples depending on the heterogeneity of the soils on the site.

End Notes

[1] In this way, offsets would complement the more traditional emissions trading that can occur between two covered sources. For example, a covered source (e.g., power plant) can make reductions beyond its compliance obligations and then sell these reductions as credits to other covered sources. This type of transaction represents the "trade" component of a cap-and-trade program.

[2] For example, in EPA's sensitivity analysis of H.R. 2454 (Waxman-Markey), the agency found that a scenario prohibiting offset use (Scenario 9e) would increase the emission allowance price by approximately 65% in 2016, compared to the core scenario (Scenario 8), which represented the bill as passed by the House. See EPA's "Data Annex" to the agency's most recent analysis of H.R. 2454, available on EPA's website at http://www.epa.gov/climatechange/economics/economicanalyses.html. Another analysis that prohibited all offset projects (domestic and international) found a price increase of 250%. For a discussion of other modeling results, see CRS Report R40809, *Climate Change: Costs and Benefits of the Cap-and-Trade Provisions of H.R. 2454*, by Larry Parker and Brent D. Yacobucci.

[3] For a discussion of these issues, see CRS Report RL34436, *The Role of Offsets in a Greenhouse Gas Emissions Cap-and-Trade Program: Potential Benefits and Concerns*, by Jonathan L. Ramseur.

[4] See EPA's Analysis of H.R. 2454 in the 111th Congress, the American Clean Energy and Security Act of 2009 (most recent version from January 2010); EIA, *Energy Market and Economic Impacts of H.R. 2454, the American Clean Energy and Security Act of 2009* (August 2009).

[5] EPA, memorandum describing the results from the Forest and Agriculture Sector Optimization Model with Greenhouse Gases (FASOMGHG), April 13, 2009.

[6] EPA, *Greenhouse Gas Mitigation Potential in U.S. Forestry and Agriculture* (2005).

[7] For a comparison between assumptions used by EPA and the United States Department of Agriculture (USDA), see CRS Report R40236, *Estimates of Carbon Mitigation Potential from Agricultural and Forestry Activities*, by Renée Johnson, Jonathan L. Ramseur, and Ross W. Gorte.

[8] This is because afforestation can generate more CO_2 sequestration per acre than soil sequestration. Indeed, the range of estimates between these project types may vary by an order of magnitude. See CRS Report R40236, *Estimates of Carbon Mitigation Potential from Agricultural and Forestry Activities*, by Renée Johnson, Jonathan L. Ramseur, and Ross W. Gorte.

[9] EPA, *Greenhouse Gas Mitigation Potential in U.S. Forestry and Agriculture*, November 2005, at http://www.epa.gov/sequestration/greenhouse_gas.html; EPA, *Updated Forestry and Agriculture Marginal Abatement Cost Curves*, March 2009, available with data annex to EPA's analysis of H.R. 2454; USDA, *Economics of Sequestering Carbon in the U.S. Agricultural Sector*, April 2004, at http://www.ers.usda.gov/publications/tb1909/.

[10] EPA, Global Mitigation of Non-CO_2 Greenhouse Gases (2006), p. I-14.

[11] See CRS Report R40556, *Market-Based Greenhouse Gas Control: Selected Proposals in the 111th Congress*, by Jonathan L. Ramseur, Larry Parker, and Brent D. Yacobucci.

[12] CRS Report R40896, *Climate Change: Comparison of the Cap-and-Trade Provisions in H.R. 2454 and S. 1733*, by Brent D. Yacobucci, Jonathan L. Ramseur, and Larry Parker.

[13] For more information, see CRS Report RL34502, *Emission Allowance Allocation in a Cap-and-Trade Program: Options and Considerations*, by Jonathan L. Ramseur.

[14] See CRS Report RL33812, *Climate Change: Action by States to Address Greenhouse Gas Emissions*, by Jonathan L. Ramseur.

[15] See http://www.arb.ca.gov/cc/landfills/landfills.htm.

[16] EPA, *Global Mitigation of Non-CO_2 Greenhouse Gases*, p. 1-23 (2006).

[17] Intergovernmental Panel on Climate Change, *Climate Change 2007: Mitigation. Contribution of Working Group III to the Fourth Assessment Report*, p. 543 (2007).

In: Energy Policies and Issues
Editors: Edgar R. Thompson

ISBN: 978-1-61122-685-0
© 2011 Nova Science Publishers, Inc.

Chapter 3

BIOCHAR: EXAMINATION OF AN EMERGING CONCEPT TO MITIGATE CLIMATE CHANGE

Kelsi S. Bracmort

SUMMARY

Biochar is a charcoal produced under high temperatures using crop residues, animal manure, or any type of organic waste material. Depending on the feedstock, biochar may look similar to potting soil or to a charred substance. The combined production and use of biochar is considered a carbon-negative process, meaning that it removes carbon from the atmosphere.

Biochar has multiple potential environmental benefits, foremost the potential to sequester carbon in the soil for hundreds to thousands of years at an estimate. Studies suggest that crop yields can increase as a result of applying biochar as a soil amendment. Some contend that biochar has value as an immediate climate change mitigation strategy. Scientific experiments suggest that greenhouse gas emissions are reduced significantly with biochar application to crop fields.

Obstacles that may stall rapid adoption of biochar production systems include technology costs, system operation and maintenance, feedstock availability, and biochar handling. Biochar research and development is in its infancy. Nevertheless, interest in biochar as a multifaceted solution to agricultural and natural resource issues is growing at a rapid pace both nationally and internationally.

Past Congresses have proposed numerous climate change bills, many of which do not directly address mitigation and adaptation technologies at developmental stages, such as biochar. However, biochar may equip agricultural and forestry producers with numerous revenue-generating products: carbon offsets, soil amendments, and energy. The American Power Act (discussion draft) contains three provisions relevant to biochar.

This chapter briefly describes biochar, its potential advantages and disadvantages, legislative support, and research and development activities underway in the United States.

INTRODUCTION

Biochar—a charcoal produced under high temperatures using crop residues, animal manure, or other organic material—has the potential to offer multiple environmental benefits. Some contend that biochar can meet pressing environmental demands by sequestering large amounts of carbon in soil. It is of interest to those seeking to sell or purchase carbon offsets, increase soil conservation efforts, improve crop yield, and produce renewable energy. However, little is known about how biochar production systems could successfully be implemented and what the effect would be on long-term operations in the U.S. agriculture and forestry sectors. Some contend that it will be a considerable amount of time before this technology reaches its full potential. Studies underway at federal government research institutions and in academia are focused on ensuring that biochar production systems are a practical and reliable technology for producers to adopt.

BIOCHAR

Biochar is a soil supplement that sequesters carbon in the soil and thus may help to mitigate global climate change. It has the potential to curtail greenhouse gas emissions and other environmental hazards in the near term and to benefit agricultural producers as a soil amendment and source of renewable energy. Thus far, biochar use in the United States has been limited to small-scale applications reflective of the limited but growing number of researchers in this area over the last few years.

Biochar is similar in appearance to potting soil or to a charred substance, depending on the feedstock (**Figure 1**). Modern biochar production is based on an ancient Amazon technique for creating a nutrient-rich soil, *terra preta*. As a charcoal containing high levels of organic matter, biochar is formed from plant and crop residues or animal manure under pyrolysis conditions (**Figure 2**). Pyrolysis is the chemical breakdown of a substance under extremely high temperatures in the absence of oxygen. The quantity and quality of biochar production depends on the feedstock, pyrolysis temperature, and pyrolysis processing time. A "fast" pyrolysis (~500°C) produces biochar in a matter of seconds, while a "slow" pyrolysis produces considerably more biochar but in a matter of hours.[1]

Biochar production via pyrolysis is considered a carbon-negative process because the biochar sequesters carbon while simultaneously enhancing the fertility of the soil on which the feedstock used to produce the bioenergy grows (**Figure 3**). The biochar production system is operated using energy produced by the system. The three main outputs of a biochar production system are syngas, bio-oil, and biochar.[2]

Source: Biochar Engineering (BEC Inc.; http://www.biocharengineering.com).
Notes: Wood chips on the right and in barrel were processed through a biochar production system.

Figure 1. Biochar

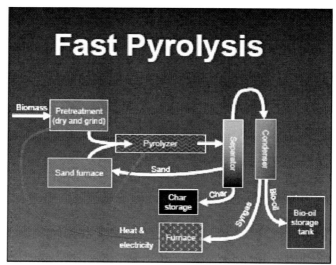

Source: U.S. Department of Agriculture (USDA) Agricultural Research Service (ARS), *ARS Biochar & Pyrolysis Initiative*, 2009.

Figure 2. Biochar Production via Pyrolysis

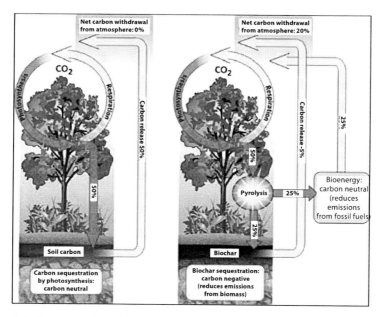

Source: J. Lehmann, "A Handful of Carbon," 2007. *Nature* 447, pp. 143-144.

Figure 3. Carbon Cycle for Soil Carbon and Biochar

Potential Advantages

Whether used as a soil amendment[3] or burned as an energy source (e.g., for cooking and heating), biochar provides numerous potential environmental benefits, some of which are not quantifiable. The three primary potential benefits are carbon sequestration, greenhouse gas emission reduction, and soil fertility.

Carbon Sequestration

Carbon sequestration is the capture and storage of carbon to prevent it from being released to the atmosphere. Studies suggest that biochar sequesters approximately 50% of the carbon available within the biomass feedstock being pyrolyzed, depending upon the feedstock type.[4] The remaining carbon is released during pyrolysis and may be captured for energy production. Large amounts of carbon may be sequestered in the soil for long time periods (hundreds to thousands of years at an estimate),[5] but precise estimates of carbon amounts sequestered as a result of biochar application are scarce. One scientist suggests that a 250-hectare farm could sequester 1,900 tons of CO_2 a year.[6]

Greenhouse Gas Emission Reduction

Primary greenhouse gases associated with the agriculture sector are nitrous oxide (N_2O) and methane (CH_4). Cropland soils and grazing lands are an agricultural source of nitrous oxide emissions.[7] Livestock manure management and enteric fermentation are leading agricultural sources of methane emissions.[8] When applied to the soil, biochar can lower greenhouse gas emissions by substantially reducing the release of nitrous oxide.[9] One report showed a 40% reduction in emissions of this greenhouse gas, which is approximately 310 times stronger than carbon dioxide in terms of global warming potential.[10] Laboratory studies suggest that nitrous oxide emission reductions from biochar-treated soil are dependent on soil moisture and soil aeration.[11] Greenhouse gas emission reductions may be 12%-84% greater if biochar is land-applied instead of combusted for energy purposes.[12]

Soil Fertility

Biochar retains nutrients for plant uptake and soil fertility. The infiltration of harmful quantities of nutrients and pesticides into groundwater and soil erosion runoff into surface waters can be limited with the use of biochar.[13] If used for soil fertility, biochar may have a positive impact on those in developing countries. Impoverished tropical and subtropical locales with abundant plant material feedstock, inexpensive cooking fuel needs, and agricultural soil replenishment needs could see an increase in crop yields.[14]

Potential Disadvantages

Recognizing that biochar technology is in its early stages of development, there are many concerns about the applicability of the technology in the United States. Three issues are feedstock availability, biochar handling, and biochar system deployment. Successful implementation of biochar technology depends on the ability of the agricultural community to afford and operate a system that is complementary to current farming and forestry practices.

Feedstock Availability

The availability of a plentiful feed supply for biochar production is an area for further study. To date, feedstock for biochar has consisted mostly of plant and crop residues, a primary domain of the agricultural community. There may be a role for the forestry community to be involved as woody biomass is deemed a cost-effective, readily available, feasible feedstock. Little is known about the advantages of using manure as a biomass feedstock. According to a group of researchers in Australia, manure-based biochar "has advantages over typically used plant-derived material because it is a by-product of another industry and in some regions is considered a waste material with little or no value. It can therefore provide a lower cost base and alleviate sustainability concerns related to using purpose-grown biomass for the process."[15]

Biochar Handling

The spreading of biochar as a soil amendment is ripe for further exploration. Specific questions concern the ideal time to apply biochar and how to ensure that it remains in place once applied and does not cause a risk to human health or degrade air quality.[16] Particulate matter, in the form of dust that is hard for the human body to filter, may be distributed in abnormal quantities if the biochar is mishandled. There are potential public safety concerns for the handling of biochar as it is a flammable substance. Additionally, the amount of land available for biochar application requires further investigation.

Biochar System Deployment

Biochar systems are designed based on the feedstock to be decomposed and the energy needs of an operation. It would be ambitious to expect a "one size fits all" standard biochar system. According to proponents, a series of mass-produced biochar systems designed for the needs of a segment of the agriculture or forestry communities might prove to be feasible (e.g., forestry community in the southeastern region, corn grower community in the midwestern region, poultry producer community in the mid-Atlantic region). Extensive deployment of biochar systems would depend on system costs, operation time, collaboration with utility providers for the sale of bio-oil, and availability of information about technology reliability.

POLICY CONTEXT

Climate Change Debate

In the 111th Congress, carbon offsets are a prominent factor in the climate change debate. The establishment of an offset program, identification of eligible projects types, and offset verification may be pertinent to the adoption of biochar production technology.[17] A carbon offset is defined as "a measurable avoidance, reduction, or sequestration of carbon dioxide ($CO2$) or other greenhouse gas (GHG) emissions."[18] Carbon sequestration projects are one type of carbon offset. In addition to direct carbon capture and sequestration activities, the 111th Congress may consider the role of biological (indirect) sequestration, such as projects that can be implemented by agricultural producers at the field level.[19] Furthermore, Congress may decide who is granted carbon offset ownership for biochar production (e.g., landlord, feedstock provider, production plant).

Congress may examine the use of biochar as an indirect carbon sequestration technology that could be used to offset carbon emissions from major emitters. In 2008, 6% of total U.S. greenhouse gas emissions were attributed to the agricultural sector.[20] While not as large as the amounts produced by some other sectors, agricultural emissions come from a large number of decentralized sources, leading many to conclude that controlling such emissions would be difficult. On the other hand, some argue that soil carbon sequestered as a result of biochar application is easily quantifiable and transparent, which may be ideal for carbon trading requirements. Others contend that ancillary benefits could include additional revenue earned by agricultural producers through the sale of carbon credits earned from biochar application or the sale of biochar as a soil amendment. Energy costs for a producer's operation may be reduced by using the energy generated from the biochar production system. Additionally, some assert that the use of biochar results in higher crop yields. This could be a criterion to consider within the larger land use debate.

Introduced Legislation

The Water Efficiency via Carbon Harvesting and Restoration (WECHAR) Act of 2009,[21] introduced in September 2009, seeks, among other things, to establish loan guarantee programs that would develop biochar technology to use excess plant biomass and establish biochar demonstration projects on public lands. The legislation is primarily focused on woody biomass as the feedstock. Some contend that the legislation addresses research and development needs for biochar production. Others argue that the legislation lacks specific actions regarding technology transfer or commercial development of biochar production systems.

The discussion draft of the American Power Act contains three provisions relevant to biochar.[22] The first provision lists projects for biochar production and use as an eligible project type under the domestic offsets program.[23] The second provision instructs the U.S. Environmental Protection Agency (EPA) to submit to Congress a report on the sources and effects of black carbon emissions, and strategies to reduce black carbon emissions, including "research and development activities needed to better characterize the feasibility of biochar techniques to decrease emissions, increase carbon soil sequestration, and improve agricultural production, and if appropriate, encourage broader application of those techniques."[24] The third provision directs the Secretary of Agriculture to provide grants for up to 60 facilities to "conduct research, develop, demonstrate and deploy biochar production technology for the purpose of sequestering carbon."[25]

Farm Bill

The 110th Congress promoted biochar development through the 2008 farm bill (P.L. 110-246), which listed it under grants for High Priority Research and Extension Areas. Noted research areas include biochar production and use, co-production with bioenergy, soil enhancements, and soil carbon sequestration. Listing biochar development as a high-priority research area in the 2008 farm bill did not authorize a specific appropriations amount. Funding for biochar development research would be determined in future appropriation bills and by the U.S. Department of Agriculture. Farm managers facing needs with respect to soil fertility, residue and manure management, energy efficiency, and additional revenue generation may benefit from a policy that further supports biochar production and use (e.g., technology practice standard, cost-share).

Long-Term Prospects

Biochar's fate as a viable component of the long-term solution to mitigate climate change by way of carbon sequestration depends upon further development by the scientific and technology transfer communities. In particular, biochar's practical application at various locations and scales using multiple feedstocks throughout the United States is an area for additional study. Policy that encourages academia and other institutions to conduct in-depth research and development could quicken the pace of technology deployment.

An assessment of external factors (e.g., feedstock transportation costs and disposal fees) associated with the economic growth of biochar production systems, similar to studies conducted for the biofuels industry, could provide guidance on the types of federal financial and technical incentives necessary to spur development (e.g., regulatory requirements, technical standards). The definition of biomass used in climate change and energy legislation will directly affect the eventual impact of biochar in limiting GHG emissions.[26] Indeed, the biomass definition would determine what sources of material are deemed acceptable and which lands would be eligible lands for biomass removal.

International Recognition

A series of presentations delivered at the United Nations Climate Change Conference in December 2008 elevated interest in biochar as an immediate response to mitigate climate change, given its carbon sequestration ability.[27] Biochar's success rate as a potential clean development mechanism (CDM) mitigation technology may provide insight on its use for U.S. carbon trading purposes.[28] A CDM, monitored by the United Nations Framework Convention on Climate Change (UNFCCC), allows developed countries to invest in and receive credit for activities that reduce greenhouse gas emissions in developing countries.

U.S. DEPARTMENT OF AGRICULTURE ACTIVITIES

According to a U.S. Department of Agriculture (USDA) Agricultural Research Service (ARS) official, an estimated $2.1 million was spent in 2009 on in-house biochar research by ARS.[29] ARS has approximately 19 projects underway to analyze the use of fast pyrolysis to convert biomass into biochar and bio-oil at various labs nationwide. ARS estimates that the United States could use biochar to sequester 139 Tg of carbon on an annual basis if it were to harvest and pyrolyze 1.3 billion tons of biomass.[30]

SELECT U.S. MANUFACTURERS

While some consider biochar research to be in its infancy, a limited number of U.S. manufacturers are selling biochar production technology to the public. CRS was not able to obtain the level of private investment in biochar technology and promotion.

Eprida, Inc.

Located in Georgia, this technology development company sells biochar production equipment. The company advocates use of both the biochar and the bio-oil produced from its patented system. Officials at Eprida, Inc., believe their technology brings value to three markets: energy, fertilizer, and carbon credit.[31]

Carbon Char Group, LLC

Agricultural grade value-added biochar is available for purchase from this New Jersey company.[32] In 2008, the company received approximately $50,000 from the USDA New Jersey Conservation Innovation Grants program (CIG) to use biochar to enhance the soil condition in sunflower fields. The CIG is a program administered by the USDA Natural Resources Conservation Service (NRCS) to encourage the development and adoption of innovative conservation technologies that work in conjunction with agricultural production.

Biochar Engineering (BEC Inc.)

Field-scale biochar production systems for research purposes are available from BEC Inc., a Colorado company. Woody biomass is the preferred feedstock for the systems. The Biochar 1000 model produces approximately 250 pounds of biochar for every 1,000 pounds of biomass on an hourly basis. BEC is designing a larger system to process a ton of biomass in an hour that may yield a quarter ton of biochar as well as 8 million British thermal units (MBTU) of heat in one hour.[33]

End Notes

[1] Institute for Governance & Sustainable Development and IGDS/INECE Climate Briefing Note, "Significant Climate Mitigation Is Available from Biochar," December 8, 2008.

[2] Syngas, or synthesis gas, consists of varying concentrations of carbon monoxide and hydrogen and can be used as a replacement to natural gas or liquid fuel. Bio-oil is a liquid fuel that can be used, once upgraded, as a motor fuel.

[3] A soil amendment improves the physical properties of soil (e.g., moisture-holding capacity, nutrient retention ability).

[4] Johannes Lehmann, John Gaunt, and Marco Rondon, "Bio-char Sequestration in Terrestrial Ecosystems—A Review," *Mitigation and Adaptation Strategies for Global Change*, vol. 11 (2006), pp. 403-427.

[5] Bruno Glaser, Johannes Lehmann, and Wolfgang Zech, "Ameliorating Physical and Chemical Properties of Highly Weathered Soils in the Tropics with Charcoal—A Review," *Biology and Fertility of Soils*, vol. 35 (2002), pp. 219-230.

[6] Emma Marris, "Black Is the New Green," *Nature*, vol. 442, no. 10 (August 2006), pp. 624-626.

[7] For more information on nitrous oxide emissions, see CRS Report R40874, *Nitrous Oxide from Agricultural Sources: Potential Role in Greenhouse Gas Emission Reduction and Ozone Recovery*, by Kelsi Bracmort.

[8] For more information on methane emissions from agricultural sources, see CRS Report R40813, *Methane Capture: Options for Greenhouse Gas Emission Reduction*, by Kelsi Bracmort et al.

[9] Johannes Lehmann, "Bio-energy in the Black," *Frontiers in Ecology and the Environment*, vol. 5, no. 7 (2007), pp. 381-387.

[10] Tyler Hamilton, "The Case for Burying Charcoal," *Technology Review*, April 26, 2007.

[11] Yosuke Yanai, Koki Toyota, and Masanori Okazaki, "Effects of Charcoal Addition on N2O Emissions from Soil Resulting from Rewetting Air-Dried Soil in Short-Term Laboratory Experiments," *Japanese Society of Soil Science and Plant Nutrition*, vol. 53 (2007), pp. 181-188.

[12] Johannes Lehmann, "A Handful of Carbon," *Nature*, vol. 447 (May 10, 2007), pp. 143-144.

[13] Johannes Lehmann, "Bio-energy in the Black," *Frontiers in Ecology and the Environment*, vol. 5, no. 7 (2007), pp. 381-387.

[14] Stephan M. Haefele, "Black Soil, Green Rice," *Rice Today*, April-June 2007, p. 27.

[15] K. Y. Chan, L. Van Zwieten, and I. Meszaros et al., "Using Poultry Litter Biochars as Soil Amendments," *Australian Journal of Soil Research*, vol. 46 (2008), pp. 437-444.

[16] David A. Laird, "The Charcoal Vision: A Win-Win-Win Scenario for Simultaneously Producing Bioenergy, Permanently Sequestering Carbon, While Improving Soil and Water Quality," *Agronomy Journal*, vol. 100, no. 1 (2008), pp. 178-181.

[17] For more information on the role of offsets in current greenhouse gas legislation, see CRS Report R40643, *Greenhouse Gas Legislation: Summary and Analysis of H.R. 2454 as Passed by the House of Representatives*, coordinated by Mark Holt and Gene Whitney.

[18] For more information on carbon offsets, see CRS Report RL34241, *Voluntary Carbon Offsets: Overview and Assessment*, by Jonathan L. Ramseur.

[19] For more information on carbon capture and sequestration, see CRS Report RL33801, *Carbon Capture and Sequestration (CCS)*, by Peter Folger; and CRS Report RL33898, *Climate Change: The Role of the U.S. Agriculture Sector*, by Renée Johnson.

[20] U.S. Environmental Protection Agency, *2010 U.S. Greenhouse Gas Inventory Report*, EPA 430-R-10-006, April 2010, *http://www.epa.gov/climatechange/emissions/usinventoryreport.html*.

[21] S. 1713.

[22] Discussion draft available at http://kerry.senate.gov/americanpoweract/pdf/APAbill.pdf.

[23] American Power Act (discussion draft), Title VII, Part D, Sec. 734.

[24] American Power Act (discussion draft), Title VII, Subtitle C, Part II, Sec. 2211.

[25] American Power Act (discussion draft), Title VII, Subtitle C, Part II, Sec. 2214.

[26] For more information on biomass definitions, see CRS Report R40529, *Biomass: Comparison of Definitions in Legislation*, by Kelsi Bracmort and Ross W. Gorte

[27] "Dangerous Sea Level Rise Imminent without Large Reductions of Black Carbon and Implementation of Other Fast-Action Mitigation Strategies," *Environmental Research Web*, December 12, 2008.

[28] For more information on the clean development mechanism, see CRS Report R41049, *Climate Change and the EU Emissions Trading Scheme (ETS): Looking to 2020*, by Larry Parker.

[29] Correspondence with USDA ARS official, May 2010.

[30] Correspondence with USDA ARS official, January 2009. A teragram (Tg) is equivalent to 1 trillion grams. A Tg C (teragram of carbon) is a unit of measurement used to compare greenhouse gases emitted from different sources on the same basis.

[31] See http://www.eprida.com.

[32] See http://www.carbonchar.com.

[33] A Btu (British thermal unit) is a unit of energy used to express the heating value of fuels.

In: Energy Policies and Issues
Editors: Edgar R. Thompson

ISBN: 978-1-61122-685-0
© 2011 Nova Science Publishers, Inc.

Chapter 4

FOREST CARBON MARKETS: POTENTIAL AND DRAWBACKS

Ross Gorte and Jonathan L. Ramseur

SUMMARY

Forests are major carbon sinks (storehouses), and activities that alter forests can release or sequester carbon dioxide (CO_2), the most common greenhouse gas (GHG). Some carbon markets have been formed under mandatory GHG reduction regimes, such as the Kyoto Protocol and various regional and state initiatives in the United States. Other markets have formed for voluntary efforts to reduce GHG emissions. Offsets, or credits for sequestering carbon or reducing emissions in unregulated sectors, are typically allowed in both mandatory and voluntary markets. Forestry activities are among the largest-volume and lowest-cost opportunities for generating offsets.

Various forestry activities may be feasible for carbon offsets. Afforestation (planting trees on open sites) and reforestation (planting trees on recently cleared sites) are the activities most commonly included for offsets. Some propose that the carbon stored in long-term wood products, such as lumber and plywood, could be credited as carbon offsets, and mill wastes often substitute for fossil fuels to produce energy; however, short-term products (e.g., paper) and the biomass left in the woods after timber harvesting release carbon, making the net carbon effects uncertain. Some forest management practices also might qualify for carbon offsets; certified sustainable forest practices provide a system of assured, long-term forests, while activities to increase tree growth face many of the same concerns as long-term wood products. Finally, deforestation is a major source of GHG emissions, accounting for as much as 17% of anthropogenic emissions. Thus, avoided deforestation, especially in the tropics, potentially provides an enormous opportunity to reduce GHG emissions. However, avoided deforestation is particularly prone to leakage (see below), as well as many of the concerns about forest carbon offsets generally.

Forestry projects may offer considerable market opportunities for carbon offsets, but several issues have generated concerns and controversy. One concern, especially for compliance markets, is whether projects are additional to business as usual. An activity that is common practice or industry standard, or a project that is required under current federal, state, or local laws, cannot be used as an offset. Functional carbon markets also require cost-effective practices to verify carbon sequestration. Current measurement and monitoring practices are costly and have several implementation challenges. Another concern is that, compared to other types of offsets, forestry projects present substantial risk of leakage. Emission leakage can occur if carbon sequestered in one location (e.g., by avoided deforestation) leads to carbon release (e.g., from increased harvesting) in another location. Product leakage could occur if forest carbon sequestration induces use of more carbon-intensive substitutes (e.g., cement or steel). Forest carbon projects are expected to generate offsets for decades. Some are concerned that the sequestration will be negated subsequently by human activity (e.g., change in land use) or a natural occurrence (e.g., forest fire or disease). Although there are legal and accounting mechanisms that can address this concern, implementing these options may present challenges, particularly for projects in developing nations. Finally, forward crediting to allow early credits for expected sequestration faces many of the same concerns about not fulfilling expectations.

Forests are major carbon sinks—repositories of vast amounts of carbon. Activities that alter Fforests—create, enhance, modify, or eliminate them— significantly affect the amount of carbon dioxide (CO_2) in the atmosphere. Forests store about 45% of terrestrial carbon, and were estimated to sequester 2.6 billion metric tons (tonnes) of CO_2 per year in the 1990s, about a third of annual anthropogenic carbon emissions from fossil fuel and land use changes.[1]

Concerns about global climate change and its impacts on the environment and the economy are encouraging policy-makers and stakeholders to explore a range of opportunities that would reduce emissions of CO_2 and other greenhouse gases (GHGs).[2] Reducing deforestation and increasing the amount of carbon stored in forests are approaches that have generated considerable interest for their ability to support climate change mitigation. Congress is considering legislation that would, among other things, provide financial incentives for parties to reduce GHGs or sequester (store) CO_2.[3] The possible use of forests to sequester CO_2 is part of this larger debate over GHGs and climate change.

This chapter describes current markets for forest carbon sequestration, the potential for using forests to offset other sources of GHG emissions, and the concerns and drawbacks related to forest carbon sequestration efforts.

FOREST CARBON MARKETS

The potential economic and environmental impacts of global climate change have led many to consider regulating GHG emissions from various sources, and to seek ways to ameliorate their own GHG emissions. Projects that sequester GHGs or reduce GHG emissions from unregulated economic sectors, such as forestry, can generate offsets, or credits, to sell to regulated entities or to those who wish to reduce their carbon footprints. In either case— for regulated entities or for voluntary reductions—forestry activities (e.g., afforestation, reforestation, and avoided deforestation) typically present opportunities to offset GHG emissions.

Offsets are commonly project-based initiatives involving specific projects or activities whose primary purpose is to reduce, avoid, or sequester GHG emissions.[4] Parties can develop offsets from a wide variety of activities, such as methane capture and agricultural soil projects,[5] but forestry-related projects offer significant potential, in the volume of GHGs that can be avoided or sequestered.[6]

Offsets, or credits earned by an offset project, would likely be the currency of most forest carbon markets. Offsets are the measurable avoidance, reduction, or sequestration of CO_2 or other GHG emissions. Forestry projects as offsets raise a number of concerns. To be credible, the emissions reduced, avoided, or sequestered must be *additional* to business as usual (i.e., what would have happened anyway), *verifiable*, and *permanent*. These concepts, and the problems that arise in assuring credible forestry, are discussed later in this chapter.

One concern for offset markets, in addition to the drawbacks discussed below, is the potential for double-counting the offsets—that is, that sellers might try to sell the same offset to multiple buyers. Thus, compliance markets, and some voluntary markets, require some type of reporting and registration for offsets. This has led to incentives for independent reporting and registry programs, as discussed below.

Compliance Offset Markets

A mandatory GHG reduction program, such as a cap-and-trade system, could allow covered entities (e.g., power plants) to use offsets to comply with their GHG emissions cap. For example, a regulated entity could purchase offsets, rather than reducing direct, onsite emissions, and might choose to do so if the offsets were less expensive. Assuming that the amount of CO_2 reduced, avoided, or sequestered through an offset project equals the amount reduced at a regulated source, the objective to reduce GHG emissions would be met. For global climate change, it does not matter where or from what source the reduction or sequestration occurs; the effect on the atmospheric concentration of GHGs would be the same.

Although forestry-related projects are eligible as offsets in several existing or developing compliance markets, forest projects have, to date, played a negligible role. If the recent cap-and-trade proposals (discussed below) are an indication, however, interest in allowing forestry offsets in a compliance regime is growing.

Kyoto Protocol[7]

The United Nations Framework Convention on Climate Change (UNFCCC) is the primary international agreement to mitigate climate change by reducing GHG emissions. The Kyoto Protocol established a framework for Annex I countries (developed countries, including the United States) for "reducing their overall emissions of such gases [GHGs] by at least 5% below 1990 levels in the commitment period 2008 to 2012." Although the United States originally signed the Kyoto Protocol, it later rejected participation, and thus is not bound by its goals.

To provide flexibility to countries in meeting their GHG reduction targets, the protocol included two mechanisms—the Clean Development Mechanism (CDM) and Joint Implementation (JI)—that allow certain forestry activities to generate offsets.

Clean Development Mechanism

The CDM is a project-based mechanism that permits Annex I countries under the Kyoto Protocol to earn credits for use in achieving their emission targets. It is the only mechanism that allows Annex I countries to earn credits for actions in non-Annex I countries (developing countries such as India or China). For forestry projects, the CDM includes only afforestation (planting trees where none were previously growing) and reforestation (replanting trees on recently cleared forest sites).[8] Further, project developers can only earn credits for additional projects—those that would not otherwise have occurred (if reforestation is required by a country's laws, for example, the reforestation project cannot earn credits under the CDM).

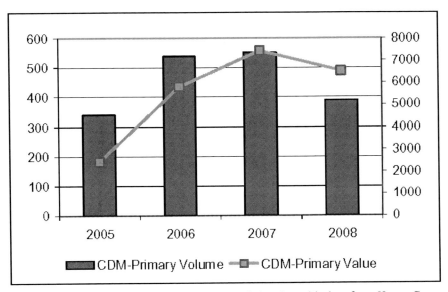

Source: Prepared by the Congressional Research Service with data from Karan Capoor and Philippe Ambrosi, *State and Trends of the Carbon Market 2009*, The World Bank, Washington, DC, May 2009, http://wbcarbonfinance.org/docs/State___Trends_of_the_Carbon_Market_2009-FINAL_26_May09.pdf.

Figure 1. Trading Volume and Market Value of Clean Development Mechanism Projects, 2005-2008

The CDM is a large and growing compliance offset market. Both the trading volume and market value of CDM projects have grown substantially in recent years, although the global recession caused a drop in 2008. (See **Figure**

1.) Forestry-sector projects were initially expected to play a significant role in the CDM, but that has not been the case. An IPCC report stated that although the forestry sector can make a "very significant contribution to a low-cost mitigation portfolio ... this opportunity is being lost in the current institutional context and lack of political will to implement and has resulted in only a small portion of this potential being realized at present."[9] Indeed, of the offsets in the pipeline under the CDM to date, afforestation and reforestation have accounted for 1.1% of the projects (55 of 5,122 CDM projects) and only 0.7% of the offsets (4.7 million tonnes of certified emission reductions—CERs—out of 709.7 million tonnes of CERs for all CDM projects).[10] Also, to date, no afforestation or reforestation projects have had CERs issues.

Joint Implementation

JI is also a project-based approach for countries to earn credits toward their emission targets under the Kyoto Protocol. JI projects are conducted jointly between two Annex I countries. A broader array of forestry activities can earn credits than under CDM; in addition to afforestation and reforestation, avoided deforestation and forest management that enhances carbon sequestration can qualify as JI projects. As with CDM projects, credits are only earned on projects that otherwise would not have occurred. JI has a much smaller market than CDM—about 86 million tonnes of emission reduction units (ERUs) compared to 709 million tonnes of CERs for CDM).[11] One JI project (with 82,000 tonnes of ERUs) is a forestry project.

Ongoing Kyoto Developments

The concerns about tropical deforestation and Third World contributions to GHG emissions were among the issues discussed at the 13th Conference of the Parties to the UNFCCC (COP-13) and the Third Meeting of the Parties to the Kyoto Protocol (MOP-3) held in Bali, Indonesia, December 3-14,2007.[12] The United States participated in discussion at Bali, as a party to the UNFCCC and as an observer to the Kyoto Protocol. Among the outcomes of the Bali negotiations was an Action Plan that included:[13]

> Policy approaches and positive incentives ... [for] reducing emissions from deforestation and forest degradation [REDD] in developing countries; and [identifying] the role of conservation, sustainable management of forests and enhancement of forest carbon stocks in developing countries ...

The negotiations also led to a decision on forests and deforestation.[14] The decision encourages various efforts, including demonstration projects, to reduce GHG emissions from deforestation and forest degradation, financial and technical support for those efforts, and improved measurement and reporting of GHG reductions that result from such efforts. Some argue that the most important result of the Bali negotiations, however, is that avoided tropical deforestation will be included in any agreement on post-Kyoto (after 2012) actions on global climate change.

COP-15 and MOP-5 were held in Copenhagen, Denmark, December 7-18, 2009. Deliberations considered multiple proposed texts, but could not reach agreement among all parties. Hence, the Copenhagen Accord set forth numerous key action points for future negotiations. One of those points is to establish a mechanism to mobilize international finance for REDD+ (reduced carbon emissions from deforestation and forest degradation plus enhanced forest carbon sequestration). However, the nature and timing of such financial tools remains to be developed.

European Union's Emission Trading Scheme

Members of the European Union (EU) are implementing the requirements of the Kyoto Protocol through the EU's Emission Trading Scheme (ETS).[15] Private parties subject to the ETS cap cannot purchase forestry offsets. However, EU governments can purchase eligible forestry offsets, from afforestation or reforestation projects, to meet their Kyoto Protocol commitments, up to 1% annually of their country's base year (1990) emissions.[16] The World Bank has reported that global transactions of land use, land use change, and forestry offsets have only accounted for 6% of this allowable limit (i.e., 0.06% of EU carbon emission reductions).

Regional Initiatives in the United States

Even though the United States is not a signatory to the Kyoto Protocol, many states are participating in regional initiatives for mandatory reduction of GHG emissions. Twenty-three states (and four Canadian provinces) have joined one of three regional partnerships that would require CO_2 (or GHG) emission reductions. Another nine states (plus two Canadian provinces and six Mexican states) are observers to the partnerships.

The first regional initiative to take effect is the Regional Greenhouse Gas Initiative (RGGI), a partnership of 10 northeastern and mid-Atlantic states that creates a cap-and-trade system aimed at limiting carbon dioxide emissions from power plants.[17] RGGI allows for five types of offset projects to generate emission credits, including afforestation.[18] RGGI participants agreed to continue to develop other offset projects, "including other types of forestry projects, and grassland revegetation projects."[19]

Two other regional initiatives have been developed, but have yet to be implemented. One is the Western Climate Initiative (WCI), a partnership of seven western states (and four Canadian provinces), with six additional states (plus two Canadian provinces and six Mexican states) as observers.[20] This partnership has agreed to a regional economy-wide GHG emissions target of 15% below 2005 levels by 2020. Although the WCI logistics are in the early stages, "in each of the opportunities for stakeholder engagement on the design of a cap-and-trade system for the Western Climate Initiative, there has been strong support for including an offset program."[21]

The other regional initiative in development is the Midwestern Greenhouse Gas Reduction Accord, signed by six states (and one Canadian province), with three additional states (and one Canadian province) as observers.[22] This accord would establish a regional multi-sector GHG cap-and-trade program. As with the WCI, this program is still in the early development stages.

Mandatory U.S. State Requirements[23]

Several U.S. states have individual programs that currently or will soon mandate reductions in CO_2 or GHG emissions. For example, the California Global Warming Solutions Act of 2006 (AB 32) established a process, with target emission reductions and implementation dates, for reducing GHG emissions within the state. However, the 2008-2009 recession and controversies over various aspects of implementation, including forest offset project protocols, have raised questions about the program's future. Hawaii and New Jersey have also passed legislation to establish mandatory statewide GHG reduction programs, but these programs are still in development. Other states have addressed the issue in a more limited fashion—for example, through restrictions on new power plants (e.g., Oregon and Washington), on existing power plants (e.g., Massachusetts and New Hampshire), and on motor vehicles.

Proposals in the 111th Congress

Members have introduced several legislative proposals that would establish a GHG emissions reduction program, such as a cap-and-trade system. Two particular bills—the American Clean Energy and Security Act of 2009 (H.R. 2454), commonly known as Waxman-Markey, and the Clean Energy

Forest Carbon Markets: Potential and Drawbacks 61

Jobs and American Power Act (S. 1733), commonly known as Kerry-Boxer—have attracted most of the attention, but other bills addressing various aspects of GHG emissions reduction and climate change have also been introduced or discussed as possible vehicles.[24] The cap-and-trade programs generally would allow the use of offsets to varying degrees, thus creating a compliance offset market.[25] Many of the proposals that allow offsets would include forestry-related activities as eligible offset projects.

Voluntary Offset Markets

Voluntary markets are exchanges of offsets by entities not subject to emissions caps. In contrast to compliance markets, forestry-related and other land use projects have played a much larger role in voluntary markets. A 2007 study found that, of the different offset categories in the voluntary market, forest sequestration accounted for the largest percentage (36%) of transaction volume.[26] The primary components of the voluntary market are "retail" offsets (also called the over-the-counter, or OTC, market) and offsets generated through the Chicago Climate Exchange (CCX), both of which include forestry projects.[27]

In the United States and elsewhere, a growing number of organizations and individuals not subject to mandatory emission caps are buying or selling offsets. These exchanges are voluntary, because there is no requirement for these parties to curtail their GHG emissions.[28] Buyers may be interested in offsetting some or all of their GHG emissions from various activities, reducing their "carbon footprint," or becoming "carbon neutral." Buyers might also be preparing for future mandatory federal GHG emission reductions, getting into the market while prices are relatively low with the expectation that today's carbon offsets will be usable to achieve future federal emission ceilings or caps. Sellers are interested in receiving income for various activities, which, without the voluntary market, would likely not occur.

There is currently no registry or tracking system that follows all exchanges in the voluntary market. For this reason, the precise size or value of the voluntary offset market is unknown. However, a series of World Bank reports provides estimates for recent years indicating that the size of the market has increased substantially since 2005. In 2008, the CCX market was 69 million tonnes of CO_2, with a market value of $309 million, and the rest of the voluntary market was 54 million tonnes of CO_2, with a market value of

$397 million.29 To put these figures in context, U.S. GHG emissions were 6,957 million tonnes of CO2 in 2008.[30]

Retail Offsets

In general, the voluntary offset market refers to retail or "over-the-counter" offsets that may be purchased by anyone. Purchasing a retail offset is as simple as online shopping. Hundreds of organizations—private and nonprofit entities—develop, provide, or sell retail offsets to businesses and individuals in the voluntary market.[31] The quality of the retail offsets in the voluntary market varies considerably, largely because there are no commonly accepted standards; one source reports 21 different standards in use.[32] Some sellers offer offsets that comply with standards generally regarded as quite rigorous, such as the CDM or the Gold Standard. Other sellers offer offsets that meet the seller's self-established guidelines, which may not be publicly available. These self-established protocols can vary considerably, raising questions of integrity.[33]

Chicago Climate Exchange

The Chicago Climate Exchange (CCX) was established in 2003 as a trading system for buyers and sellers of offset projects to reduce GHG emissions.[34] Buyers (i.e., GHG emitters) make voluntary but legally binding commitments to meet GHG emission reduction targets; those who emit more than their targets comply by purchasing CCX Carbon Financial Instrument (CFI) contracts, which can be generated by qualifying carbon offset projects (from sellers). CCX has standardized rules for CFI contracts, including forestry projects, and requires third-party verification for projects. Eligible forestry projects include afforestation, reforestation, reduced deforestation and forest degradation, forest management to increase stand-level and landscape-level carbon density, and long-term carbon storage in wood products. CCX has guidelines and rules for determining eligible projects and their resulting carbon offsets. However, studies have also criticized the quality of the offsets generated by the CCX.[35]

Reporting and Registry Programs

In general, GHG reporting and registry programs allow facilities to submit and officially record emissions data. The primary incentive appears to be the

Forest Carbon Markets: Potential and Drawbacks   63

opportunity for participants to create an official record of reduced or sequestered emissions, which the parties hope will count as emissions credits in future mandatory reduction programs. At a minimum, participants typically receive some public recognition for their efforts, which may help promote an organization's environmental stewardship profile.

1605(b) Reporting Program

Section 1605(b) of the Energy Policy Act of 1992 (P.L. 102-486; 42 U.S.C. §§ 13201, et seq.) created a program of voluntary reporting of GHG emissions, reductions, and sequestration. The U.S. Department of Energy, with assistance from other departments, established guidelines for reporting estimated emissions, reductions, and sequestration; the guidelines were revised and updated in 2006.

The program has been criticized, because facilities need only report reductions and/or sequestration, instead of reporting all emissions.[36] In other words, a company can submit a record of tons sequestered at one location, but continue to increase emissions at other sites. This may present a concern in subsequent years, if these companies are allowed to receive credit for these reductions or sequestration, and apply the credit towards compliance with an emissions cap.

California Registry

The California Climate Action Registry is a private, nonprofit organization for voluntary reporting of GHG emissions and reductions, initially formed by the State of California in 2001. Registry members (currently more than 300 corporations, government agencies, and other organizations) voluntarily measure, verify, and report emissions using registry standards and tools. The Climate Action Reserve is a division of the registry to establish standards for voluntary carbon reductions. The registry and reserve include forestry protocols for the forest sector (for organizations and landowners to account for entity-wide forest carbon stocks and emissions), for forest projects (for carbon sequestration projects by landowners), and for certification (for third-party verifiers to assess reported GHG data).[37]

The Climate Registry

The Climate Registry was launched on May 8, 2007. As of February, 2009, 41 states,[38] all Canadian provinces and territories (except Nunavut), and the six northernmost Mexican states have joined the registry to support both voluntary and mandatory reporting schemes. The Climate Registry is modeled on the California Climate Action Registry, with a goal of providing "an accurate, complete, consistent, transparent and verified set of greenhouse gas emissions data supported by a robust reporting and verification infrastructure."[39] Neither the California Registry nor the Climate Registry directly facilitate market transactions, but the information provided could provide a consistent basis for calculating carbon offsets.

USDA Guidelines[40]

The 2008 farm bill (the Food, Conservation, and Energy Act of 2008, P.L. 110-246) contains a new conservation provision to facilitate the development of markets in environmental services. It directs the U.S. Department of Agriculture to develop technical guidelines for measuring environmental services from farms and forests. The provision specifically includes carbon in environmental services, in recognition of the need for uniform standards and consistent measures of emissions reduction and carbon sequestration in the agricultural and forestry sectors. These technical guidelines could provide a consistent basis for carbon reporting and for offset projects in both voluntary and compliance markets.

FORESTRY PROJECTS FOR OFFSETS

Several types of forestry projects might qualify as offsets for compliance or voluntary carbon markets. The capacity of forestry projects to provide offsets is substantial, with higher carbon prices increasing the number of economically feasible projects. One study estimated that U.S. forestry projects could sequester more than 100 million tonnes of CO_2 at a carbon price of $5 per tonne or as much as 1,200 million tonnes at $50, as shown in **Figure 2**.[41] Subsequent changes in law and policy, as well as changes in energy, carbon, and forestry markets and different assumptions, would likely lead to different conclusions. Still, this potential is significant when compared to the 6,957 million tonnes of U.S. CO_2 emissions in 2008.[42]

The inclusion of projects in other countries would affect the quantity and price of offsets. This is particularly significant for forestry, since tropical deforestation and forest degradation have been estimated to cause as much as 17% of anthropogenic carbon emissions.[43] Whether to include international projects in compliance schemes has been subject of extensive debate. (See "Avoided Deforestation," below.) In addition, international forestry projects

Forest Carbon Markets: Potential and Drawbacks 65

may face more significant problems than domestic projects, as discussed below.

Afforestation and Reforestation

Establishing stands of trees is one of the most basic objectives of forestry. *Afforestation* is planting tree seedlings or preparing an area for tree seeding on sites that have been without trees for several years (generally a decade or more), such as pastures or recently abandoned or retired cropland. *Reforestation* is similar, but applies to sites recently cleared of trees, due to timber harvesting or a natural disaster.

Afforestation and reforestation are common forestry activities included in trading schemes for forest carbon sequestration offsets. Successful projects must result in established stands to qualify as an offset. Planting failures sometimes occur due to diseases or adverse conditions (e.g., drought). Forest stands generally sequester more carbon than sites without forest cover.[44] Forest biomes store as much as 10 times more carbon in their vegetation than do non-forest biomes, usually at least for decades, and for centuries in some ecosystems. Afforestation will generally sequester more carbon than reforestation because of the carbon release from the site clearing prior to reforestation. (See "Long-Term Wood Products," below.) Afforestation can provide a broad array of other environmental benefits (e.g., improved water quality and habitat for native animal species), especially if the newly established tree stands restore a historically native mix of species. Plantations, including plantations of exotic species, probably provide less carbon storage than natural mixed forests, but can still be beneficial, especially if fast-growing species are used for products to displace harvests of natural forests (reducing deforestation).

The opportunities for afforestation are best in areas with long histories of land clearing for agriculture and other uses—Europe, North America, China, India, and the like. Some countries or regions with substantial open land may have limited opportunities for afforestation because of their arid conditions (e.g., central Asia, north Africa). In other areas (such as the United States), strong demand for corn and other agricultural products (e.g., soybeans, oil palms, or switchgrass) to produce ethanol or biodiesel may also limit afforestation opportunities.

Long-Term Wood Products

Some have suggested that harvesting timber for long-term wood products should be included as possible carbon offsets. Lumber, plywood, and other solid wood products can store carbon for many years, ranging from 10 years for shipping pallets to 100 years or more for buildings.[45] Sawmill wastes are almost entirely used for paper or energy (burned as a substitute for fossil fuels). Paper products have a relatively brief duration, often releasing their carbon in less than a year, but paper is commonly recycled, reducing the carbon release as well as reducing the demand for wood from the forest.[46]

The wood left on the site after harvesting timber for wood products is more problematic. Some carbon may be added to the soil through decomposition, but much of the carbon left on the site returns to the atmosphere over time—a few minutes if the slash (tree tops and limbs) is burned; weeks, months, or even years if the slash rots.

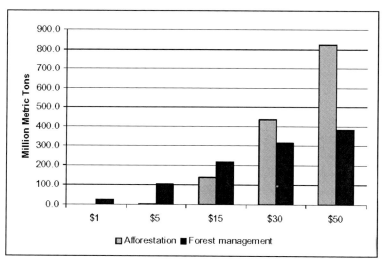

Source: Prepared by Congressional Research Service with data from U.S. Environmental Protection Agency, Office of Atmospheric Programs, *Greenhouse Gas Mitigation Potential in U.S. Forestry and Agriculture*, EPA 430-R-05-006 (Washington, DC: November 2005), pp. 4-21.

Figure 2. Estimated U.S. GHG Mitigation Totals by Activity: Annualized Averages, 2010-2110

Wood product harvests from natural tropical forests generally release more carbon than do harvests from plantations and temperate and boreal forests. Native tropical forests have much greater tree species diversity, and thus generally have a greater percentage of the biomass on a site remaining after a timber harvest. *Reduced impact logging* (RIL) is a collection of practices and techniques intended to reduce the environmental damage of logging, especially in the tropics, that can ameliorate the carbon release from tropical logging.[47] One source reported that RIL reduces wood waste by more than 60% and soil disturbance in roads, landings, and skid trails by almost 50%.[48] However, one barrier to increased use of RIL is illegal logging in the tropics.[49]

The net carbon consequences of timber harvesting for wood products have been debated extensively, with little resolution. Some argue that harvesting increases carbon sequestration by storing carbon in long-term products and sequestering large amounts of carbon in reforestation.[50] Others have determined that the carbon released in harvesting operations substantially exceeds the additional carbon sequestered by reforestation.[51] Both conclusions may be valid in certain circumstances; the consequences probably depend on many factors, such as the products made and the amount and treatment of the carbon left on the site. Thus, whether timber harvesting for wood products could be a carbon offset is uncertain.

Forest Management

Forest management includes a variety of practices. Some are aimed at enhancing growth of the commercially desirable trees. Other plants compete for space, light, water, and nutrients. The undesirable vegetation can be killed chemically (with herbicides), mechanically (with machines or tools), or sometimes by fire (with prescribed burning). The net result, regardless of the tool, is that the carbon from the dead vegetation is released by burning or decomposition. One study found that mechanical thinning increased total carbon storage in dense, young stands, where competition had significantly reduced growth rates; elsewhere, it released carbon by reducing canopy cover and disturbing soils.[52] This is significant because many forest carbon models project carbon sequestration as a fixed percentage of commercial timber volume, not of total biomass on the site. In contrast, using fertilizers can enhance total vegetative growth without disturbing the soil, although many fertilizers are derived from fossil fuels and thus might not result in total net carbon storage. In sum, forestry practices to enhance growth apparently increase carbon sequestration in some circumstances, but not in others. This limits generalizations about potential of forestry practices to offset GHG emissions and raises questions about including growth enhancement for carbon offset projects.

One particular forest management practice that can enhance carbon sequestration is delayed timber harvesting. As noted above, whether harvests for long-term wood products represent a net storage or release of carbon is disputed. However, few dispute that allowing trees to continue to grow will continue to sequester additional carbon. Many of the estimates of the potential carbon benefits from forest management are based on the relatively low cost to induce landowners to delay the harvest of their timber to sequester additional carbon in the short run. However, the lack of harvest planning for many landowners raises questions about additionality from delayed harvesting, as discussed below.

Another significant practice is certified sustainable forestry. The sustainability of forests has long been an issue of environmental concern. In 1994, the Working Group on Criteria and Indicators for the Conservation and Sustainable Management of Temperate and Boreal Forests was formed to develop internationally accepted measures of sustainable forestry.[53] The 12 member countries, representing 90% of the world's temperate and boreal forests, agreed in 1995 on a set of criteria and indicators to measure forest conservation and sustainable management; these are presented in the Santiago Declaration.[54]

Several systems have been developed to certify that forests are being managed sustainably, consistent with the criteria and indicators developed through the Montreal Process and similar processes for other forested regions. The systems include programs from the Forest Stewardship Council (FSC), the Sustainable Forestry Initiative (SFI), and the Programme for the Endorsement of Forest Certification (PEFC). Although the programs differ in many details, they have many elements in common, such as using RIL, reforesting after harvests, protecting water quality, maintaining habitats for rare species, and preserving native peoples' rights. Furthermore, most require long-term planning for forested areas and independent, third-party monitoring to assure that implementation is consistent with the system's requirements. Most systems also require chain-of-custody reporting to assure that wood products claiming to be from sustainable forests actually come from certified forest lands.

Forest certification clearly provides a legally enforceable standard for forest management that could establish a permanent contract for sustainable production. It clearly produces environmental benefits and provides carbon sequestration when compared to unregulated timber harvesting. However, quantification of the carbon offsets that might result from forest certification, reflecting the variation in forest types and traditional forestry practices, poses a challenge.

Avoided Deforestation[55]

As noted above, tropical deforestation is estimated to account for about 17% of global anthropogenic GHG emissions. Thus, avoiding tropical deforestation has great potential to reduce GHG emissions. Since tropical deforestation is currently external to carbon compliance requirements, it could be a substantial source of forest carbon offsets. At the project level, preventing deforestation is a relatively simple, straightforward action—contracts, easements, and other legal instruments can be created to assure that a site is not cleared of its timber. However, avoiding deforestation is particularly prone to leakage—deforestation of another site to provide the desired products or outcomes. This issue is discussed below.

Some of the leakage problem can be addressed by determining offsets for avoided deforestation at the national or regional level; this approach is used for some CDM and JI offsets. Proponents of including aggregate national total for avoided deforestation argue that (a) it lowers compliance costs, since avoiding deforestation can be substantially less expensive than active forestry or other emission reduction or sequestration efforts; and (b) it provides compensation to developing tropical Third World nations. Opponents argue that (a) it would be a disincentive to, and would raise eventual costs for, developing countries to participate in global GHG emission reduction efforts; (b) it would benefit the political elite of developing nations, while their indigenous peoples would be further disenfranchised; and (c) it would delay technological development and implementation to reduce GHG emissions in the industries that cause the emissions.[56]

POTENTIAL DRAWBACKS OF FORESTRY-RELATED PROJECTS

Although forestry-related projects may offer considerable opportunities to mitigate climate change, several issues with offsets generally and with forestry projects in particular have generated controversy. The primary concern is the integrity and credibility of offsets generated by forestry activities. To be credible, a forestry offset should provide a net CO_2 reduction or sequestration equal to an emission reduction from a direct emission source, such as a smokestack or exhaust pipe. This issue is critical, particularly if the offsets are to be used in an emissions trading program.

Implementing this objective imposes challenges for all offset types, but forest offsets generally present more hurdles than other projects. To generate credible offsets, projects must be *additional* to what would have occurred without the incentive supplied by the carbon market; they must be *verifiable* (i.e., measurable and enforceable); they must control or adjust for *leakage*; and they must address the issue of *permanence*. *Forward crediting* is proposed by some to accommodate the long period of carbon accumulation in forests, but others are concerned about assuring payments only for actual carbon sequestration. These issues are discussed below.

Additionality

Additionality is a significant factor in determining offset integrity. Indeed, if a project is not *additional*, it cannot qualify as an offset in a compliance market. Additionality means that the offset project is an activity beyond what would have occurred under a business-as-usual scenario. In other words, in the case of a forestry project, would the sequestration have happened anyway?

A test of additionality would examine whether the offset project would have gone forward in the absence of the forest carbon market. For instance, does the activity represent a common practice or conform to an industry standard? Is the forestry project required under other federal, state, or local laws? Would the sequestration project generate financial gain (i.e., be profitable) due to revenues from outside the offset market?[57] For example, in the United States and Canada, reforestation following a timber harvest would generally not qualify as an offset, because most states and provinces require reforestation. Similarly, disposal of sawmill waste by burning to produce energy, and displace the use of fossil fuel, would not qualify as an offset, because all U.S. sawmills burn their waste (except for what is sold for paper production) for energy.

Additionality is at the crux of an offset's integrity, but applying the additionality criterion may present practical challenges. Assessing a project's additionality may involve some degree of subjectivity, which may lead to inconsistent additionality determinations. For instance, it may be impossible to accurately determine "what would have happened anyway" for some projects. Data on historic deforestation are sketchy, at best, making it difficult to assess whether an avoided deforestation program would be additional. In addition, offsets from forest management via delayed timber harvests might be difficult

Forest Carbon Markets: Potential and Drawbacks

to document as additional, since many landowners do not have explicit plans for the exact timing of future harvests.

Verifiability

The forest carbon sequestration must be real and measurable. That is, the forestry project—afforestation, avoided deforestation, etc.—must actually occur and have a quantifiable amount of carbon sequestered. Meeting these objectives requires measurement, monitoring, and enforcement.[58]

Measurement

Measuring forest carbon sequestration can be problematic. Various approaches have been taken, including tables, models, and protocols for estimating carbon sequestration by various practices in different locales. A common limitation is that many estimators use commercial timber volume as the basis for carbon stored, but the relationship between commercial volume and carbon sequestered might not be linear. For example, thinning is a forestry practice intended to increase commercial volume by concentrating the same total growth on fewer commercial stems.[59] Total growth also varies widely from site to site, depending on a host of localized physical and environmental factors. Thus, many observers recommend, and some existing carbon markets require, field measurements to adjust the estimated carbon storage to on-the-ground reality.[60] One problem is that field measurements are expensive and subject to sampling error.

Monitoring

To verify that sequestration projects are meeting their stated level of sequestration, some level of monitoring is required. For enforceable contracts, periodic monitoring is essential to assure that the contract is fulfilled. For agreements larger than projects, such as avoided deforestation for an entire landholding or country, periodic monitoring becomes more important and more difficult. Remote sensing (e.g., satellite imagery) and field sampling are common practices for monitoring large-scale changes, but both are expensive and both are subject to sampling and other possible errors. The two practices are commonly used together, with field sampling to assure the on-the-ground accuracy of remotely sensed data.

Enforcement

Often, the reality of a project is assured through an enforceable contract, such as an easement attached to the forested property to require continued forest cover. Many existing forest carbon markets require third-party verification for forest carbon credits. For some markets and practices, assurance of sustainable forest management can be obtained through forest certification. A number of organizations, such as the Forest Stewardship Council (FSC), the Programme for the Endorsement of Forest Certification (PEFC), and the Sustainable Forestry Initiative (SFI), have set standards and rely on independent third parties for certification of sustainable forest management.

Leakage

Leakage "occurs when economic activity is shifted as a result of the emission control regulation and, as a result, emission abatement achieved in one location that is subject to emission control regulation is [diminished] by increased emissions in unregulated locations."[61] In the context of forestry-related offsets, the opportunity for leakage exists on two fronts: emissions leakage and product leakage.

Emissions Leakage

Compared to other offset types, forestry projects, particularly those that sequester carbon by curbing logging, likely present the greatest risk of leakage.[62] For example, if large landowners or countries agree to preserve their forests, wood processors might simply shift their harvests to neighboring landowners or countries. As a result, the total harvest (total deforestation) might be unchanged, even though particular landowners or countries might have avoided deforestation of their forests. The only recognized solution is for a majority of landowners or countries to agree to participate in a program to reduce deforestation.[63]

Product Leakage

Forest products face another type of leakage: product leakage. Producing long-term wood products, such as lumber and plywood, uses much less energy—and thus emits fewer GHGs—than comparable quantities of alternative products used to build homes and other structures, such as concrete

Forest Carbon Markets: Potential and Drawbacks

and masonry walls and steel and aluminum framing.[64] Thus, avoided deforestation might lead builders to replace wood with other more energy-intensive, GHG-emitting products. The net carbon consequences of such a shift are unclear.

Permanence

For forestry projects, one concern is that the projected sequestration will be halted or reversed. Forest offset projects are typically expected to generate offsets (via sequestration) for decades. Some are concerned that the emission offsets will be subsequently negated by human activity (e.g., change in land use) or a natural occurrence (e.g., forest fire, disease, or pestilence).

Permanence is especially problematic for forests, because forests are composed of living organisms—they are born (seeds germinate), they grow, and eventually they die. This life cycle varies widely, depending on the tree species; for example, aspen and Southern yellow pines rarely grow older than 200 years, while Douglas-fir and many live oak species commonly grow for more than 1,000 years, and bristlecone pines can live for more than 4,000 years. Nevertheless, trees die eventually, and their carbon is converted to wood products, contributed to the soil, or sent into the atmosphere.

Permanence can be achieved for forest projects by providing for mitigation or a buffer against natural losses. An analysis of four particular carbon offset market standards found that one required a 10% buffer (i.e., only 90% of the estimated carbon offset could be sold); another required a 30% buffer, while the other two used variable buffers (from 5% to 60%) depending on an assessment of the risk of the project.[65] For landowners or countries, carbon sequestration permanence can be achieved through sustainable forestry practices, with reforestation following any and all carbon removals to assure stable or increasing carbon storage.

An alternative for achieving permanence is to use regional or national accounting, such that a reversal on one project or site is balanced by additional sequestration from other projects or sites. This relies on accurate measurement and monitoring to assure that payments are for *net* carbon sequestration.

Forward Crediting

Many biological sequestration projects, such as afforestation or reforestation, present a unique challenge because of the significant time gap between the initial project activity (e.g., planting trees) and the actual carbon sequestration. Although the project may generate considerable offsets in aggregate, the offsets are produced gradually, over the course of many years or decades. Tree growth patterns follow a traditional S-shape, with slow growth in the early years, accelerating for many years to decades, before tapering off to an eventual maximum. The age at which growth has reached its maximum varies widely among species—as short as 100 years for short-lived species (e.g., aspen and Southern pines), and more than 1,000 years for long-lived species (e.g., western hemlock and Douglas-fir). However, even old-growth forests that have little or no additional tree growth apparently continue to sequester carbon in the soils.[66]

This aspect of sequestration projects raises the question of how sequestration offsets should be distributed. Should they be allotted as they are produced—on an annual basis—or should they be allotted up front in an aggregate sum, based on expected future sequestration? The latter option is referred to as forward crediting.

Forward crediting entails risk, because there is some uncertainty about whether the offsets will actually be realized. This risk can be addressed through discounting, much as the permanence risk is addressed through buffers: by retaining a percentage of the offsets that are expected over the course of the project to accommodate unexpected events (e.g., slower vegetative growth than anticipated). Whether such discounting is necessary for forest carbon offsets, and if so how much the discount should be, are as yet undetermined.

End Notes

[1] Gordon B. Bonan, "Forests and Climate Change: Forcings, Feedbacks, and the Climate Benefits of Forests," *Science*, v. 320 (2008): 1444-1449.

[2] Other greenhouse gases include methane (CH4), nitrous oxide (N_2O), hydrofluorocarbons (HFCs), perfluorocarbons (PFCs), and sulfur hexafluoride (SF_6). In general, emissions of these gases are measured in carbon-equivalents or CO_2 equivalents.

[3] See CRS Report RL34436, *The Role of Offsets in a Greenhouse Gas Emissions Cap-and-Trade Program: Potential Benefits and Concerns*, by Jonathan L. Ramseur.

[4] Because offset projects can involve various GHGs, they are quantified and described with a standard form of measure, usually metric tons (tonnes) of CO_2-equivalents ($mtCO_2$-e).

Forest Carbon Markets: Potential and Drawbacks 75

[5] See CRS Report RL34436, *The Role of Offsets in a Greenhouse Gas Emissions Cap-and-Trade Program: Potential Benefits and Concerns*, by Jonathan L. Ramseur.

[6] See CRS Report R40236, *Estimates of Carbon Mitigation Potential from Agricultural and Forestry Activities*, by Renée Johnson, Jonathan L. Ramseur, and Ross W. Gorte.

[7] See CRS Report RL33826, *Climate Change: The Kyoto Protocol, Bali "Action Plan," and International Actions*, by Jane A. Leggett.

[8] See UNFCCC, Conference of the Parties, Seventh Session—"the Marrakesh Accords"—2001, Decision 11.

[9] Intergovernmental Panel on Climate Change, *Climate Change 2007: Mitigation. Contribution of Working Group III to the Fourth Assessment Report* (2007), p. 543.

[10] United Nations Environment Programme, *UNEP Risoe CDM/JI Pipeline Analysis and Database*, May 1, 2010, http://cdmpipeline.org/.

[11] United Nations Environment Programme, *UNEP Risoe CDM/JI Pipeline Analysis and Database*, May 1, 2010, http://cdmpipeline.org/.

[12] See CRS Report RS22806, *The Bali Agreements and Forests*, by Ross W. Gorte and Pervaze A. Sheikh.

[13] UNFCCC, *Decision -/CP.13—Bali Action Plan*, at http://unfccc.int/files/meetings/cop_13/application/pdf/ cp_bali_action.pdf.

[14] UNFCCC, *Decision -/CP.13—Reducing Emissions From Deforestation in Developing Countries: Approaches to Stimulate Action*, at http://unfccc.int/files/meetings/cop_13/application/pdf/cp_redd.pdf.

[15] See CRS Report RL34150, *Climate Change and the EU Emissions Trading Scheme (ETS): Kyoto and Beyond*, by Larry Parker.

[16] See European Union Directive 2004/101/EC (October 27, 2004); Kyoto Protocol, Decision 17/CP.7 (November 2001).

[17] The 10 states are Connecticut, Delaware, Maine, Massachusetts, New Hampshire, New Jersey, New York, Pennsylvania, Rhode Island, and Vermont. Also participating are the District of Columbia, the Canadian province of New Brunswick, and "Eastern Canadian Provinces." See http://www.rggi.org/home.

[18] http://www.rggi.org/offsets.

[19] http://rggi.org/docs/mou_final_12_20_05.pdf.

[20] Participants are the states of Arizona, California, Montana, New Mexico, Oregon, Utah, and Washington, and the Canadian provinces of British Columbia, Manitoba, Ontario, and Quebec. Observers include the states of Alaska, Colorado, Idaho, Kansas, Nevada, and Wyoming, the Canadian provinces of Saskatchewan and Yukon Territory, and the Mexican border states of Baja California, Chihuahua, Coahuila, Nuevo León, Sonora, and Tamaulipas. For the text of the agreement, see http://www.westernclimateinitiative.org/.

[21] Western Climate Initiative, *Design Recommendations* (Sept. 23, 2008), *http://www.weste rnclimateinitiative.org/the-wci-cap-and-trade-program/design-recommendations*.

[22] Participants are the states of Illinois, Iowa, Kansas, Michigan, Minnesota, and Wisconsin, and the Canadian province of Manitoba. Observers include Indiana, Ohio, and South Dakota, and the Canadian province of Ontario (which is also a participant in the WCI). The text of the accord is available at http://www.midwesterngovernors.org/publications.htm.

[23] For more information see CRS Report RL33812, *Climate Change: Action by States to Address Greenhouse Gas Emissions*, by Jonathan L. Ramseur.

[24] For relevant CRS reports on these bills and issues, visit the CRS website.

[25] See CRS Report RL34436, *The Role of Offsets in a Greenhouse Gas Emissions Cap-and-Trade Program: Potential Benefits and Concerns*, by Jonathan L. Ramseur.

[26] Katherine Hamilton, Ricardo Bayon, Guy Turner, and Douglas Higgins, *State of the Voluntary Carbon Markets 2007: Picking Up Steam* (Washington, DC: Ecosystem Marketplace and New Carbon Finance, 2007).

[27] Katherine Hamilton, Milo Sjardin, and Alison Shapiro, and Thomas Marcello, *Fortifying the Foundation: State of the Voluntary Carbon Markets 2009*, Ecosystem Marketplace and New

Carbon Finance, May 20, 2009, http://www.forest-trends.org/documents/files/doc_2343.pdf.

[28] See CRS Report RL34241, *Voluntary Carbon Offsets: Overview and Assessment*, by Jonathan L. Ramseur.

[29] Karan Capoor and Philippe Ambrosi, *State and Trends of the Carbon Market 2009*. The World Bank, Washington, DC, May 2009, http://wbcarbonfinance.org/docs/State___Trends_of_the_Carbon_Market_2009-FINAL_26_May09.pdf.

[30] U.S. Environmental Protection Agency, *Inventory of U.S. Greenhouse Gas Emissions and Sinks: 1990-2008*, U.S. EPA # 430-R-10-006, Washington, DC, April 2010, http://epa.gov/climatechange/emissions/usinventoryreport.html.

[31] Haymarket Publications, ENDS Carbon Offsets: The Independent Guide to the Voluntary Carbon Market, 2010, http://www.endscarbonoffsets.com/.

[32] *ENDS Carbon Offsets.*

[33] Studies have analyzed offset sellers and provided recommendations; see, for example, Anja Kollmuss, Helge Zink, and Clifford Polycarp, *Making Sense of the Voluntary Carbon Market: A Comparison of Carbon Offset Standards*, WWF Germany (Stockholm Environment Institute and Tricorona, March 2008), http://www.globalcarbonproject.org/global/pdf/WWF_2008_A%20comparison%20of%20C%20offset%20Standards.pdf; and Clean Air-Cool Planet, *A Consumer's Guide to Retail Carbon Offset Providers* (December 2006), prepared by Trexler Climate + Energy Services, http://www.aceee.org/consumerguide/CleanCool_06Report.pdf.

[34] See http://www.chicagoclimatex.com/content.jsf?id=821.

[35] See, for example, Kollmuss, Zink, and Polycarp, *Making Sense of the Voluntary Carbon Market*.

[36] See Pew Center on Climate Change, *Greenhouse Gas Reporting and Disclosure: Key Elements of a Prospective U.S. Program*, In Brief (Number 3), at http://www.pewclimate.org/docUploads/policy_inbrief_ghg.pdf.

[37] See http://www.climateregistry.org/tools/protocols/project-protocols/forests.html.

[38] The nine states that are not members are Alaska, Arkansas, Indiana, Louisiana, Mississippi, Nebraska, North Dakota, South Dakota, and Texas.

[39] See http://www.theclimateregistry.org/principles.html.

[40] See CRS Report RL34042, *Provisions Supporting Ecosystem Services Markets in U.S. Farm Bill Legislation*, by Renée Johnson.

[41] U.S. Environmental Protection Agency, Office of Atmospheric Programs, *Greenhouse Gas Mitigation Potential in U.S. Forestry and Agriculture*, EPA 430-R-05-006 (Washington, DC: November 2005), p. 4-21.

[42] EPA, *Inventory of U.S. Greenhouse Gas Emissions and Sinks: 1990-2008*.

[43] Intergovernmental Panel on Climate Change, "Summary for Policymakers," *Climate Change 2007: The Physical Science Basis—Contribution of Working Group I to the Fourth Assessment Report of the Intergovernmental Panel on Climate Change*, p. 3, http://www.ipcc-wg1.unibe.ch/publications/wg1-ar4/wg1-ar4.html.

[44] Intergovernmental Panel on Climate Change, "Table 1: Global Carbon Stocks in Vegetation and Carbon Pools Down to a Depth of 1 m [meter]," *IPCC Special Report on Land Use, Land-Use Change and Forestry: Summary for Policymakers* (2000), *http://www.ipcc.ch/ipccreports/sres/land_use/003.htm*.

[45] Kenneth E. Skog and Geraldine A. Nicholson, "Carbon Sequestration in Wood and Paper Products," in *The Impact of Climate Change on America's Forests: A Technical Document Supporting the 2001 USDA Forest Service RPA Assessment* (Linda Joyce and Richard Birdsey, tech. eds.), Gen. Tech. Rept. RMRS-GTR-59 (Ft. Collins, CO: USDA Forest Service, 2000), pp. 79-88.

[46] Skog and Nicholson, "Carbon Sequestration in Wood and Paper Products."

[47] See Dennis P. Dykstra, *Reduced Impact Logging: Concepts and Issues*, FAO Corporate Document Repository, at http://www.fao.org/docrep/005/ac805e/ac805e04.htm.

Forest Carbon Markets: Potential and Drawbacks

[48] Tropical Forest Foundation, "Reduced Impact Logging," at *http://www.tropica lforestfoundation.org/ril.html*.

[49] See CRS Report RL33932, *Illegal Logging: Background and Issues*, by Pervaze A. Sheikh. See also Patrick B. Durst and Thomas Enters, "Illegal Logging and the Adoption of Reduced Impact Logging," paper presented at *Forest Law Enforcement and Governance: East Asia Regional Ministerial Conference* (Denpasar, Indonesia: September 11-13, 2001), at http://wbla0018.worldbank.org/eap/eap.naf/Attachments/FLEG_S6-5/$File/6+5+Durst+FAO.pdf.

[50] John Perez-Garcia, Chadwick D. Oliver, and Bruce R. Lippke, "How Forests Can Help Reduce Carbon Dioxide Emissions to the Atmosphere," in U.S. House Resources Subcommittee on Forests and Forest Health, *Hearing on H.Con.Res. 151*, September 18, 1997 (Washington, DC: GPO, 1998), Serial No. 105-61, pp. 46-68.

[51] Mark E. Harmon, William K. Ferrell, and Jerry F. Franklin, "Effects on Carbon Storage of Conversion of Old-Growth Forests to Young Forests," *Science*, v. 247 (Feb. 9, 1990): 699-702; and Peter M. Vitousek, "Can Planted Forests Counteract Increasing Atmospheric Carbon Dioxide?" *Journal of Environmental Quality*, v. 20 (Apr.-June 1991): pp. 348-354.

[52] Paul Schroeder, "Can Intensive Management Increase Carbon Storage in Forests?" *Environmental Management*, v. 15, no. 4 (1991): pp. 475-481.

[53] See http://www.rinya.maff.go.jp/mpci/.

[54] See http://www.rinya.maff.go.jp/mpci/rep-pub/1995/santiago_e.html. The Montreal Process excludes the forests of Europe (except for the Russian Federation), which have been addressed separately, under the Helsinki or Pan-European Process.

[55] See CRS Report R41144, *Deforestation and Climate Change*, by Ross W. Gorte and Pervaze A. Sheikh.

[56] See CRS Report RL34436, *The Role of Offsets in a Greenhouse Gas Emissions Cap-and-Trade Program: Potential Benefits and Concerns*, by Jonathan L. Ramseur.

[57] See World Resources Institute, *The Greenhouse Gas Protocol for Project Accounting* (December 2005), at http://www.ghgprotocol.org.

[58] See CRS Report RS22964, *Measuring and Monitoring Carbon in the Agricultural and Forestry Sectors*, by Ross W. Gorte and Renée Johnson.

[59] See David M. Smith, Bruce C. Larson, Matthew J. Kelty, and P. Mark S. Ashton, *The Practice of Silviculture: Applied Forest Ecology*, 9th ed. (New York, NY: John Wiley & Sons, Inc., 1997).

[60] See, for example, The Wilderness Society, Ecology and Economics Research Department, *Measuring Forest Carbon: Strengths and Weaknesses of Available Tools*, Science & Policy Brief, No. 1 (Washington, DC: April 2008).

[61] U.S. Environmental Protection Agency, Office of Air and Radiation, *Tools of the Trade: A Guide To Designing and Operating a Cap and Trade Program For Pollution Control*, EPA430-B-03-002 (June 2003), Glossary.

[62] Nicholas Institute for Environmental Policy Solutions, *Harnessing Farms and Forests in the Low-Carbon Economy: How to Create, Measure, and Verify Greenhouse Gas Offsets*, Zach Wiley and Bill Chameides, eds. (Durham, ND: Duke Univ. Press, 2007), pp. 18-19.

[63] Brian Murray and Lydia Olander, *A Core Participation Requirement for Creation of a REDD Market*, Nicholas Institute for Environmental Policy Solutions, Short Policy Brief (Durham, NC: Duke Univ. Press, May 2008).

[64] Jim Bowyer, Steve Bratkovich, Alison Lindberg, and Kathryn Fernholz, *Wood Products and Carbon Protocols: Carbon Storage and Low Energy Intensity Should Be Considered* (Dovetail Partners, Inc., April 28, 2008).

[65] Eduard Merger and Alwyn Williams, *Comparison of Carbon Offset Standards for Climate Forestation Projects Participating in the Voluntary Carbon Market: A Comparison of Climate, Community & Biodiversity Standard (CCBS), CarbonFix Standard (CFS), Plan Vivo Systems and Standard, and AFOLU Voluntary Carbon Standard (VCS)* (Christchurch, New Zealand: Univ. of Canterbury, May 2008).

[66] See, for example, Mark E. Harmon, William K. Ferrell, and Jerry F. Franklin, "Effects on Carbon Storage of Conversion of Old-Growth Forests to Young Forests," *Science*, v. 247 (February 9, 1990): pp. 699-702.

In: Energy Policies and Issues
Editors: Edgar R. Thompson

ISBN: 978-1-61122-685-0
© 2011 Nova Science Publishers, Inc.

Chapter 5

ANAEROBIC DIGESTION: GREENHOUSE GAS EMISSION REDUCTION AND ENERGY GENERATION

Kelsi S. Bracmort

SUMMARY

Anaerobic digestion technology may help to address two congressional concerns that have some measure of interdependence: development of clean energy sources and reduction of greenhouse gas emissions. Anaerobic digestion technology breaks down a feedstock—usually manure from livestock operations—to produce a variety of outputs including methane. An anaerobic digestion system may reduce greenhouse gas emissions because it captures the methane from manure that might otherwise be released into the atmosphere as a potent greenhouse gas. The technology may contribute to the development of clean energy because the captured methane can be used as an energy source to produce heat or generate electricity.

Anaerobic digestion technology has been implemented sparingly, with 151 anaerobic digestion systems operating nationwide. Some barriers to adoption include high capital costs, questions about reliability, and varying payment rates for the electricity generated by anaerobic digestion systems. Two sources of federal financial assistance that may make the technology more attractive are the Section 9007 Rural Energy for America Program of the

Food, Conservation, and Energy Act of 2008 (2008 farm bill, P.L. 110-246), and the Renewable Electricity Production Tax Credit (26 U.S.C. §45).

Congress could decide to encourage development and use of the technology by (1) identifying the primary technology benefit, so as to determine whether it should be pursued in the framework of greenhouse gas emission reduction or clean energy development; (2) determining if the captured methane will count as a carbon offset; and (3) considering additional financing options for the technology.

This chapter provides information on anaerobic digestion systems, technology adoption, challenges to widespread implementation, and policy interventions that could affect adoption of the technology.

INTRODUCTION

An anaerobic digestion system (AD system) captures the methane that may otherwise be released from conventional manure handling methods, and has the potential to reduce greenhouse gas emissions and produce clean energy. Absent such technology, confined animal feeding operations typically collect and store manure (e.g., in a waste storage facility) under anaerobic conditions, which produces the potent greenhouse gas methane. The methane is released into the atmosphere as the manure decomposes while being stored. Livestock producers handle large quantities of manure on a daily basis that emit methane.[1] Some estimate that livestock operations produce more than a billion tons of manure yearly[2] and that 0.7% of total U.S. methane emissions are from managed manure.[3] Through methane capture, anaerobic digestion has the potential to reduce these emissions.

In addition, anaerobic digestion of manure produces biogas—a combination of methane, carbon dioxide, and trace amounts of other gases that can be used for renewable energy purposes or flared.[4] Recent legislation pertaining to agricultural sources of renewable energy has focused primarily on corn-based ethanol and cellulosic ethanol for liquid fuel purposes, and not biogas.[5] The economic environment is not currently favorable to profit from the investment required to compress biogas[6] produced from an AD system into a liquid fuel. There are, however, several successful cases where an engine-generator set has been used to generate electricity from the biogas or the biogas is burned in a boiler to produce heat. Biogas from an AD system could be used to assist livestock producers in an effort to have an energy self-sufficient operation as well as, potentially, to sell electricity to the local utility.

There are 151 AD systems operating nationally (see Figure 1). Some factors that may be responsible for the low technology adoption rates are high capital costs, reliability concerns, and payment rates for the electricity generated. Congress may consider encouraging increased adoption of the technology by (1) identifying the primary technology benefit, so as to determine whether AD should be pursued in the framework of greenhouse gas emission reduction or clean energy development; (2) determining if the captured methane will count as a carbon offset; and (3) considering additional financing options for the technology. Moreover, Congress may receive insight on collaborative techniques by monitoring the first public-private partnership agreement between the U.S. Department of Agriculture and the Innovation Center for U.S. Dairy to reduce greenhouse gas emissions from dairy operations by 25% by 2020.[7] One goal of the agreement is to "accelerate and streamline the process for adopting anaerobic digesters by the United States dairy farm operators through various USDA programs."[8]

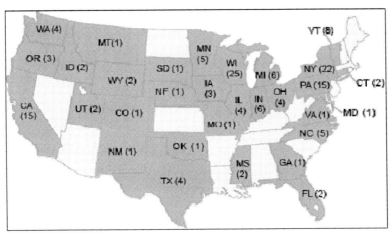

Source: Environmental Protection Agency, 2010. The AgSTAR Program. http://www.epa.gov/agstar/ accomplish.html.

Notes: The AgSTAR Program is a voluntary effort jointly sponsored by the U.S. Environmental Protection Agency, the U.S. Department of Agriculture, and the U.S. Department of Energy. The program encourages biogas capture and utilization at animal feeding operations that manage manures as liquids and slurries.

Figure 1. Operational Anaerobic Digesters

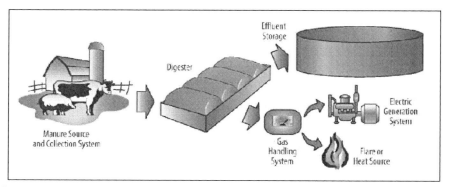

Source: U.S. EPA, The AgSTAR Program.

Figure 2. Anaerobic Digestion System Schematic

This chapter provides information on AD systems, technology adoption, and challenges to widespread technology implementation, and explores the issues facing Congress concerning adoption of the technology.

WHAT IS AN ANAEROBIC DIGESTION SYSTEM?

Most manure management systems used on livestock operations store the manure in an open facility, allowing the manure to decompose naturally, which releases the potent greenhouse gas methane into the atmosphere. By contrast, an AD system feeds manure into a digester that breaks it down in a closed facility in the absence of oxygen (see Figure 2). The digested feedstock[9] is contained for a period of time[10] as anaerobic bacteria decompose the manure to produce several outputs, including biogas, liquid effluent, and dry matter. The captured biogas is flared (see footnote 4) or used for energy. The liquid effluent may be applied to the land as a fertilizer. The digested dry matter may be sold as a soil amendment product or used for animal bedding. AD systems have other benefits (e.g., odor reduction) that may curb negative impacts of livestock operations, including environmental pollution.[11]

An AD system is designed and constructed to suit the needs of an individual livestock operation and is typically selected based on the total solids (TS) content[12] of the manure and the manure handling system (see **Figure 3**). Other criteria taken into consideration when building an AD system include the feedstock quantity, feedstock quality, feedstock availability, feedstock handling, demand for effluent, use of captured biogas, and transportation logistics (e.g., feedstock may be transported to an AD system if it is not available on-site, or effluent transported to a receiving entity if not used on-site).

AD systems in the United States are in use on dairy cow, swine, and poultry operations. More than 80% of the operating AD systems are located on dairy cow operations. Some argue that less complex AD systems could be constructed on dairy cow operations at a lower cost and that the manure could be easily transported to the AD system, thus making them more economically appealing. Others contend that fewer AD systems are installed on swine operations because many swine operations currently store liquid manure in pits beneath the livestock; the producer would need to redesign the swine operation to incorporate an AD system. Installation of an AD system on a swine operation may also be more expensive if a storage facility must be constructed to contain the digested feedstock. Some assert that AD systems are not a favorable addition to a poultry operation partly because the litter is dry and may require more resources for transport to an AD system and additional inputs to digest.

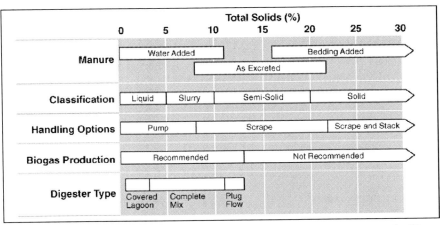

Source: U.S. Environmental Protection Agency, *Managing Manure with Biogas Recovery Systems: Improved Performance at Competitive Costs*, EPA-430-F-02-004, 2002, http://www.epa.gov/agstar/pdf/manage.pdf.

Figure 3. Manure Characteristics and Handling Systems for Specific Types of Anaerobic Digestion Systems

THREE COMMON AD SYSTEM TYPES FOUND IN THE UNITED STATES

Covered lagoon AD system:

- Usually an earthen structure containing manure affixed with a flexible geosynthetic cover (e.g., high density polyethylene).
- Typically operated at ambient temperature.
- Biogas production may occur seasonally when weather is warmer.
- Ideal for manure with 0.5%-2% TS content.
- Time required to treat manure ranges from approximately 30 to 60 days.
- Low capital costs.

Plug flow AD system (see **Figure 4**):

- Usually a rectangular concrete tank affixed with a flexible geosynthetic cover.
- Digestion occurs in a plug fashion where the digested manure exits the system as raw manure enters the system.
- Heated structure.
- Ideal for manure with 11%-13% TS content.
- Time required to treat manure ranges from approximately 18 to 20 days.

Complete mix AD system (see **Figure 5**):

- Usually a round concrete or steel tank.
- Heated structure.
- Capable of digesting a range of feedstock with varying total solids content.
- Ideal for manure with 3%-10% TS content.
- Time required to treat manure ranges from approximately 5 to 20 days.
- High capital costs.

Anaerobic Digestion: Greenhouse Gas Emission Reduction and... 85

Source: EPA, The AgSTAR Program.

Figure 4. Plug Flow AD System

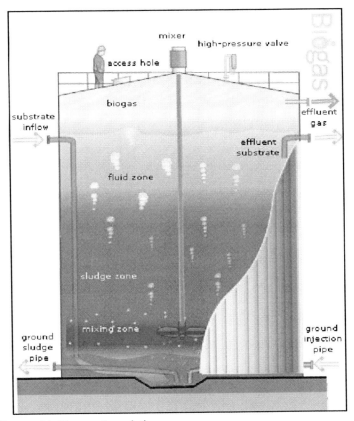

Source: Renewable Energy Association.

Figure 5. Complete Mix AD System Schematic

CHARACTERISTICS OF ANAEROBIC DIGESTION SYSTEMS

Methane Capture

Methane (CH_4) is one of the primary greenhouse gases associated with the agricultural sector.[13] The odorless, colorless, flammable gas is potent because it is 21 times more effective at trapping heat in the atmosphere than carbon dioxide (CO_2) over a 100-year timeframe.[14] In other words, it takes 21 tons of CO_2 to equal the effect of 1 ton of CH4. Methane has a relatively short atmospheric lifetime (approximately 12 years) when compared to the atmospheric lifetime for carbon dioxide, which has a half-life of roughly 100 years; thus some argue that efforts to capture methane from anthropogenic sources may provide near-term climate change abatement.

Major sources of methane emissions from animal agriculture are enteric fermentation[15] and manure management (see **Table 1**). While enteric fermentation emissions are much larger than manure management emissions, they are also much more difficult (nearly impossible) to control. Emission factors[16] affiliated with methane released from enteric fermentation, and conversion factors[17] affiliated with methane released from a manure management system, are used to estimate overall methane emissions from animal agriculture. Estimation incorporates a multi-step process that takes into account livestock population data, waste characteristics, waste management system data, and other variables.

Table 1. Methane Emissions from Animal Agriculture ($TgCO_2e$)

Source	2006	2007	2008
Enteric fermentation	139.0	141.2	140.8
Manure management	42.3	45.9	45.0

Source: Environmental Protection Agency, 2010 U.S. Greenhouse Gas Inventory Report.

Notes: Select values obtained from EPA, 2010 U.S. Greenhouse Gas Inventory Report, Table 6-1. A teragram (Tg) is equivalent to 1 trillion grams. A Tg CO_2e (teragram of carbon dioxide equivalent) is a principal unit of measurement across greenhouse gases. Agricultural activities and livestock emit an assortment of greenhouse gases in various quantities given numerous factors. CO_2e is used to compare greenhouse gases emitted from different sources on the same basis.

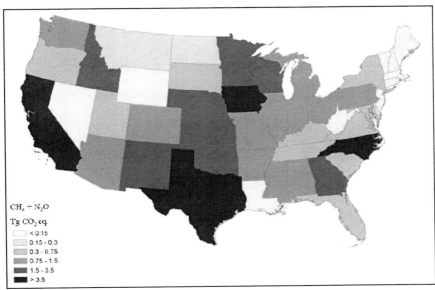

Source: USDA, U.S. Agriculture and Forestry Greenhouse Gas Inventory: 1990-2005.

Figure 6. Greenhouse Gas Emissions (Methane and Nitrous Oxide) from Managed Waste in 2005

Table 2. Methane Emissions from Manure Management (TgCO₂e)

Animal Type	2006	2007	2008
Swine	18.5	20.1	19.6
Dairy cattle	17.5	19.5	19.4
Poultry	2.7	2.7	2.6
Beef cattle	2.6	2.6	2.5
Horses	0.9	0.9	0.8
Sheep	0.1	0.1	0.1
Goats	+	+	+

Source: Environmental Protection Agency, 2010 U.S. Greenhouse Gas Inventory Report.

Notes: Select values obtained from EPA, 2010 U.S. Greenhouse Gas Inventory Report, Table 6-6. The + symbol denotes a value that does not exceed 0.05 Tg CO_2e. A Tg CO_2e (teragram of carbon dioxide equivalent) is a principal unit of measurement across greenhouse gases. Agricultural activities and livestock emit an assortment of greenhouse gases in various quantities given numerous factors. CO_2e is used to compare greenhouse gases emitted from different sources on the same basis.

Capturing methane with an AD system is beneficial because it reduces emissions of a harmful greenhouse gas from an agricultural source of methane: managed manure (e.g., manure stored in pit storage, an anaerobic lagoon, or a storage facility).[18] Swine and dairy cattle are the two dominant livestock emitters of methane for managed manure (see **Table 2**). Emissions from managed manure vary on a statewide basis depending on the livestock population and the manure handling systems in place (see **Figure 6**).

Captured methane may qualify as a carbon offset because the methane would no longer be released directly into the atmosphere. Carbon offsets[19] are a facet of the climate change cap-and-trade program debate currently underway in the 111th Congress. Accurate quantification and verification of the methane captured from an AD system requires robust data, observed or inferred, to ensure that actual reductions are occurring as projected.

Biogas Quality and Use

Another AD system benefit is the production of biogas, which can be used as a renewable energy source. Biogas consists of 60%-70% methane, 30%-40% carbon dioxide, and trace amounts of other gases (e.g., hydrogen sulfide, ammonia, hydrogen, nitrogen gas, carbon monoxide). Biogas can be explosive if exposed to air, depending on the concentration of methane in a confined space. The quality (i.e., heat value) and amount of biogas produced varies based on the hydraulic retention time of the AD system, the manure total solids content, and temperature.

Biogas can be used to produce heat or generate electricity. The biogas may be burned in a boiler for space heating or water heating on-site. Another option is to use an engine-generator set to create electricity from the biogas. Biogas that is upgraded to pipeline quality[20] may be sold to a natural gas utility. Typically a producer will decide on only one use for the biogas—either generating electricity or producing heat—due to the expense associated with energy generation and boiler equipment. Few choose to sell the biogas to a natural gas utility.[21]

If electricity is generated from the captured biogas, it may be sold to a utility in addition to its on-site use.[22] A rule of thumb is that manure from approximately five Holstein milking cows supplies fuel for 1 kilowatt capacity.[23] Sales to a utility require a contractual agreement between the producer and the local utility provider that typically outlines safety, reliability, and performance standards. Additionally, any federal and state environmental

Anaerobic Digestion: Greenhouse Gas Emission Reduction and...   89

requirements must be met (e.g., AD system generators may have to meet Best Available Control Technology[24] requirements). Net metering,[25] a preferred form of billing for many renewable electricity generators, is an option for producers selling the electricity generated to electric utilities in 43 states.[26]

Biogas may be used as a fuel if it contains at a minimum a 50% concentration of methane (CH_4).[27] The biogas must be cleaned, upgraded, and compressed if it is to be used in a mobile engine. Cleaning biogas removes hydrogen sulfide. Removing any moisture and carbon dioxide upgrades the biogas and increases the British thermal unit (Btu) value.[28] With an energy content of 600 Btu/ft^3 for biogas with approximately a 60% methane concentration, biogas is a low-Btu fuel compared to other fuels (see **Table 3**). A high-Btu fuel is necessary for energy applications requiring greater amounts of power.

Biogas is flared if not used for energy purposes. Flaring the biogas destroys the methane and yields the greenhouse gas carbon dioxide (CO_2) and water.[29] Carbon dioxide has a longer atmospheric lifetime (~100 years) and is less effective at trapping heat in the atmosphere when compared to methane, which has an approximate atmospheric lifetime of 12 years. Some view the release of the carbon dioxide due to biogas flaring as more environmentally acceptable than releasing unused biogas into the atmosphere.[30] Environmental impacts of flaring methane require further investigation to determine flare efficiency under varying wind speeds and various biogas compositions.

Table 3. Energy Content for Select Fuels

Fuel	Energy Content
Biogas[a]	600 Btu/ft^3
Natural gas	1,000 Btu/ft^3
Propane	92,000 Btu/gallon
Diesel fuel	138,000 Btu/gallon
Coal	25,000,000 Btu/ton

Source: James C. Barker. *Methane Fuel Gas from Livestock Wastes: A Summary.* North Carolina State University Cooperative Extension Service, EBAE 071-80, 2001.

a. Assumes a 60% methane concentration.

U.S. Adoption of Anaerobic Digestion Technology

Federal funding (discussed in the following section) has supported the installation of 151 AD systems nationwide, operating with a total energy production of approximately 374,000 megawatt-hours (MWh) in 2009.[31] These AD systems restricted roughly 900,000 metric tons of carbon dioxide equivalent (CO2e) in direct emissions from entering the atmosphere, which is comparable to the annual greenhouse gas emissions from approximately 172,000 passenger vehicles.[32]

Startup Financing

Congress as well as states have enacted legislation that provides financial assistance for AD system installation. Loans, grants, tax credits, tax exemptions, and production incentives are common financial assistance tools available at the federal and state levels.[33] One principal source of federal funding is the Section 9007 Rural Energy for America Program (REAP) of the Food, Conservation, and Energy Act of 2008 (2008 farm bill, P.L. 110-246).[34] Section 9007 authorizes $255 million in mandatory funding for 2009-2012, with an additional $25 million per year in discretionary funding. For FY2009, $55 million is available, part of which is to be distributed to eligible applicants for AD system projects. Grants dispensed to applicants are not to exceed 25% of the cost of the activity. Loan guarantees dispensed to applicants are not to exceed $25 million. The maximum amount of a combined loan and grant can be no more than 75% of the cost of the activity. Approximately $40 million in loans and grants from Section 9006 of the 2002 farm bill was allocated for the construction of AD systems.

Another source of financial assistance offered for anaerobic digestion projects is the Renewable Electricity Production Tax Credit (REPTC; 26 U.S.C. §45).[35] The REPTC grants a one cent per kilowatt-hour tax credit for electricity generated from open-loop biomass (e.g., agricultural livestock waste nutrients).[36] The tax credit period is five years for an open-loop biomass facility using agricultural livestock waste placed in service after October 22, 2004, and before August 9, 2005. The tax credit period is 10 years for a facility placed in service after August 8, 2005.

ANAEROBIC DIGESTION OBSTACLES

Some technology deployment and adoption barriers exist because of the complexity involved in designing and operating an AD system. Thus far, a significant number of successful AD systems are operated by producers who have sophisticated anaerobic digestion technology knowledge. Some assert that the technology will reach its full potential when an array of concerns are addressed. Some challenges include:[37]

- *Lack of economic return.* AD systems are capital-intensive.[38] The cost fluctuates depending upon the system type, system size, livestock operation type, and factors specific to the site. Capital costs generally include the AD system cost, the engine-generator set, the engineering design process, and installation. Extra costs are incurred for additional elements (e.g., a post-digestion solids separator, utility and interconnection fees). System costs range from a few hundred thousand dollars to a few million dollars.[39] A covered lagoon AD system could cost at a minimum a few hundred thousand dollars.[40] A complete mix AD system or plug flow AD system can cost a few million dollars. An analysis of 38 AD systems indicates that approximately one-third of the total system cost is estimated to be spent on the electrical generation equipment.[41] A producer may find it feasible to forgo producing electricity to save money and to use the biogas produced on-site for heating purposes, which still requires a boiler. A general approximation is that 300-500 head for a dairy cow operation and 2,000 head for a swine operation is the minimum number of head necessary to produce electricity with an AD system at a possible profit.[42]
- *Reliability.* Some argue that producers hesitate to adopt anaerobic digestion technology due to the poor performance rate observed in the 1970s. AD system performance has improved over time due to better engineering, construction materials, and management. Communicating current performance rates may provide producers with the information needed to gain more confidence in the improved technology. AD system performance data may be expanded with mandatory reporting on a periodic basis by an independent third party, which might bolster performance claims made by some AD system construction companies. Information (e.g., demonstration projects, long-term performance records) that communicates recent

performance may mitigate producers' doubts about technology reliability and may verify energy generation and greenhouse gas emission reduction data reported.[43] Some producers and construction companies are opposed to a national reporting program because of the release of potentially proprietary information.

- *Lack of an engineering practice standard.* A national practice standard that lists performance criteria, safety precautions, technical components, and design elements and has undergone review from a standards developing organization is not available for anaerobic digestion technology. Some producers may be reluctant to make a financial investment in a technology that may or may not meet future environmental and technical requisites. The USDA Natural Resources Conservation Service (NRCS) issued a revised anaerobic digester conservation practice standard in 2009.[44]
- *Utility collaboration.* Rates paid by utilities for the electricity generated from AD systems vary by state and within each utility. It may not be economically attractive for a producer to sell the renewable energy generated depending on the cost per kilowatt-hour offered. Some net-metering agreements pay wholesale rates instead of retail rates for the electricity generated, thus limiting potential profitability. Some gas utility companies may be reluctant to accept a renewable energy fuel originating from a technology with no official standard that may contaminate an otherwise clean energy source.
- *Unquantifiable co-benefits.* Certain benefits (e.g., odor reduction) may not be quantifiable in dollar terms but may add to the value of an AD system.
- *Operation and maintenance.* AD systems perform optimally when they are well maintained. Some estimate that daily AD system operation and maintenance may require 30 minutes to an hour. The producer may have to acquire a level of technical expertise not previously necessary.

ISSUES FOR CONGRESS

The 111th Congress is faced with proposed legislation centered on clean energy and climate change mitigation. There may be an opportunity for the agricultural community, particularly the livestock industry, to participate in forthcoming efforts for energy generation and greenhouse gas emission reduction with anaerobic digestion technology. Prior to incorporating anaerobic digestion technology into legislation, Congress may choose to consider:

- *Identifying the primary benefit offered by an AD system.* Selecting a primary benefit (renewable energy generation or greenhouse gas emission reduction) may assist with determining which policy vehicle could support technology deployment (e.g. energy legislation, climate change legislation, agricultural legislation). A single message regarding the technology benefit may encourage producers to adopt the technology to achieve the policy goal.
- *Determining if the methane captured from the technology will be included as a carbon offset.* The climate change debate underway in the 111th Congress includes carbon offsets as a potential greenhouse gas emission reduction strategy. Producers may find it economically worthwhile to invest in AD technology if it produces an additional revenue source in the form of carbon offsets. If the methane captured and combusted is not treated as a carbon offset, will the 111th Congress consider regulating the methane captured as a pollutant?
- *Identifying whether alternate sources of financial support for technology implementation are appropriate.* Most of the federal financial assistance available comes in loans and grants for AD system construction. A shorter payback period for an AD system may occur if producers receive a more substantial monetary sum for the energy generated and transferred to a utility company via a federal electricity rate premium. Additional tax credits may also improve the economic return for AD technology (e.g., raising the tax credit value for agricultural livestock waste nutrients to that of closed-loop biomass for the Renewable Electricity, Refined Coal, and Indian Coal Production Credit).

End Notes

[1] For example, the amount of manure excreted from one lactating dairy cow is estimated at 150 pounds per day based on the American Society of Agricultural and Biological Engineers (ASABE) Manure Production and Characteristics Standard D384.2, March 2005.

[2] Amanda D. Cuellar and Michael E. Webber, "Cow Power: The Energy and Emissions Benefits of Converting Manure to Biogas," *Environmental Research Letters*, vol. 3 (2008).

[3] The agriculture sector was responsible for roughly 6% of all U.S. greenhouse gas emissions in 2008, approximately 11% of which is attributable to methane emissions from managed manure. U.S. Environmental Protection Agency, *2010 U.S. Greenhouse Gas Inventory Report*, EPA 430-R-10-006, April 2010, http://www.epa.gov/climatechange/ emission s/usinventoryreport.html.

[4] Flaring is the combustion of gas without commercial purposes. Flaring emits fewer greenhouse gases than simply releasing the biogas as is into the atmosphere. See the "Biogas Quality and Use" section for additional details.

[5] For more information on agriculture-based renewable energy, see CRS Report RL34130, *Renewable Energy Programs in the 2008 Farm Bill*, by Megan Stubbs, CRS Report RL34738, *Cellulosic Biofuels: Analysis of Policy Issues for Congress*, by Kelsi Bracmort et al., and CRS Report RL32712, *Agriculture-Based Renewable Energy Production*, by Randy Schnepf.

[6] Biogas consists of 60%-70% methane, 30%-40% carbon dioxide, and trace amounts of other gases.

[7] U.S. Department of Agriculture, "Agriculture Secretary Vilsack, Dairy Producers Sign Historic Agreement to Cut Greenhouse Gas Emissions by 25% by 2020," press release, December 15, 2009, http://www.usda.gov/wps/portal/ !ut/p/_s.7_0_A/7_0_1OB?contentidonly=true& contentid=2009/12/0613.xml.

[8] *Memorandum of Understanding between the United States Department of Agriculture and The Innovation Center for U.S. Dairy*, December 15, 2009, http://www.usda.gov/documents/ FINAL_USDA_DAIRY_GHG_AGREEMENT.pdf.

[9] The feedstock is usually manure, but can also include other organic matter. The digestion of two or more types of organic matter is referred to as co-digestion.

[10] The time required for the manure to be treated is referred to as the hydraulic retention time (HRT). HRT is normally expressed in days.

[11] For more information on environmental issues facing the livestock community, see CRS Report RL32948, *Air Quality Issues and Animal Agriculture: A Primer*, by Claudia Copeland, and CRS Report RL33691, *Animal Waste and Hazardous Substances: Current Laws and Legislative Issues*, by Claudia Copeland.

[12] Total solids content for manure is the amount of solid material remaining after all moisture has been removed from a sample.

[13] For additional information on agricultural greenhouse gas emissions, see CRS Report RL33898, *Climate Change: The Role of the U.S. Agriculture Sector*, by Renée Johnson. For more information on methane capture, see CRS Report R40813, *Methane Capture: Options for Greenhouse Gas Emission Reduction*, by Kelsi Bracmort et al.

[14] The IPCC Second Assessment Report issued in 1996 assigned methane a Global Warming Potential of 21. Global Warming Potential is an estimate of how much a greenhouse gas affects climate change over a quantity of time relative to CO_2, which has a GWP value of 1.

[15] Enteric fermentation is the production and release of methane via eructation (burping) and flatulence as ruminant animals digest their feed.

[16] The amount of methane produced by an animal expressed per mass unit for one year (kg CH_4/head/year).

[17] The potential amount of methane produced from a manure management system for a given animal expressed in percent. The factor for dry manure management systems may vary according to climate.

[18] Manure that is not managed (e.g., manure deposited in a pasture from livestock grazing) has low methane emissions, but relatively high nitrous oxide emissions. The greenhouse gas nitrous oxide is 310 times more effective at trapping heat in the atmosphere than carbon dioxide over a 100-year timeframe.

[19] A carbon offset is a measurable reduction, avoidance, or sequestration of GHG emissions from a source not covered by an emission reduction program. For more information on carbon offsets, see CRS Report RL34705, *Estimating Offset Supply in a Cap-and-Trade Program*,

by Jonathan L. Ramseur, and CRS Report RL34436, *The Role of Offsets in a Greenhouse Gas Emissions Cap-and-Trade Program: Potential Benefits and Concerns*, by Jonathan L. Ramseur.

[20] Pipeline quality is achieved by the removal of carbon dioxide and other contaminants so that only the methane is sold to the natural gas utility.

[21] Elizabeth R. Leuer, Jeffrey Hyde, and Tom L. Richard, "Investing in Methane Digesters on Pennsylvania Dairy Farms: Implications of Scale Economics and Environmental Programs," *Agricultural and Resources Economics Review*, vol. 37, no. 2 (October 2008), pp. 188-203.

[22] The quality of the biogas, measured by its Btu value, necessary to generate electricity varies depending on the engine.

[23] Wisconsin Focus on Energy, *Farm Anaerobic Digesters: Producing Energy from Waste*, REN2003-0709, 2009, http://www.focusonenergy.com/files/document_management_system/renewables/farmenerg yfrommanure_factsheet.pdf.

[24] Best Available Control Technology (BACT) is a pollution control standard mandated by the Clean Air Act.

[25] Net metering is an energy metering method that uses a bidirectional meter, thus allowing the meter to run backwards if a customer generates more electricity than being consumed.

[26] Interstate Renewable Energy Council, *Map of state net metering rules*, 2010, http://www.dsireusa.org.

[27] Jenifer Beddoes, Kelsi Bracmort, and Robert Burns et al., *An analysis of energy production costs from anaerobic digestion systems on U.S. livestock production facilities*, USDA Natural Resources Conservation Service, October 2007.

[28] A Btu (British thermal unit) is a unit of energy used to express the heating value of fuels.

[29] Stoichiometric equation for biogas combustion: $CH_4 + 2O_2 \rightarrow CO_2 + 2H_2O$.

[30] According to the California Climate Action Registry, *Livestock Project Reporting Protocol Version 2.1*, August 2008, the CO_2 released from flaring the biogas is considered biogenic and therefore more environmentally acceptable. See http://www.climateregistry.org/resources/docs/protocols/project/livestock/ CCARLivestock ProjectReportingProtocol2.1.pdf.

[31] U.S. Environmental Protection Agency, The AgSTAR Program, online *AgSTAR Digest*, spring 2009. One megawatt-hour (MWh) is equivalent to 1,000 kWh. The energy generated could provide approximately 33,887 average homes with electricity for one year assuming the average residential home uses 11,040 kWh on a monthly basis. EIA estimates that the average annual electricity consumption for a U.S. residential utility customer in 2008 was 11,040 kWh.

[32] Passenger vehicle estimate computed using the EPA Greenhouse Gas Equivalencies Calculator available at http://www.epa.gov/rdee/energy-resources/calculator.html#results http://www.epa.gov/solar/energy-resources/calculator.html. Calculation based on 2007 average fuel economy assumptions and average vehicle miles traveled at 20.4 mpg and 11,720 miles per year, respectively. Additional information on passenger vehicle calculation available at website provided.

[33] For a comprehensive list of AD system financing tools, visit the EPA AgSTAR Program Federal Incentives for Developing Anaerobic Digester Systems, at *http://www.epa.g ov/agstar/pdf/agstar_federal_incentives.pdf*; and consult the EPA AgSTAR Funding Database website at http://www.epa.gov/agstar/resources/funding.html document.

[34] REAP is an extension of the Farm Security and Rural Investment Act of 2002 (2002 farm bill, P.L. 107-171).

[35] For more information on renewable energy policy, see CRS Report R40999, *Energy Tax Policy: Issues in the 111th Congress*, by Donald J. Marples and Molly F. Sherlock, and CRS Report R40412, *Energy Provisions in the American Recovery and Reinvestment Act of 2009 (P.L. 111-5)*, coordinated by Fred Sissine.

[36] For more information about the Renewable Electricity, Refined Coal, and Indian Coal production credit visit http://www.irs.gov/pub/irs-pdf/f8835.pdf

[37] No relative importance is intended by the order in which challenges are listed.

[38] William F. Lazarus, *Farm-Based Anaerobic Digesters as an Energy and Odor Control Technology: Background and Policy Issues*, USDA Office of the Chief Economist Office of Energy Policy and New Uses, Agricultural Economic Report Number 843, February 2008, http://www.usda.gov/oce/reports/energy/AnerobicDigesters0308.pdf.

[39] AgSTAR Program, *Estimating Anaerobic Digestion Capital Costs for Dairy Farms*, February 2009, http://www.epa.gov/agstar/pdf/conf09/crenshaw_digester_cost.pdf.

[40] Assuming the producer is only purchasing the cover and the biogas recovery equipment to add to an existing lagoon.

[41] Jenifer Beddoes, Kelsi Bracmort, and Robert Burns et al., *An analysis of energy production costs from anaerobic digestion systems on U.S. livestock production facilities*, USDA Natural Resources Conservation Service, October 2007.

[42] U.S. Environmental Protection Agency, *Market Opportunities for Biogas Recovery Systems*, EPA-430-8-06-004; The Minnesota Project, *Profits from Manure Power*, http://www.mnproject.org/pdf/AD%20economics.pdf; Wisconsin Focus on Energy, Farm anaerobic digesters: producing energy from waste, REN2003-0709, 2009, http://www.focusonenergy.com/files/document_management_system/renewables/farmenergyfrommanure_factsheet.pdf.

[43] For an example of reporting criteria to communicate technology performance, see John H. Martin, *A Protocol for Quantifying and Reporting the Performance of Anaerobic Digestion Systems for Livestock Manures*, January 2007.

[44] The conservation practice standard must be adhered to for AD systems that will be constructed with financial or technical support from USDA NRCS. Conservation practice standards are provided at http://www.nrcs.usda.gov/ technical/standards/nhcp.html.

In: Energy Policies and Issues
Editors: Edgar R. Thompson

ISBN: 978-1-61122-685-0
© 2011 Nova Science Publishers, Inc.

Chapter 6

GAS HYDRATES: RESOURCE AND HAZARD

Peter Folger

SUMMARY

Solid gas hydrates are a potentially huge resource of natural gas for the United States. The U.S. Geological Survey estimated that there are about 85 trillion cubic feet (TCF) of technically recoverable gas hydrates in northern Alaska. The Minerals Management Service estimated a mean value of 21,000 TCF of in-place gas hydrates in the Gulf of Mexico. By comparison, total U.S. natural gas consumption is about 23 TCF annually. The in-place estimate disregards technical or economical recoverability, and likely overestimates the amount of commercially viable gas hydrates. Even if a fraction of the U.S. gas hydrates can be economically produced, however, it could add substantially to the 1,300 TCF of technically recoverable U.S. conventional natural gas reserves. To date, however, gas hydrates have no confirmed commercial production.

Gas hydrates are both a potential resource and a risk, representing a significant hazard to conventional oil and gas drilling and production operations. If the solid gas hydrates dissociate suddenly and release expanded gas during offshore drilling, they could disrupt the marine sediments and compromise pipelines and production equipment on the seafloor. The tendency of gas hydrates to dissociate and release methane, which can be a hazard, is the same characteristic that research and development efforts strive to enhance so that methane can be produced and recovered in commercial quantities. Gas hydrates have hindered attempts to plug the Deepwater Horizon oil well blowout in the Gulf of Mexico, and may have had some role in contributing to anomalous gas pressure in the wellbore that caused the blowout itself.

Developing gas hydrates into a commercially viable source of energy is a goal of the U.S. Department of Energy (DOE) methane hydrate program, initially authorized by the Methane Hydrate Research and Development Act of 2000 (P.L. 106-193). The Energy Policy Act of 2005 (P.L. 109-58, Subtitle F, § 968) extended the authorization through FY2010 and authorized total appropriations of $155 million over a five-year period. Congress appropriated $15 million for the gas hydrate research and development (R&D) program in FY2009. The Obama Administration requested $25 million for the natural gas technologies program for FY2010, which includes gas hydrate R&D. Congress appropriated $17.8 million for the program in FY2010, which would also fund research and development into unconventional gas production from basins containing tight gas sands, shale gas, and coal bed methane, as well as for gas hydrates.

Gas hydrates occur naturally onshore in permafrost, and at or below the seafloor in Gsediments where water and gas combine at low temperatures and high pressures to form an ice-like solid substance.[1] Methane, or natural gas, is typically the dominant gas in the hydrate structure. In a gas hydrate, frozen water molecules form a cage-like structure around high concentrations of natural gas. The gas hydrate structure is very compact. When heated and depressurized to temperatures and pressures typically found on the Earth's surface (one atmosphere of pressure and 70° Fahrenheit), its volume expands by 150 to 170 times. Thus, one cubic foot of solid gas hydrate found underground in permafrost or beneath the seafloor would produce between 150 to 170 cubic feet of natural gas when brought to the surface.

Gas hydrates are a potentially huge global energy resource. The United States and other countries with territory in the Arctic or with offshore gas hydrates along their continental margins are interested in developing the resource. Countries currently pursuing national research and development programs include Japan, India, Korea, and China, among others. Although burning natural gas produces carbon dioxide (CO_2), a greenhouse gas, the amount of CO_2 liberated per unit of energy produced is less than 60% of the CO_2 produced from burning coal.[2] In addition, the United States imports 20% of its natural gas consumed each year.[3] Increasing the U.S. supply of natural gas from gas hydrates would decrease reliance on imported gas and reduce

U.S. emissions $^{of\ CO}2$ if domestically produced gas hydrates substitute for coal as an energy source.

GAS HYDRATE RESOURCES

There are several challenges to commercially exploiting gas hydrates. How much and where gas hydrate occurs in commercially viable concentrations are not well known, and how the resource can be extracted safely and economically is a current research focus. Estimates of global gas hydrate resources, which range from at least 100,000 TCF to possibly much more, may greatly overestimate how much gas can be extracted economically. Reports of vast gas hydrate resources can be misleading unless those estimates are qualified by the use of such terms as *in-place* resources, technically recoverable resources, and proved reserves:

- The term in-place is used to describe an estimate of gas hydrate resources without regard for technical or economical recoverability. Generally these are the largest estimates.
- Undiscovered technically recoverable resources are producible using current technology, but this does not take into account economic viability.
- Proved reserves are estimated quantities that can be recovered under existing economic and operating conditions.

For example, the U.S. Department of Energy's Energy Information Agency (EIA) estimates that total undiscovered technically recoverable conventional natural gas resources in the United States are approximately 1,300 TCF, but proved reserves are only 200 TCF.[4] This is an important distinction because there are no proved reserves for gas hydrates at this time. Gas hydrates have no confirmed past or current commercial production.

Until recently, the Department of the Interior's U.S. Geological Survey (USGS) and Minerals Management Service (MMS) have reported only in-place estimates of U.S. gas hydrate resources. However, a November 12, 2008, USGS estimate of undiscovered technically recoverable gas hydrates in northern Alaska probably represents the most robust effort to identify gas hydrates that may be commercially viable sources of energy.[5] Despite a lack of a production history, the USGS report cites a growing body of evidence indicating that some gas hydrate resources, such as those in northern Alaska, might be produced with existing technology despite only limited field testing.

Gas Hydrates on the North Slope, Alaska

The USGS assessment indicates that the North Slope of Alaska may host about 85 TCF of undiscovered technically recoverable gas hydrate resources (Figure 1). According to the report, technically recoverable gas hydrate resources could range from a low of 25 TCF to as much as 158 TCF on the North Slope. Total U.S. consumption of natural gas in 2007 was slightly more than 23 TCF.

Of the mean estimate of 85 TCF of technically recoverable gas hydrates on the North Slope, 56% is located on federally managed lands, 39% on lands and offshore waters managed by the state of Alaska, and the remainder on Native lands.[6] The total area comprised by the USGS assessment is 55,894 square miles, and extends from the National Petroleum Reserve in the west to the Arctic National Wildlife Refuge (ANWR) in the east (**Figure 1**). The area extends north from the Brooks Range to the state-federal offshore boundary three miles north of the Alaska coastline. Gas hydrates might also be found outside the assessment area; the USGS reports that the gas hydrate stability zone—where favorable conditions of temperature and pressure coexist for gas hydrate formation—extends beyond the study boundaries into federal waters beyond the three-mile boundary (**Figure 1**).

Gas Hydrates in the Gulf of Mexico

On February 1, 2008, the MMS released an assessment of gas hydrate resources for the Gulf of Mexico.[7] The report gives a statistical probability of the volume of undiscovered *in-place* gas hydrate resources, with a mean estimate of over 21,000 TCF. The MMS report estimates how much gas hydrate may occur in sandstone and shale reservoirs, using a combination of data and modeling, but does not indicate how much is recoverable with current technology. The report notes that porous and permeable sandstone reservoirs have the greatest potential for actually producing gas from hydrates, and gives a mean estimate of over 6,700 TCF of sandstone-hosted gas hydrates, about 30% of the total mean estimate for the Gulf of Mexico.[8] Even for sandstone reservoirs, however, the in-place estimates for gas hydrates in the Gulf of Mexico likely far exceed what may be commercially recoverable with current technology. The MMS is planning similar in-place gas hydrate assessments for other portions of the U.S. Outer Continental Shelf (OCS), including Alaska.

Gas Hydrates along Continental Margins

Globally, the amount of gas hydrate to be found offshore along continental margins probably exceeds the amount found onshore in permafrost regions by two orders of magnitude, according to one estimate.[9] With the exception of the assessments discussed above, none of the global gas hydrate estimates is well defined, and all are speculative to some extent.[10] One way to depict the potential size and producibility of global gas hydrate resources is by using a resource pyramid (**Figure 2**).[11] The apex of the pyramid shows the smallest but most promising gas hydrate reservoir—arctic and marine sandstones—which may host tens to hundreds of TCF. The bottom of the pyramid shows the largest but most technically challenging reservoir—marine shales.

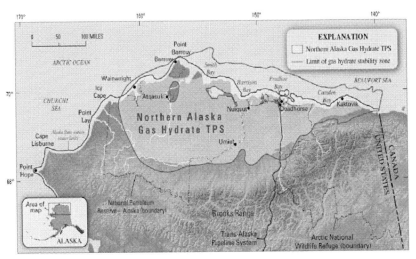

Source: USGS Fact Sheet 2008-3073, Assessment of Gas Hydrate Resources on the North Slope, Alaska, 2008, at http://pubs.usgs.gov/fs/2008/3073/.
Note: TPS refers to total petroleum system, which refers to geologic elements that control petroleum generation, migration, and entrapment.

Figure 1. Gas Hydrate Assessment Area, North Slope, Alaska

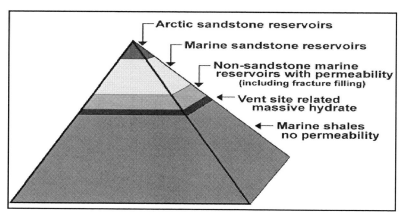

Source: Roy Boswell and Timothy S. Collett, "The Gas Hydrate Resource Pyramid," Fire in the Ice, Methane Hydrate R&D Program Newsletter, Fall 2006.

Figure 2. Gas Hydrate Reservoir Pyramid

Sandstones are considered superior reservoirs because they have much higher permeability—they allow more gas to flow—than shales, which can be nearly impermeable. The marine shale gas hydrate reservoir may host hundreds of thousands of TCF, but most or all of that resource may never be economically recoverable. It is likely that continued research and development efforts in the United States and other countries will focus on producing gas hydrates from arctic and marine sandstone reservoirs.

GAS HYDRATE HAZARDS

Gas hydrates are a significant hazard for drilling and production operations.[12] Gas hydrate production is hazardous in itself, as well as for conventional oil and gas activities that place wells and pipelines into permafrost or marine sediments. For activities in permafrost, two general categories of problems have been identified: (1) uncontrolled gas releases during drilling; and (2) damage to well casing during and after installation of a well. Similar problems could occur during offshore drilling into gas hydrate-bearing marine sediments. Offshore drilling operations that disturb gas hydrate-bearing sediments could fracture or disrupt the bottom sediments and compromise the wellbore, pipelines, rig supports, and other equipment involved in oil and gas production from the seafloor.[13]

Problems may differ somewhat between onshore and offshore operations, but they stem from the same characteristic of gas hydrates: decreases in pressure and/or increases in temperature can cause the gas hydrate to dissociate and rapidly release large amounts of gas into the well bore during a drilling operation.

Oil and gas wells drilled through permafrost or offshore to reach conventional oil and gas deposits may encounter gas hydrates, which companies generally try to avoid because of a lack of detailed understanding of the mechanical and thermal properties of gas hydrate-bearing sediments.[14] However, to mitigate the potential hazard in these instances, the wells are cased—typically using a steel pipe that lines the wall of the borehole—to separate and protect the well from the gas hydrates in the shallower zones as drilling continues deeper. Unless precautions are taken, continued drilling may heat up the sediments surrounding the wellbore, causing gas from the dissociated hydrates to leak and bubble up around the casing. Once oil production begins, hot fluids flowing through the well could also warm hydrate-bearing sediments and cause dissociation. The released gas may pool and build up pressure against the well casing, possibly causing damage.[15] Some observers suggest that exploiting the gas hydrate resources by intentionally heating or by depressurization poses the same risks—requiring mitigation—as drilling through gas hydrates to reach deeper conventional oil and gas deposits.[16]

GAS HYDRATES AND THE DEEPWATER HORIZON OIL SPILL IN THE GULF OF MEXICO

On April 20, 2010, a well drilled by the Deepwater Horizon semisubmersible oil platform "blew out," igniting a fire on board the platform, which eventually sank. The blowout has resulted in an uncontrolled leak of oil and gas from the broken off pipe, or "riser," that led from the top of the well to the drilling platform. In one of the early attempts to plug the well, a heavy steel and concrete box was lowered atop the leaking riser in an attempt to capture the oil and gas and siphon it to the surface. The attempt failed because hydrates clogged the valves and pipes leading to the surface from the steel box as methane converted from a gas phase to solid phase methane hydrate.

The Deepwater Horizon had drilled an "ultradeep" exploratory well in the Gulf of Mexico in approximately 5,000 feet of water. At 5,000 feet

104   Peter Folger

below the surface, seawater is approximately 40° F (4.4° C), and the pressure is approximately 2,500 pounds per square inch (psi). Gas hydrates are stable at that depth and pressure, and can form as long as sufficient quantities of natural gas and water are present—as was the case for the Deepwater Horizon blowout.

Indeed, gas hydrates may have had some role in the original blowout. If a sufficient amount of methane were present in the seafloor sediments, gas hydrates could have formed at the temperatures and pressures in the sediments 1,000 or perhaps 1,500 feet below the seafloor at the Deepwater Horizon drill site (depending on the geothermal gradient—how rapidly the earth changes temperature with depth in that part of the Gulf of Mexico). As discussed in the text of this chapter, drilling and well completion activities may have disturbed hydrate-bearing sediments, resulting in depressurization or heating that could have caused the hydrate to dissociate into a gas. If the gas were able to enter the wellbore through some defect in the casing or cement, it may have contributed to the anomalous gas pressure inside the wellbore that led to the April 20 blowout. Pending an analysis of the causes for the blowout, however, it is currently unknown whether gas hydrates were involved.

Sources: personal communication, Carolyn Ruppel, Gas Hydrates Project, U.S. Geological Survey, Reston, VA, May 17, 2010; MMS Report 2008-004, Preliminary Evaluation of In-Place Gas Hydrate Resources: Gulf of Mexico Outer Continental Shelf.

GAS HYDRATE RESEARCH AND DEVELOPMENT

A goal of the DOE methane hydrate research and development (R&D) program is to develop knowledge and technology to allow commercial production of methane from gas hydrates by 2015.[17] Since the Methane Hydrate Research and Development Act of 2000 (P.L. 106-193) was enacted, DOE has spent $102.3 million through FY2009, or approximately 67% of the $152.5 million authorized by law. The Omnibus Appropriations Act, 2009 (P.L. 111-8), provided $20 million in FY2009 for natural gas technologies R&D, which included $15 million for gas hydrates R&D. The Obama Administration requested $25 million for the natural gas technologies program in FY2010, or half of the $50 million authorized for methane hydrates R&D by the Energy Policy Act of 2005 (P.L. 109-58). Congress appropriated $17.8

Gas Hydrates: Resource and Hazard

million for natural gas technologies in FY2010, giving DOE direction to fund research into unconventional gas production from basins containing tight gas sands, shale gas, and coal bed methane, as well as for gas hydrates.[18] The gas hydrate R&D program is authorized through FY2010 under current law.

The DOE program completed a Gulf of Mexico offshore expedition in May 2009 and an Alaska production test in the summer of 2009. The Gulf of Mexico program was aimed at validating techniques for locating and assessing commercially viable gas hydrate deposits.[19] In Alaska, a two-year production test is expected to provide critical information about methane flow rates and sediment stability during gas hydrate dissociation.[20] Results from the two-year test in Alaska may be crucial to companies interested in producing gas hydrates commercially. Both projects have international and industry partners.

Researchers identify a need to better understand how geology in the permafrost regions and on continental margins controls the occurrence and formation of methane hydrates.[21] They underscore the need to understand fundamental aspects—porosity, permeability, reservoir temperatures—of the geologic framework that hosts the gas hydrate resource to improve assessment and exploration, to mitigate the hazard, and to enhance gas recovery.

Together with advances in R&D, economic viability will depend on the relative cost of conventional fuels, as well as other factors such as pipelines and other infrastructure needed to deliver gas hydrate methane to market. Additionally, price volatility will likely affect the level of private sector investment in commercial production of gas hydrates.

End Notes

[1] The terms *methane hydrate* and *gas hydrate* are often used interchangeably, and refer to the methane-water crystalline structure called a clathrate.

[2] U.S. Department of Energy, Energy Information Agency (EIA), at http://www.eia.doe.gov/cneaf/coal/quarterly/ co2_article/co2.html.

[3] In 2007, the United States consumed approximately 23 TCF of natural gas, of which 4.6 TCF were imported. See EIA at http://tonto.eia.doe.gov/dnav/ng/ng_sum_lsum_dcu_nus_a.htm.

[4] These estimates are as of 2006. Global proved reserves of conventional natural gas are over 6,185 TCF. See EIA at http://www.eia.doe.gov/emeu/aer/pdf/pages/sec4_3.pdf and http://www.eia.doe.gov/emeu/international/reserves.html.

[5] USGS Fact Sheet 2008-3073, Assessment of Gas Hydrate Resources on the North Slope, Alaska, 2008, at http://pubs.usgs.gov/fs/2008/3073/.

[6] USGS presentation, Timothy S. Collett, October 2008, at http://energy.usgs.gov/flash/AlaskaGHAssessment_slideshow.swf.

[7] U.S. Department of the Interior, Minerals Management Service, Resource Evaluation Division, "Preliminary evaluation of in-place gas hydrate resources: Gulf of Mexico outer continental

shelf," OCS Report MMS 2008-004 (Feb. 1, 2008), at http://www.mms.gov/revaldiv/GasHydrateFiles/MMS2008-004.pdf.

[8] Ibid., table 16.

[9] George J. Moridis et al., "Toward production from gas hydrates: current status, assessment of resources, and simulation-based evaluation of technology and potential," 2008 SPE Unconventional Reservoirs Conference, Keystone, CO, February 10, 2008, p. 3, at http://www.netl.doe.gov/technologies/oil-gas/publications/Hydrates/reports/G308_SPE114163_Feb08.pdf.

[10] Ibid.

[11] Roy Boswell and Timothy S. Collett, "The Gas Hydrate Resource Pyramid," Fire in the Ice, Methane Hydrate R&D Program Newsletter, Fall 2006, pp. 5-7, at http://www.netl.doe.gov/technologies/oil-gas/FutureSupply/ MethaneHydrates/newsletter/newsletter.htm.

[12] Timothy S. Collett and Scott R. Dallimore, "Detailed analysis of gas hydrate induced drilling and production hazards," Proceedings of the Fourth International Conference on Gas Hydrates, Yokohama, Japan, April 19-23, 2002.

[13] George J. Moridis and Michael B. Kowalsky, "Geomechanical implications of thermal stresses on hydrate-bearing sediments," Fire in the Ice, Methane Hydrate R&D Program Newsletter, Winter 2006.

[14] Moridis and Kowalski (2006).

[15] Collett and Dallimore (2002).

[16] Personal communication, Ray Boswell, Manager, Methane Hydrate R&D Programs, DOE National Energy Technology Laboratory, Morgantown, WV, Nov. 5, 2008.

[17] DOE methane hydrate R&D program, at http://www.netl.doe.gov/technologies/oil-gas/FutureSupply/MethaneHydrates/rd-program/rd-program.htm.

[18] See H.Rept. 111-278.

[19] See DOE, National Energy Technology Laboratory, "Fire in the Ice," Summer 2009, at http://www.netl.doe.gov/technologies/oil-gas/publications/Hydrates/Newsletter/MHNews Summer09.pdf.

[20] See http://www.netl.doe.gov/technologies/oil-gas/FutureSupply/MethaneHydrates/projects/DOEProjects/Alaska-41332.html.

[21] Collett and Dallimore (2002); Moridis and Kowalski (2006).

In: Energy Policies and Issues
Editors: Edgar R. Thompson

ISBN: 978-1-61122-685-0
© 2011 Nova Science Publishers, Inc.

Chapter 7

OFFSHORE OIL AND GAS DEVELOPMENT: LEGAL FRAMEWORK

Adam Vann

SUMMARY

The development of offshore oil, gas, and other mineral resources in the United States is impacted by a number of interrelated legal regimes, including international, federal, and state laws. International law provides a framework for establishing national ownership or control of offshore areas, and domestic federal law mirrors and supplements these standards.

Governance of offshore minerals and regulation of development activities are bifurcated between state and federal law. Generally, states have primary authority in the three-geographical-mile area extending from their coasts. The federal government and its comprehensive regulatory regime govern those minerals located under federal waters, which extend from the states' offshore boundaries out to at least 200 nautical miles from the shore. The basis for most federal regulation is the Outer Continental Shelf Lands Act (OCSLA), which provides a system for offshore oil and gas exploration, leasing, and ultimate development. Regulations run the gamut from health, safety, resource conservation, and environmental standards to requirements for production based royalties and, in some cases, royalty relief and other development incentives.

In 2008, both the President and the 110th Congress removed previously existing moratoria on offshore leasing on most areas of the outer continental shelf. As of the date of this chapter, the 111th Congress has not reinstated the appropriations-based moratoria that were not renewed by the 110th Congress, and the President has advocated moving forward with oil and natural gas exploration and production in some areas previously under moratoria.

Other recent legislative and regulatory activity also suggests an increased willingness to allow offshore drilling in the U.S. Outer Continental Shelf. In 2006, Congress passed a measure that would allow new offshore drilling in the Gulf of Mexico. Areas of the North Aleutian Basin off the coast of Alaska have also been recently made available for leasing by executive order. The five-year plan for offshore leasing for 2007-2012 adopted by the Minerals Management Service (MMS) in December of 2007 proposed further expansion of offshore leasing. At the same time, the role of the coastal states in deciding whether to lease in areas adjacent to their shores has also received recent attention.

In addition to these legislative and regulatory efforts, there has also been significant litigation related to offshore oil and gas development. Cases handed down over a number of years have clarified the extent of the Secretary of the Interior's discretion in deciding how leasing and development are to be conducted.

The development of offshore oil, gas, and other mineral resources in the United States is impacted by a number of interrelated legal regimes, including international, federal, and Tstate laws. International law provides a framework for establishing national ownership or control of offshore areas, and U.S. domestic law has, in substance, adopted these internationally recognized principles. U.S. domestic law further defines U.S. ocean resource jurisdiction and ownership of offshore minerals, dividing regulatory authority and ownership between the states and the federal government based on the resource's proximity to the shore. This chapter explains the nature of U.S. authority over offshore areas pursuant to international and domestic law. It also describes the laws, at both the state and federal levels, governing the development of offshore oil and gas and the litigation that has flowed from development under these legal regimes. Also included is an outline of the changes to the authorities regulating offshore development wrought by the Energy Policy Act of 2005 and subsequent legislation and executive action, as well as a discussion of recent executive action and legislative proposals that would allow for further offshore exploration and production.

OCEAN RESOURCE JURISDICTION

Under the United Nations Convention on the Law of the Sea,[1] coastal nations are entitled to exercise varying levels of authority over a series of adjacent offshore zones. Nations may claim a 12-nautical-mile territorial sea, over which they may exercise rights comparable to, in most significant respects, sovereignty. An additional area, termed the contiguous zone and extending 24 nautical miles from the coast (or baseline), may also be claimed. In this area, coastal nations may regulate, as necessary, to protect the territorial sea and to enforce their customs, fiscal, immigration, and sanitary laws. Further, in the contiguous zone and an additional area, the exclusive economic zone (EEZ), coastal nations have sovereign rights to explore, exploit, conserve, and manage marine resources and jurisdiction over:

(i) the establishment and use of artificial islands, installations and structures;
(ii) marine scientific research; and
(iii) the protection and preservation of the marine environment.[2]

The EEZ extends 200 nautical miles from a nation's recognized coastline. This area overlaps substantially with another offshore area designation, the continental shelf. International law defines a nation's continental shelf as the seabed and subsoil of the submarine areas that extend beyond either "the natural prolongation of [a coastal nation's] land territory to the outer edge of the continental margin, or to a distance of 200 nautical miles from the baselines from which the breadth of the territorial sea is measured where the outer edge of the continental margin does not extend up to that distance."[3] In general, however, under the Convention, a nation's continental shelf cannot extend beyond 350 nautical miles from its recognized coastline regardless of submarine geology.[4] In this area, as in the EEZ, a coastal nation may claim "sovereign rights" for the purpose of exploring and exploiting the natural resources of its continental shelf.[5]

Federal Jurisdiction

While a signatory to UNCLOS, the United States has not ratified the treaty. Regardless, many of its provisions are now generally accepted principles of customary international law and, through a series of Executive Orders, the United States has claimed offshore zones that are virtually identical to those described in the treaty.[6] In a series of related cases, the U.S. Supreme Court confirmed federal control of these offshore areas.[7] Federal statutes also refer to these areas and, in some instances, define them as well. Of particular relevance, the primary federal law governing offshore oil and gas development indicates that it applies to the "outer Continental Shelf," which it defines as "all submerged lands lying seaward and outside of the areas ... [under state control] and of which the subsoil and seabed appertain to the United States and are subject to its jurisdiction and control...."[8] Thus, the U.S. Outer Continental Shelf (OCS) would appear to comprise an area extending at least 200 nautical miles from the official U.S. coastline and possibly farther where the geological continental shelf extends beyond that point. The federal government's legal authority to provide for and to regulate offshore oil and gas development therefore applies to all areas under U.S. control except where U.S. waters have been placed under the primary jurisdiction of the states.

State Jurisdiction

In accordance with the federal Submerged Lands Act of 1953 (SLA),[9] coastal states are generally entitled to an area extending three geographical miles[10] from their officially recognized coast (or baseline).[11] In order to accommodate the claims of certain states, the SLA provides for an extended three-marine-league[12] seaward boundary in the Gulf of Mexico if a state can show such a boundary was provided for by the state's "constitution or laws prior to or at the time such State became a member of the Union, or if it has been heretofore approved by Congress."[13] After enactment of the SLA, the Supreme Court of the United States held that the Gulf coast boundaries of Florida and Texas do extend to the three-marine-league limit; other Gulf coast states were unsuccessful in their challenges.[14]

Within their offshore boundaries, coastal states have "(1) title to and ownership of the lands beneath navigable waters within the boundaries of the respective states, and (2) the right and power to manage, administer, lease, develop and use the said lands and natural resources...."[15] Accordingly, coastal states have the option of developing offshore oil and gas within their waters; if they choose to develop, they may regulate that development.

Coastal State Regulation

State laws governing oil and gas development in state waters vary significantly from jurisdiction to jurisdiction. Some state laws are limited to a single paragraph and do not differentiate between onshore and offshore state resources; other states do not distinguish between oil and gas and other types of minerals. In addition to regulation aimed specifically at oil and gas development, it should be noted that a variety of other laws could impact offshore development, such as environmental and wildlife protection laws and coastal zone management regulation. Finally, in states that authorize offshore oil and gas leasing, the states decide which offshore areas under their jurisdiction will be opened for development. The **Appendix** of this chapter contains a table of state laws regulating and sometimes banning offshore mineral development. The table indicates which state agency is primarily responsible for authorizing oil and gas development and if state oil and gas leasing is limited to specific areas by statute.

FEDERAL RESOURCES

The primary federal law governing development of oil and gas in federal waters is the Outer Continental Shelf Lands Act (OCSLA).[16] As stated above, the OCSLA codifies federal control of the OCS, declaring that the submerged lands seaward of the state's offshore boundaries appertain to the U.S. federal government. More than simply declaring federal control, the OCSLA has as its primary purpose "expeditious and orderly development [of OCS resources], subject to environmental safeguards, in a manner which is consistent with the maintenance of competition and other national needs...."[17] To effectuate this purpose, the OCSLA extends application of federal laws to certain structures and devices located on the OCS;[18] provides that the law of adjacent states will apply to the OCS when it does not conflict with federal law;[19] and, significantly, provides a comprehensive leasing process for certain OCS mineral resources and a system for collecting and distributing royalties from the sale of these federal mineral resources.[20] The OCSLA thus provides comprehensive regulation of the development of OCS oil and gas resources.

Moratoria

In general, the OCSLA requires the federal government to prepare, revise, and maintain an oil and gas leasing program. Until recently, however, many offshore areas were withdrawn from disposition under the OCSLA pursuant to two broad categories of moratoria applicable to OCS oil and gas leasing: those imposed by the President under authority granted by the OCSLA,[21] and those imposed directly by Congress, which have most often taken the form of limitations on the use of appropriated funds.[22]

Appropriations-based congressional moratoria first appeared in the appropriations legislation for FY1982. The language of the appropriations legislation barred the expenditure of funds by the Department of the Interior (DOI) for leasing and related activities in certain areas in the OCS.[23] Similar language appeared in every DOI appropriations bill through FY2008. However, starting with FY2009, Congress has not included this language in appropriations legislation. As a result, the Minerals Management Service (MMS) is free to use appropriated funds to fund all leasing, preleasing, and related activities in most OCS areas (where such activities are not prohibited by other legislation). Language used in the legislation that funds DOI in the future will determine whether, and in what form, budget-based restrictions on OCS leasing might return.

In addition to the congressional moratoria, for most of the last 20 years there have been moratoria issued by the executive branch on offshore drilling. The first of these was issued by President George H. W. Bush on June 26, 1990.[24] This memorandum, issued pursuant to the authority vested in the President under Section 12(a) of the OCSLA, placed under presidential moratoria those areas already under an appropriations-based moratorium pursuant to P.L. 105-83, the Interior Appropriations legislation in place at that time. That appropriations-based moratorium prohibited "leasing and related activities" in the areas off the coast of California, Oregon, and Washington, and the North Atlantic and certain portions of the eastern Gulf of Mexico. The legislation further prohibited leasing, preleasing, and related activities in the North Aleutian basin, other areas of the eastern Gulf of Mexico, and the Mid- and South Atlantic. The Presidential moratorium was extended by President Bill Clinton by memorandum dated June 12, 1998.[25]

On July 14, 2008, President George W. Bush issued an executive memorandum that rescinded the executive moratorium on offshore drilling created by the 1990 order of President George H. W. Bush and renewed by President Bill Clinton in 1998.[26] The memorandum revised the language of the

Offshore Oil and Gas Development: Legal Framework   113

previous memorandum so that only areas designated as marine sanctuaries are withdrawn from disposition. The withdrawal has no expiration date.

The July 14, 2008, memorandum, taken together with the expiration of the congressional moratorium, has the effect of opening up areas of the OCS for consideration for exploration and production where such activities had not previously been allowed. OCS acreage not protected by other statutory measures can now be considered by MMS for leasing, as described *infra*. However, it is important to note that other prohibitions and moratoria on development on exploration and production in certain areas of the OCS exist. For example, the Gulf of Mexico Energy Security Act of 2006, enacted as part of H.R. 6111, the Omnibus Tax Relief and Health Care Act of 2006,[27] created a new congressional moratorium over leasing in portions of the OCS that do not depend on annual renewal in appropriations legislation. The 2006 legislation explicitly permits oil and gas leasing in areas of the Gulf of Mexico,[28] but also established a new moratorium on preleasing, leasing, and related activity in the eastern Gulf of Mexico through June 30, 2022.[29] This moratorium is independent of any appropriations-based congressional moratorium, and thus would continue even if Congress reinstated the annual appropriations-based moratorium.

On March 31, 2010, President Barack Obama issued an executive memorandum pursuant to his authority under section 12(a) of the OCSLA creating a new moratorium on oil and natural gas leasing in the Bristol Bay area of the North Aleutian Basin of Alaska.[30] This withdrawal runs through June 30, 2017. No other offshore areas are affected by this memorandum.

Leasing and Development

In 1978, the OCSLA was significantly amended so as to increase the role of the affected coastal states in the leasing process.[31] The amendments also revised the bidding process and leasing procedures, set stricter criteria to guide the environmental review process, and established new safety and environmental standards to govern drilling operations.

The OCS leasing process consists of four distinct stages: (1) the five-year planning program;[32] (2) preleasing activity and the lease sale;[33] (3) exploration;[34] and (4) development and production.[35]

The Five-Year Plan

The Secretary of the Interior is required to prepare a five-year leasing plan, subject to annual revisions, that governs any offshore leasing that takes place during the period of plan coverage.[36] Each five-year plan establishes a schedule of proposed lease sales, providing the timing, size, and general location of the leasing activities. This plan is to be based on multiple considerations, including the Secretary's determination as to what will best meet national energy needs for the five-year period and the extent of potential economic, social, and environmental impacts associated with development.[37]

During the development of the plan, the Secretary must solicit and consider comments from the governors of affected states, and at least 60 days prior to publication of the plan in the *Federal Register*, the plan is to be submitted to the governor of each affected state for further comments.[38] After publication, the Attorney General is also authorized to submit comments regarding potential effects on competition.[39] Subsequently, at least 60 days prior to its approval, the plan is to be submitted to Congress and the President, along with any received comments and an explanation for the rejection of any comment.[40] Once the leasing plan is approved, areas included in the plan are to be available for leasing, consistent with the terms of the plan.[41]

The development of the five-year plan is considered a major federal action significantly affecting the quality of the human environment and as such requires preparation of an environmental impact statement (EIS) under the National Environmental Policy Act (NEPA).[42] Thus, the NEPA review process complements and informs the preparation of a five-year plan under the OCSLA.[43]

The current Five-Year Plan took effect on July 1, 2007.[44] The Plan contemplated leasing in areas off the coast of Alaska and in the Central and Western Gulf of Mexico, as well as the possibility of leasing in the mid-Atlantic Ocean Planning Area off the coast of Virginia. In response to calls to expand offshore exploration and production leasing, in July of 2008 MMS took the unprecedented step of initiating a new Five-Year Plan that is expected to commence before the expiration of the previous plan. MMS published notice and a request for comments in the Federal Register regarding a proposed new Five-Year Plan for mid-2010 to mid-2015 that would have replaced the existing Plan.[45] The notice sought "comments on areas that ... were removed from Presidential Withdrawal on July 14, 2008."[46] However, those efforts appear to have stalled. Instead, the current Administration is focusing on expanding offshore exploration and production efforts under the Five-Year Plan that will cover mid-2012 to mid-2017.

Offshore Oil and Gas Development: Legal Framework 115

According to plans recently publicized by the Obama Administration, the scoping evaluation for the 2012-2017 Five-Year Plan will include eight different OCS areas, some of which are not currently available for leasing for purposes of oil and natural gas exploration and production.[47] These areas are: the Beaufort Sea, Chukchi Sea, and Cook Inlet in Alaska, the Western, Central and Eastern Gulf of Mexico, and the South Atlantic and Mid-Atlantic Ocean.[48] While the full extent of the 2012-2017 Five-Year Plan will not be known for some time, this likely will represent an expansion of current OCS leasing activities into areas not previously leased for purposes of oil and natural gas exploration and production. The scope of the initial evaluation of the 2012-2017 Five Year Plan, as well as President Obama's moratorium on oil and natural gas exploration and production in Bristol Bay and the decision to move forward with leasing off the coast of Virginia as permitted under the 2007-2012 Five-Year Plan, is depicted in **Figure 1** and **Figure 2** below.

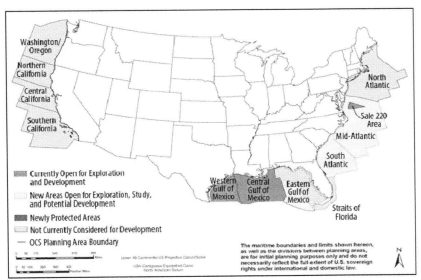

Source: http://www.doi.gov/whatwedo/energy/ocs/lower48-strategy.cfm. Adapted by CRS.

Figure 1. Atlantic, Gulf of Mexico, and Pacific Strategies as of April 6, 2010
Department of the Interior Outer Continental Shelf Oil and Gas Strategy

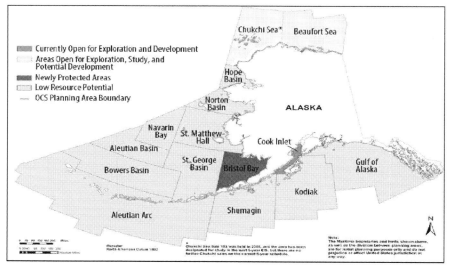

Source: http://www.doi.gov/whatwedo/energy/ocs/AlaskaRegion.cfm. Adapted by CRS.

Figure 2. Alaska Strategy as of April 6, 2010 Department of the Interior Outer Continental Shelf Oil and Gas Strategy

Leasing

The lease sale process involves multiple steps as well. Leasing decisions are impacted by a variety of federal laws; however, it is section 8 of the OCSLA and its implementing regulations that establish the mechanics of the leasing process.[49]

The process begins when the Director of MMS publishes a call for information and nominations regarding potential lease areas. The Director is authorized to receive and consider these various expressions of interest in lease areas and comments on which areas should receive special concern and analysis.[50] The Director is then to consider all available information and perform environmental analysis under NEPA in crafting both a list of areas recommended for leasing and any proposed lease stipulations.[51] This list is submitted to the Secretary of the Interior and, upon the Secretary's approval, published in the *Federal Register* and submitted to the governors of potentially affected states.[52]

The OCSLA and its regulations authorize the governor of an affected state and the executive of any local government within an affected state to submit to the Secretary any recommendations concerning the size, time, or location[53] of a proposed lease sale within 60 days after notice of the lease sale.[54] The Secretary must accept the governor's recommendations (and has discretion to accept a local government executive's recommendations) if the Secretary determines that the recommendations reasonably balance the national interest and the well-being of the citizens of an affected state.[55]

The Director of MMS publishes the approved list of lease sale offerings in the *Federal Register* (and other publications) at least 30 days prior to the date of the sale.[56] This notice must describe the areas subject to the sale and any stipulations, terms, and conditions of the sale.[57] The bidding is to occur under conditions described in the notice and must be consistent with certain baseline requirements established in the OCSLA.[58]

Although the statute establishes base requirements for the competitive bidding process and sets forth a variety of possible bid formats,[59] some of these requirements are subject to modification at the discretion of the Secretary.[60] Before the acceptance of bids, the Attorney General is also authorized to review proposed lease sales to analyze any potential effects on competition, and may subsequently recommend action to the Secretary of the Interior as may be necessary to prevent violation of antitrust laws.[61] The Secretary is not bound by the Attorney General's recommendation, and likewise, the antitrust review process does not affect private rights of action under antitrust laws or otherwise restrict the powers of the Attorney General or any other federal agency under other law.[62] Assuming compliance with these bidding requirements, the Secretary may grant a lease to the highest bidder, although deviation from this standard may occur under some circumstances.[63]

In addition, the OCSLA prescribes many minimum conditions that all lease instruments must contain. The statute supplies generally applicable minimum royalty or net profit share rates, as necessitated by the bidding format adopted, subject, under certain conditions, to secretarial modification. Several provisions authorize royalty reductions or suspensions. Royalty rates or net profit shares may be reduced below the general minimums or eliminated to promote increased production.[64] For leases located in "the Western and Central Planning Areas of the Gulf of Mexico and the portion of the Eastern Planning Area of the Gulf of Mexico encompassing whole lease blocks lying west of 87 degrees, 30 minutes West longitude and in the Planning Areas offshore Alaska," a broader authority is also provided, allowing the Secretary, with the lessee's consent, to make "other modifications" to royalty or profit share requirements to encourage increased production.[65] Royalties may also be suspended under certain conditions by MMS pursuant to the Outer Continental Shelf Deep Water Royalty Relief Act, discussed *infra*.

The OCSLA generally requires successful bidders to furnish a variety of up-front payments and performance bonds upon being granted a lease.[66] Additional provisions require that leases provide that certain amounts of production be sold to small or independent refiners. Further, leases must contain the conditions stated in the sale notice and provide for suspension or cancellation of the lease in certain circumstances.[67] Finally, the law indicates that a lease entitles the lessee to explore for, develop, and produce oil and gas, conditioned on applicable due diligence requirements and the approval of a development and production plan, discussed below.[68]

Exploration

Exploration for oil and gas pursuant to an OCSLA lease must comply with an approved exploration plan.[69] Detailed information and analysis must accompany the submission of an exploration plan, and, upon receipt of a complete proposed plan, the relevant MMS regional supervisor is required to submit the plan to the governor of an affected state and the state's Coastal Zone Management agency.[70]

Under the Coastal Zone Management Act (CZMA), federal actions and federally permitted projects, including those in federal waters, must be submitted for state review.[71] The purpose of this review is to ensure consistency with state coastal zone management programs as contemplated by the federal law. When a state determines that a lessee's plan is inconsistent with its coastal zone management program, the lessee must either reform its plan to accommodate those objections and resubmit it for MMS and state approval or succeed in appealing the state's determination to the Secretary of Commerce.[72] Simultaneously, the MMS regional supervisor is to analyze the environmental impacts of the proposed exploration activities under NEPA; however, regulations prescribe that MMS complete its action on the plan review within thirty days. Hence, extensive environmental review at this stage may be constrained or rely heavily upon previously prepared NEPA documents.[73] If the regional supervisor disapproves the proposed exploration plan, the lessee is entitled to a list of necessary modifications and may resubmit the plan to address those issues.[74] Once a plan has been approved, drilling associated with exploration remains subject to the relevant MMS district supervisor's approval of an application for a permit to drill, which involves analysis of even more specific drilling plans.

Offshore Oil and Gas Development: Legal Framework

Development and Production

While exploration often will involve drilling wells, the scale of such activities will significantly increase during the development and production phase. Accordingly, additional regulatory review and environmental analysis are required by the OCSLA before this stage begins.[75] Operators are required to submit a Development and Production Plan for areas where significant development has not occurred before[76] or a less extensive Development Operations Coordination Document for those areas, such as certain portions of the Western Gulf of Mexico, where significant activities have already taken place.[77] The information required to accompany submission of these documents is similar to that required at the exploration phase, but must address the larger scale of operations.[78] As with the processes outlined above, the submission of these documents complements the department's and MMS's environmental analysis under NEPA. It may not always be necessary to prepare a new EIS at this stage, and environmental analysis may be tied to previously prepared NEPA documents.[79] In addition, affected states are allowed, under the OCSLA, to submit comments on proposed Development and Production Plans and to review these plans for consistency with state Coastal Zone Management Programs.[80] Additionally, if the drilling project involves "non-conventional production or completion technology, regardless of water depth," applicants must also submit a Deepwater Operations Plan (DWOP) and a Conceptual Plan.[81] These additional documents allow MMS to adequately review the engineering, safety, and environmental impacts associated with these technologies.[82]

As with the exploration stage, actual drilling requires approval of an Application for Permit to Drill (APD).[83] An APD focuses on the specifics of particular wells and associated machinery. Thus, an application must include a plat indicating the well's proposed location, information regarding the various design elements of the proposed well, and a drilling prognosis, among other things.[84]

Lease Suspension and Cancellation

The OCSLA authorizes the Secretary of the Interior to promulgate regulations on lease suspension and cancellation.[85] The Secretary's discretion over the use of these authorities is specifically limited to a set number of circumstances established by the OCSLA. These circumstances are described below.

Suspension of otherwise authorized OCS activities may generally occur at the request of a lessee or at the direction of the relevant MMS Regional

Supervisor, given appropriate justification.[86] Under the statute, a lease may be suspended (1) when it is in the national interest; (2) to facilitate proper development of a lease; (3) to allow for the construction or negotiation for use of transportation facilities; or (4) when there is "a threat of serious, irreparable, or immediate harm or damage to life (including fish and other aquatic life), to property, to any mineral deposits (in areas leased or not leased), or to the marine, coastal, or human environment...."[87] The regulations also indicate that leases may be suspended for other reasons, including (1) when necessary to comply with judicial decrees; (2) to allow for the installation of safety or environmental protection equipment; (3) to carry out NEPA or other environmental review requirements; or (4) to allow for "inordinate delays encountered in obtaining required permits or consents...."[88] Whenever suspension occurs, the OCSLA generally requires that the term of an affected lease or permit be extended by a length of time equal to the period of suspension.[89] This extension requirement does not apply when the suspension results from a lessee's "gross negligence or willful violation of such lease or permit, or of regulations issued with respect to such lease or permit...."[90]

If a suspension period reaches five years,[91] the Secretary may cancel a lease upon holding a hearing and finding that (1) continued activity pursuant to a lease or permit would "probably cause serious harm or damage to life (including fish and other aquatic life), to property, to any mineral (in areas leased or not leased), to the national security or defense, or to the marine, coastal, or human environment"; (2) "the threat of harm or damage will not disappear or decrease to an acceptable extent within a reasonable period of time"; and (3) "the advantages of cancellation outweigh the advantages of continuing such lease or permit in force...."[92]

Upon cancellation, the OCSLA entitles lessees to certain damages. The statute calculates damages at the lesser of (1) the fair value of the canceled rights on the date of cancellation[93] or (2) the excess of the consideration paid for the lease, plus all of the lessee's exploration- or development-related expenditures, plus interest, over the lessee's revenues from the lease.[94]

The OCSLA also indicates that the "continuance in effect" of any lease is subject to a lessee's compliance with the regulations issued pursuant to the OCSLA, and failure to comply with the provisions of the OCSLA, an applicable lease, or the regulations may authorize the Secretary to cancel a lease as well.[95] Under these circumstances, a nonproducing lease can be canceled if the Secretary sends notice by registered mail to the lease owner and the noncompliance with the lease or regulations continues for a period of 30 days after the mailing.[96] Similar noncompliance by the owner of a

Offshore Oil and Gas Development: Legal Framework 121

producing lease can result in cancellation after an appropriate proceeding in any United States district court with jurisdiction as provided for under the OCSLA.[97]

Legal Challenges to Offshore Leasing

Multiple statutes govern aspects of offshore oil and gas development, and therefore, may give rise to legal challenges. Certainly, violations of the Marine Mammal Protection Act,[98] Endangered Species Act,[99] and other environmental laws have provided mechanisms for challenging actions associated with offshore oil and gas production in the past.[100] Of primary interest here, however, are legal challenges to agency action with respect to the planning, leasing, exploration, and development phases under the procedures mandated by the OCSLA itself and the related environmental review required by the National Environmental Policy Act.

Suits under the Outer Continental Shelf Lands Act

The OCSLA provides for judicial review of agency action alleged to be in violation of federal law, including the OCSLA, its implementing regulations, and the terms of any permit or lease.[101] The following paragraphs provide an overview of the existing case law and address the limitations applicable to relief at each phase of the leasing and development process.

Jurisdiction to review agency actions taken in approving the five-year plan is vested in the U.S. Court of Appeals for the D.C. Circuit, subject to appellate review by writ of certiorari to the U.S. Supreme Court.[102] A few challenges to five-year plans have been brought in federal courts. The first, *California ex. rel. Brown v. Watt*,[103] involved a variety of challenges to the 1980-1985 plan, and, while the court ultimately found that the Secretary had failed to comply with certain procedural requirements in making determinations, the court established a relatively deferential standard of review, which it has continued to apply in later challenges. When reviewing "findings of ascertainable fact made by the Secretary," the court will require the Secretary's decisions to be supported by "substantial evidence."[104] However, the court noted that many of the decisions required in the formulation of the five-year plan will involve the determination of policy in the face of disputed facts, and that such determinations should be subject to a less searching standard. In such instances, a court will examine agency action and determine whether "the decision is based on a consideration of the relevant factors and whether there has been a clear error of judgment."[105]

The standards for review outlined in *Watt* have been upheld in subsequent litigation related to the five-year plan.[106] In these subsequent cases, the Court of Appeals for the D.C. Circuit applied a deferential standard in reviewing the Secretary's decisions, particularly in reviewing the Secretary's environmental impact determinations, such that the Secretary could perform environmental analysis using "any methodology so long as it is not irrational."[107] Further, these cases indicate that the Secretary is vested with significant discretion in determining which areas are to be offered for leasing and which areas will not. Thus, while the Secretary must receive and consider comments related to excluding areas from leasing, the court has clearly stated that the Secretary need only identify the legal or factual basis for leasing determinations at this stage and explain those determinations. More searching judicial review of the Secretary's analysis is not required.[108]

Litigation under the OCSLA has also challenged actions taken during the leasing phase. As described above, the OCSLA authorizes states to submit comments during the notice of lease sale stage and directs the Secretary to accept a state's recommendations if they "provide for a reasonable balance between the national interest and the well-being of the citizens of the affected State."[109] Courts have typically applied the deferential "arbitrary and capricious" standard to the Secretary's decisions with respect to these recommendations. According to the cases from the Ninth Circuit Court of Appeals, because the OCSLA does not provide clear guidance as to how balancing of national interest and a state's considerations is to be performed, agency action will generally be upheld so long as "some consideration of the relevant factors ..." takes place.[110] Cases from the federal courts in Massachusetts, including a decision affirmed by the First Circuit Court of Appeals, have, while embracing the arbitrary and capricious standard, found the Secretary's balancing of interests insufficient.[111] However, it should be noted that the Massachusetts cases reviewed agency action that was not supported by explicit analysis of the sort challenged in the Ninth Circuit. Thus, it is possible that, given a more thorough record of the Secretary's decision, these courts may afford more significant deference to the Secretary's determination.

Apart from matters relating primarily to the authority of the Secretary to authorize the various stages of leasing, recent litigation has focused on the authority of MMS to require royalty payments on certain offshore leases allegedly subject to mandatory royalty relief provisions. In *Kerr-McGee Oil &*

Gas Corp. v. Allred, the plaintiff, an oil and gas company operating offshore wells in the Gulf of Mexico pursuant to federal leases, challenged actions by the department to collect royalties on deepwater oil and gas production.[112] The plaintiff alleged the department does not have authority to assess royalties based on an interpretation of the 1995 Outer Continental Shelf Deepwater Royalty Relief Act (DWRRA), that the act requires royalty-free production until a statutorily prescribed threshold volume of oil or gas production has been reached, and does not permit a price-based threshold for this royalty relief.[113]

The DWRRA separates leases into three categories based on date of issuance. These categories are (1) leases in existence on November 28, 1995; (2) leases issued after November 28, 2000; and (3) leases issued in between those periods, during the first five years after the act's enactment. The third category of leases is the source of current controversy. According to Kerr-McGee, its leases, which were issued during the initial five-year period after the DWRRA's enactment, are subject to different legal requirements than those applicable to the other two categories. Kerr-McGee argued that the department has a nondiscretionary duty under the DWRRA to provide royalty relief on its deepwater leases, and that the statute does not provide an exception to this obligation based on any preset price threshold. To the extent any price threshold has been included in these leases, Kerr-McGee argued that such provisions are contrary to DOI's statutory authority and unenforceable.

Section 304 of the DWRRA, which addresses deepwater leases[114] issued within five years after the DWRRA's enactment, directs that such leases use the bidding system authorized in section 8(a)(1)(H) of the OCSLA, as amended by the DWRRA. Section 304 of the DWRRA also stipulates that leases issued during the five-year post-enactment time frame must provide for royalty suspension on the basis of volume. Specifically, section 304 states:

> [A]ny lease sale within five years of the date of enactment of this title, shall use the bidding system authorized in section 8(a)(1)(H) of the Outer Continental Shelf Lands Act, as amended by this title, except that the suspension of royalties shall be set at a volume of not less than the following:
>
> (1) 17.5 million barrels of oil equivalent for leases in water depths of 200 to 400 meters;
>
> (2) 52.5 million barrels of oil equivalent for leases in 400 to 800 meters of water; and
>
> (3) 87.5 million barrels of oil equivalent for leases in water depths greater than 800 meters.[115]

It is possible to interpret this provision as authorizing leases issued during the five-year period to contain *only* royalty suspension provisions that are based on production volume with no allowance at all for a price-related threshold in addition. Such an intent might be gleaned from the language of the quoted section alone; indeed, in this provision, Congress provides for a specific royalty suspension method and does not clearly authorize the Secretary to alter or supplement it. Kerr-McGee's challenge to the Secretary's authority to impose price-based thresholds on royalty suspension was based on this interpretation of the statutory language above.

The U.S. District Court for the Western District of Louisiana agreed with Kerr-McGee's interpretation of the language discussed above. The court found that the DWRRA allowed only for volumetric thresholds on royalty suspension for leases issued between 1996 and 2000, and that the Secretary did not have authority under the DWRRA to attach price-based thresholds to royalty suspension for those leases.[116] On January 12, 2009, the U.S. Court of Appeals for the Fifth Circuit issued a decision affirming the district court's ruling,[117] and on October 5, 2009, the U.S. Supreme Court denied a petition for writ of certiorari.

Suits under the National Environmental Policy Act

In the context of proposed OCS development, NEPA generally requires publication of notice of an intent to prepare an Environmental Impact Statement (EIS), acceptance of comments on what should be addressed in the EIS, agency preparation of a draft EIS, a comment period on the draft EIS, and publication of a final EIS addressing all comments at each stage of the leasing process where government action will significantly affect the environment.[118] As described above, NEPA figures heavily in the OCS planning and leasing process and requires various levels of environmental analysis prior to agency decisions at each phase in the leasing and development process.[119] Lawsuits brought under NEPA are thus indirect challenges to agency decisions in that they typically question the adequacy of the environmental analysis performed prior to a final decision.

In *Natural Resources Defense Council v. Hodel*,[120] the plaintiff challenged the adequacy of the alternatives examined in the EIS and the level of consideration paid to cumulative effects of offshore drilling activities. The court held that not every possible alternative needed to be examined, and that the determination as to adequacy was subject to the "rule of reason."[121] This standard appears to afford some level of deference to the Secretary, and his choice of alternatives was found to be sufficient by the court in this

Offshore Oil and Gas Development: Legal Framework 125

instance.[122] However, without significant explanation of the standard of review to be applied, the court found that the Secretary's failure to analyze certain cumulative impacts was a violation of NEPA.[123] Thus, the Secretary was required to include this analysis, although final decisions based on that analysis remained subject to the Secretary's discretion, with review only under the arbitrary and capricious standard.[124]

As mentioned above, NEPA plays a role in the leasing phase as well. MMS often uses NEPA and its tiering option to evaluate lease sales.[125] The NEPA procedures and standard of review remain the same at this phase; however, due to the structure of the OCSLA process, more specific information is generally required.[126] Still, courts are deferential at the lease sale phase. In challenges to the adequacy of environmental review, courts have stressed that inaccuracies and more stringent NEPA analysis will be available at later phases.[127] Thus, because there will be an opportunity to cure any defects in the analysis as the OCSLA process continues, challenges under NEPA at this phase are often unsuccessful.[128]

It is also possible to challenge exploration and development plans under NEPA. In *Edwardsen v. U.S. Department of the Interior*, the Ninth Circuit Court of Appeals applied the typical "rule of reason" to determine if the EIS adequately addressed the probable environmental consequences of the development and production plan, and held that, despite certain omissions in the analysis and despite an MMS decision to tier its NEPA analysis to an EIS prepared for a similar lease sale, the requirements of NEPA were satisfied.[129] Thus, while additional analysis was required to account for the greater specificity of the plans and to accommodate the "hard look" at environmental impacts NEPA mandates, the reasonableness standard applied to what must be examined in an EIS did not allow for a successful challenge to agency action.

APPENDIX. STATE LAWS THAT BAN OR REGULATE OFFSHORE RESOURCE DEVELOPMENT

Table A-1. State Laws That Ban or Regulate Offshore Resource Development: Policy and Statutes

State	Policy	Statutes
AL	Drilling is authorized in Alabama's state waters. The State Lands Division of the	**Authorization:** Ala. Code §§ 9-15-18;

Table A-1. (Continued)

State	Policy	Statutes
	Department of Conservation & Land Resources is charged with leasing offshore oil and gas in state waters. In addition, the Alabama State Oil and Gas Board regulates oil and gas production to ensure the conservation and proper development of oil and gas resources.	9-17-1 *et seq.*; 40-20-1 *et seq.*
AK	The Alaska Department of Natural Resources is responsible for leasing oil and gas on state lands, including offshore areas. Certain areas are specifically designated as off limits to oil and gas leasing, and administrative decisions may further limit access.	**Ban:** Alaska Stat. §§ 38.05.140(f); 38.05.184. **Authorization:** Alaska Stat. §§ 38.05.131 *et seq.*
CA	The State Lands Commission is generally responsible for oil and gas leasing. California currently has a general ban in place restricting any state agency from issuing new offshore leases, unless the President of the United States determines that there is a "severe energy supply interruption and has ordered distribu-tion of the Strategic Petroleum Reserve ... , the Governor finds that the energy resources of the sanctuary will contribute significantly to the alleviation of that interruption, and the Legislature subsequently acts to amend...[the law] to allow that extraction." The ban is limited to areas that are not currently subject to a lease.	**Ban:** Cal. Pub. Res. Code §§ 6871.1-.2 (repealed 1994); 6870 (Santa Barbara limitations); 6243 (general ban). **Authorization:** Cal. Pub. Res. Code §§ 6870 *et. seq.*; 6240 *et seq.*
CT	Connecticut does not appear to have laws addressing oil and gas development in state waters.	
DE	The governor and the secretary of the Department of Natural Resources and Environmental Control are authorized to lease oil and gas in state waters. Lands "administered by the Dep-artment of Natural Resources and Environm-ental Control" may not be leased by the secretary.	**Ban:** Del. Code Ann. tit. 7 ch. 61 § 6102(e). **Authorization:** Del. Code. Ann. tit. 7 ch. 61.
FL	In general, the Department of Natural Resources is vested with the authority to permit oil and gas development on state lands and sub-merged lands; in 1990, Florida enacted a broad ban on offshore oil and gas	**Ban:** Fla. Stat. Ann. § 377.242. **Authorization:** Fla. Stat. Ann. §§

Offshore Oil and Gas Development: Legal Framework 127

Table A-1. (Continued)

State	Policy	Statutes
	development by prohibiting oil and gas drilling structures in a variety of locations, including Florida's terri-torial waters. The development ban provides an exception for valid existing rights.	377.01 *et seq.*; 253.001 *et seq.*
GA	The State Properties Commission is authori-zed to issue leases for state-owned oil and gas. The statute does not distinguish between onshore and offshore minerals.	**Authorization:** Ga. Stat. § 50-16-43.
HI	The Board of Land and Natural Resources is authorized to lease oil and gas on state lands, including submerged lands. There would not appear to be a statutory ban in place.	**Authorization:** Hawaii Rev. Stat. §§ 182-1 *et seq.*
LA	The state Mineral Board is responsible for leasing oil and gas in Louisiana and its off-shore territory. Development is limited to areas offered by the Board for leasing.	**Authorization:** La. Rev. Stat. §§ 30:121 *et seq.*
ME	The Bureau of Geology and Natural Areas has primary authority over oil and gas development on state lands, including tidal and submerged lands. The Bureau is authorized to issue exploration permits and mineral leases.	**Authorization:** Me. Rev. Stat. tit. 12 §§ 549 *et seq.*
MD	The Department of the Environment regulates oil and gas development. The areas underlying the Chesapeake Bay, its tributa-ries, and the Chesapeake Bay Critical Area are unavailable for oil and gas development.	**Ban:** Md. Code, Envt. § 14-107. **Authorization:** Md. Code, Envt. §§ 14-101 *et seq.*
MA	The Division of Mineral Resources is charged with administering the leasing of oil and gas on state lands. The law requires a public hearing before any license to explore or lease for extraction is issued for mineral resources located in coastal waters. Many of the state's offshore areas are designated as ocean sanctuaries in which oil and gas development is prohibited.	**Authorization:** Mass. Gen. Laws Ann. Ch. 21 §§ 54 *et seq.* **Ban:** Mass. Gen. Laws Ann. Ch. 132A § 15.
MS	The Mississippi Major Economic Impact Authority is responsible for administering oil and gas leases on state lands. Offshore oil and gas development is generally permissible. Specific areas are not available for leasing. No	**Authorization:** Miss. Code. Ann. §§ 29-7-1 *et seq.* **Ban:** Miss. Code. Ann. § 29-7-3.

Table A-1. (Continued)

State	Policy	Statutes
	development may occur in areas north of the coastal barrier islands, except in Blocks 40, 41, 42, 43, 63, 64, and 66 through 98. Further, "surface offshore drilling operations" may not be conducted within one mile of Cat Island.	
NH	New Jersey does not appear to have laws addressing offshore oil and gas development in state waters.	
NJ	State law authorizes the removal of sand and other materials from lands under tidewaters and below the high water mark if approved by the Tidelands Resource Council. Offshore oil and gas development is not addressed.	**Authorization:** N.J. Stat. Ann. §§ 12:3-12-1 *et seq.*
NY	Leases and permits for the right to use state-owned submerged lands for navigation, commerce, fishing, bathing, and recreation are authorized for specified submerged areas. General authority for issuing oil and gas leases is vested in the Department of Environmental Conservation. Certain submerged lands underlying specified lakes are excluded from exploration and leasing, but offshore areas would not appear to be subject to a similar ban.	**Authorization:** N.Y. Pub. Lands Law § 75; N.Y. Envt'l & Conserv. Law §§ 23- 0101 *et seq.*
NC	State law authorizes the sale or lease of any state-owned mineral underlying the bottoms of any sounds, rivers, creeks, or other waters of the state. The state is authorized to sell, lease, or otherwise dispose of oil and gas at the request of the Department of Environment and Natural Resources.	**Authorization:** N.C. Gen. Stat. § 146-8.
OR	The Department of State Lands is generally responsible for leasing state owned minerals, including oil and gas. Leasing of tidal and submerged lands is governed by separate provisions of law. There does not appear to be a ban in place.	**Authorization:** Or. Rev. Stat. §§ 274.705 *et seq.*; 273.551 (for submerged lands seaward more than 10 miles easterly of the 124th West Meridian).
RI	The Coastal Resources Management Council is charged with identifying, evaluating, and determining which uses are appropriate for the state's coastal resources and submerged lands.	**Authorization:** R.I. Gen. Laws §§ 46-23-1 *et seq.*

Offshore Oil and Gas Development: Legal Framework 129

Table A-1. (Continued)

State	Policy	Statutes
SC	The State Budget and Control Board is authorized to "negotiate for leases of oil, gas and other mineral rights upon all of the lands and waters of the State, including offshore marginal and submerged lands."	**Authorization:** S.C. Code. Ann. §§ 10-9-10 *et seq.*
TX	The School Land Board is authorized to lease those portions of the Gulf of Mexico under the state's jurisdiction for oil and gas development.	**Authorization:** Tex. Nat. Res. Code §§ 52.011 *et seq.*
VA	The Marine Resources Commission is authorized to grant easements or to lease "the beds of the waters of the Commonwealth outside of the Baylor Survey" for oil and gas development.	**Authorization:** Va. Code Ann. § 28.2-1208.
WA	In general, the Department of Natural Resources is responsible for mineral development on state lands. State law prohibits leasing of tidal or submerged lands "extending from mean high tide seaward three miles along the Washington coast from Cape Flattery south to Cape Disappointment, nor in Grays Harbor, Willapa Bay, and the Columbia river downstream from the Longview bridge, for purposes of oil or gas exploration, development, or production."	**Ban:** Wash. Rev. Code Ann. §§ 43.143.005 *et seq.*

End Notes

[1] United Nations Convention on the Law of the Sea III (entered into force November 16, 1994) (hereinafter UNCLOS).

[2] Id. at Art. 56.1.

[3] Id. at Art. 76.1.

[4] Id. at Art. 76.4-76.7.

[5] Id. at Art. 77.1.

[6] Policy of the United States with Respect to the Natural Resources of the Subsoil and Sea Bed of the Continental Shelf, Proclamation No. 2667, 10 *Fed. Reg.* 12,303 (September 28, 1945); Exclusive Economic Zone of the United States of America, Proclamation No. 5030, 48 *Fed. Reg.* 10,605 (March 14, 1983); Territorial Sea of the United States of America, Proclamation No. 5928, 54 *Fed. Reg.* 777 (December 27, 1988); Contiguous Zone of the United States, Proclamation No. 7219, 64 *Fed. Reg.* 48,701 (August 2, 1999).

[7] *See* United States v. Texas, 339 U.S. 707 (1950); United States v. Louisiana, 339 U.S. 699 (1950); United States v. California, 332 U.S. 19 (1947). In accordance with the Submerged Lands Act, states generally own an offshore area extending three geographical miles from the shore. Florida (Gulf coast) and Texas, by virtue of their offshore boundaries prior to admission to the Union, have an extended, three-marine-league offshore boundary. *See*

United States v. Louisiana, 363 U.S. 1, 36-64 (1960); United States v. Florida, 363 U.S. 121, 121-129 (1960).

[8] 43 U.S.C. § 1331(a).

[9] 43 U.S.C. §§ 1301 *et seq.*

[10] A geographical or nautical mile is equal to 6,080.20 feet, as opposed to the typical statute mile, which is equal to 5,280 feet.

[11] 43 U.S.C. §1301(b).

[12] A marine league is equal to 18,228.3 feet.

[13] 43 U.S.C. §§ 1312, 1301(b).

[14] United States v. Louisiana, 363 U.S. 1, 66 ("[P]ursuant to the Annexation Resolution of 1845, Texas' maritime boundary was established at three leagues from its coast for domestic purposes.... Accordingly, Texas is entitled to a grant of three leagues from her coast under the Submerged Lands Act."); United States v. Florida, 363 U.S. 121, 129 (1960) ("We hold that the Submerged Lands Act grants Florida a three-marine-league belt of land under the Gulf, seaward from its coastline, as described in Florida's 1868 Constitution.").

[15] 43 U.S.C. § 1311.

[16] 43 U.S.C. §§ 1331-1356.

[17] 43 U.S.C. § 1332(3).

[18] 43 U.S.C. § 1333. The provision also expressly makes the Longshore and Harbor Workers' Compensation Act, the National Labor Relations Act, and the Rivers and Harbors Act applicable on the OCS, although application is limited in some instances.

[19] Id.

[20] 43 U.S.C. §§ 1331(a), 1332, 1333(a)(1).

[21] 43 U.S.C. § 1341(a).

[22] *See, e.g.*, P.L. 108-447, §§ 107-109.

[23] P.L. 97-100, § 109. The Minerals Management Service (MMS), an agency that is part of DOI, administers the OCS exploration and production program.

[24] Statement on Outer Continental Shelf Oil and Gas Development, 26 Weekly Comp. Pres. Doc. 1006 (June 26, 1990).

[25] Memorandum on Withdrawal of Certain Areas of the United States Outer Continental Shelf from Leasing Disposition, 34 Weekly Comp. Pres. Doc. 1111 (June 12, 1998).

[26] Memorandum on Modification of the Withdrawal of Certain Areas of the United States Outer Continental Shelf from Leasing Disposition, 44 Weekly Comp. Pres. Doc. 986 (July 14, 2008).

[27] P.L. 109-432.

[28] Id. at § 103.

[29] P.L. 109-432, § 104(a).

[30] Memorandum on the Withdrawal of Certain Areas of the United States Outer Continental Shelf from Leasing Disposition (March 31, 2010).

[31] P.L. 95-372.

[32] 43 U.S.C. § 1344.

[33] 43 U.S.C. §§ 1337, 1345.

[34] 43 U.S.C. § 1340.

[35] 43 U.S.C. § 1351.

[36] 43 U.S.C. § 1344(a), (e).

[37] Id.

[38] "Affected state" is defined in the act as any state:

(1) the laws of which are declared, pursuant to section 1333(a)(2) of this title, to be the law of the United States for the portion of the outer Continental Shelf on which such activity is, or is proposed to be, conducted;

(2) which is, or is proposed to be, directly connected by transportation facilities to any artificial island or structure referred to in section 1333(a)(1) of this title;

Offshore Oil and Gas Development: Legal Framework

(3) which is receiving, or in accordance with the proposed activity will receive, oil for processing, refining, or transshipment which was extracted from the outer Continental Shelf and transported directly to such State by means of vessels or by a combination of means including vessels;

(4) which is designated by the Secretary as a State in which there is a substantial probability of significant impact on or damage to the coastal, marine, or human environment, or a State in which there will be significant changes in the social, governmental, or economic infrastructure, resulting from the exploration, development, and production of oil and gas anywhere on the outer Continental Shelf; or

(5) in which the Secretary finds that because of such activity there is, or will be, a significant risk of serious damage, due to factors such as prevailing winds and currents, to the marine or coastal environment in the event of any oil spill, blowout, or release of oil or gas from vessels, pipelines, or other transshipment facilities....

43 U.S.C. § 1331(f).

[39] 43 U.S.C. § 1344(d).

[40] Id.; *see also* 30 C.F.R. §§ 256.16-256.17.

[41] 43 U.S.C. §1344(d).

[42] 42 U.S.C. § 4332(2)(C). In general, NEPA and the regulations that govern its administration require various levels of environmental analysis depending on the circumstances and the type of federal action contemplated. Certain actions that have been determined to have little or no environmental effect are exempted from preparation of NEPA documents entirely and are commonly referred to as "categorical exclusions." In situations where a categorical exclusion does not apply, an intermediate level of review, an environmental assessment (EA), may be required. If, based on the EA, the agency finds that an action will not have a significant effect on the environment, the agency issues a "finding of no significant impact" (FONSI), thus terminating the NEPA review process. On the other hand, major federal actions that are found to significantly affect the environment require the preparation of an environmental impact statement (EIS), a document offering detailed analysis of the project as proposed as well as other options, including taking no action at all. NEPA does not direct an agency to choose any particular course of action; the primary purpose of an EIS is to ensure that environmental consequences are considered. For additional information, see CRS Report RS20621, *Overview of National Environmental Policy Act (NEPA) Requirements*, by Kristina Alexander.

[43] *See* Natural Resources Defense Council v. Hodel, 865 F.2d 288, 310 (D.C. Cir.1988).

[44] The Plan is available on MMS's website at http://www.mms.gov/offshore/PDFs/OMMStrategicPlan2007-2012.pdf.

[45] 73 Fed. Reg. 45065 (August 1, 2008).

[46] Id.

[47] *Notice of Intent to Prepare and Scope an Environmental Impact Statement (EIS) for the Outer Continental Shelf (OCS) Oil and Gas Leasing Program for 2012-2017*, 75 Fed. Reg. 16828 (April 2, 2010).

[48] Id.

[49] 43 U.S.C. § 1337.

[50] 30 C.F.R. §§ 256.23, 256.25.

[51] 30 C.F.R. § 256.26.

[52] 30 C.F.R. § 256.29.

[53] It should be noted that the OCSLA establishes certain minimum requirements applicable to these subjects. For instance, lease tracts are, in general, to be limited to 5,760 acres, unless the Secretary determines that a larger area is necessary to comprise a "reasonable economic production unit...." *Id.* § 1337(b). The law and its implementing regulations also set the range of initial lease terms and baseline conditions for lease renewal.

[54] 43 U.S.C. § 1345(a); *see also* 30 C.F.R. § 256.31.

[55] 43 U.S.C. § 1345(c).

[56] 43 U.S.C. § 1337(*l*).

[57] 30 C.F.R. § 256.32(1).

[58] 43 U.S.C. § 1337.

[59] 43 U.S.C. § 1337(a)(1)(A)-(H). For example, bids may be on the basis of "cash bonus bid with a royalty at not less than 12 ½ per centum fixed by the Secretary in amount or value of the production saved, removed, or sold...." *See also* 30 C.F.R. §§ 256.35 - 256.47.

[60] 43 U.S.C. 1337(a)(1)-(3), (8)-(9).

[61] 43 U.S.C. § 1337(c); 30 C.F.R. § 256.47(d).

[62] 43 U.S.C. § 1337(c), (f).

[63] Restrictions include a statutory prohibition on issuance of a new lease to a bidder that is not meeting applicable due diligence requirements with respect to the bidder's other leases. *See* 43 U.S.C. § 1337(d).

[64] Id. at § 1337(a)(3).

[65] 43 U.S.C. § 1337(a)(3)(B).

[66] 43 U.S.C § 1337(a)(7); 30 C.F.R. §§ 256.52 - 256.59.

[67] 43 U.S.C. § 1337.

[68] 43 U.S.C. § 1337(b)(4).

[69] 43 U.S.C. § 1340(b), (c).

[70] 30 C.F.R. §§ 250.226, 250.227, 250.232, 250.235.

[71] 16 U.S.C. § 1456(c).

[72] 30 C.F.R. § 250.235.

[73] 30 C.F.R. § 250.232(c).

[74] 30 C.F.R. §§ 250.231 - 250.233.

[75] 43 U.S.C. § 1351.

[76] 30 C.F.R. § 250.201.

[77] Id.

[78] 30 C.F.R. §§ 250.24 - 250.262.

[79] The regulations indicate that "at least once in each planning area (other than the western and central Gulf of Mexico planning areas) we [MMS] will prepare an environmental impact statement (EIS)...." 30 C.F.R. § 250.269.

[80] 30 C.F.R. § 250.267.

[81] 30 C.F.R. §§ 250.286, 250.287.

[82] 30 C.F.R.§§ 250.289, 250.292.

[83] 30 C.F.R. §§ 250.410 - 250.469.

[84] 30 C.F.R. § 250.411.

[85] 43 U.S.C. § 1334; *see also* 30 C.F.R. §§ 250.168 - 250.185.

[86] 30 C.F.R. §§ 250.168, 250.171-250.175.

[87] 43 U.S.C. § 1334(a)(1).

[88] 30 C.F.R. § 250.173 - 250.175.

[89] 43 U.S.C. § 1334(a)(1).

[90] Id.

[91] 43 U.S.C. § 1334(a)(2)(B). The requisite suspension period may be reduced upon the request of the lessee.

[92] 43 U.S.C. § 1334(a)(2)(A)(i)-(iii). For regulations implementing the cancellation provisions, see 30 C.F.R. §§ 250.180 - 250.185.

[93] The statute requires "fair value" to take account of "anticipated revenues from the lease and anticipated costs, including costs of compliance with all applicable regulations and operating orders, liability for cleanup costs or damages, or both, in the case of an oil spill, and all other costs reasonably anticipated on the lease...." 43 U.S.C. § 1334(a)(2)(C).

[94] Exceptions from this method of calculation are carved out for leases issued before September 18, 1978, and for joint leases that are canceled due to the failure of one or more partners to exercise due diligence. 43 U.S.C. § 1334(a)(2)(C)(ii)(I), (II); *see also* 30 C.F.R. §§ 250.184 - 250.185.

Offshore Oil and Gas Development: Legal Framework 133

[95] 43 U.S.C. § 1334(b).

[96] 43 U.S.C. § 1334(c).

[97] 43 U.S.C. § 1334(d).

[98] 16 U.S.C. §§ 1361-1423.

[99] 16 U.S.C. §§ 1531-1544.

[100] Village of Akutan v. Hodel, 869 F.2d 1185 (9th Cir. 1988); Village of False Pass v. Clark, 733 F.2d 605 (9th Cir. 1984); North Slope Borough v. Andrus, 642 F.2d 589 (D.C. Cir. 1980); Conservation Law Foundation v. Andrus, 623 F.2d 712 (1st Cir. 1979).

[101] 43 U.S.C. § 1349.

[102] 43 U.S.C. § 1349(c).

[103] 668 F.2d 1290 (D.C. Cir. 1981).

[104] Watt, 668 F.2d at 1302; *see also* 43 U.S.C. § 1349(c)(6).

[105] Watt, 668 F.2d at 1301-1302 (*quoting* Citizens to Preserve Overton Park v. Volpe, 401 U.S. 402, 416 (1971) (internal quotations omitted)).

[106] *See* California v. Watt, 712 F.2d 584 (D.C. Cir. 1983); Natural Resources Defense Council v. Hodel, 865 F.2d 288 (D.C. Cir. 1988).

[107] California, 715 F.2d at 96 (internal quotations omitted).

[108] Hodel, 865 F.2d at 305.

[109] 43 U.S.C. § 1345(d).

[110] California v. Watt, 683 F.2d 1253, 1269 (9th Cir. 1982); *see also* Tribal Village of Akutan v. Hodel, 869 F.2d 1185 (9th Cir. 1988).

[111] Conservation Law Foundation v. Watt, 560 F.Supp. 561 (D.Mass. 1983), aff'd sub nom. Massachusetts v. Watt, 716 F.2d 946 (1st Cir. 1983); Massachusetts v. Clark, 594 F.Supp. 1373 (D.Mass. 1984).

[112] Kerr-McGee v. Allred, No, 2:06 CV 0439, 2007 WL 3231634 (W.D. La. Oct. 30, 2007).

[113] P.L. 104-58.

[114] This term refers to "tracts located in water depths of 200 meters or greater in the Western and Central Planning Area of the Gulf of Mexico, including that portion of the Eastern Planning Area of the Gulf of Mexico encompassing whole lease blocks lying west of 87 degrees, 30 minutes West longitude...." 43 U.S.C. § 1337 note.

[115] P.L. 104-58.

[116] Kerr-McGee v. Allred, slip. op. at 8-9.

[117] Kerr-McGee Oil & Gas Corp. v. U.S. Dep't of Interior, 554 F.3d 1082 (5th Cir. 2009).

[118] 40 C.F.R. §§ 1501.7, 1503.1, 1503.4, 1506.10.

[119] 42 U.S.C. § 4332.

[120] Natural Resources Defense Council, Inc. v. Hodel, 865 F.2d 288 (D.C. Cir. 1988).

[121] Id. at 294.

[122] Id. at 296.

[123] Id. at 297-300.

[124] *See* California ex. rel. Brown v. Watt, 668 F.2d 1290, 1301-1302 (D.C. Cir. 1981).

[125] *See* 30 C.F.R. § 256.26(b); 40 C.F.R. § 1508.28.

[126] Tribal Village of Akutan v. Hodel, 869 F.2d 1185, 1191 (9th Cir. 1988).

[127] Id. at 1192; Alaska v. Andrus, 580 F.2d 465, 473 (D.C. Cir. 1978); Village of False Pass v. Clark, 733 F.2d 605, 612-616 (9th Cir. 1984); North Slope Borough v. Andrus, 642 F.2d 589, 594-905 (D.C. Cir. 1980).

[128] *But see* Conservation Law Foundation v. Clark, 560 F.Supp. 561 (D. Mass. 1983).

[129] Edwardsen v. U.S. Department of the Interior, 268 F.3d 781, 784-790 (9th Cir. 2001).

In: Energy Policies and Issues
Editors: Edgar R. Thompson

ISBN: 978-1-61122-685-0
© 2011 Nova Science Publishers, Inc.

Chapter 8

OUTER CONTINENTAL SHELF MORATORIA ON OIL AND GAS DEVELOPMENT

Curry L. Haggerty

SUMMARY

Moratoria provisions for the outer continental shelf (OCS), enacted as part of the Department of the Interior appropriations over 26 years, prohibited federal spending on oil and gas development in certain locations and for certain activities. These annual congressional moratoria expired on September 30, 2008. While the expiration of the restrictions does not make leasing and drilling permissible in all offshore areas, it is a significant development in conjunction with other changes in offshore leasing activity. The ending of the moratoria signals a shift in policy that may affect other OCS policies as well.

The chief policy goal in not continuing annual moratoria beyond FY2008 was to increase domestic OCS energy production. Also influential were policies to diversify domestic energy production, including by launching renewable energy programs in the OCS, and the availability of new technology that would allow OCS activity in deeper waters beyond clear jurisdictional boundaries. These developments, taken together, reflect a transformative change in OCS policy alternatives. Their impact during periods of volatility in oil markets and in an exceptionally weak economy focuses congressional attention on federal priorities for OCS development.

In the past, Congress has addressed OCS oil and gas development by balancing numerous factors, including economic feasibility, environmental risk, technology, and ocean sovereignty. Disagreements tend to arise in each of these four issue areas between those in favor of offshore oil and gas development and those opposed. Positions are sharply divided on national and coastal state goals for OCS activities in former moratorium areas, and in areas in the Gulf of Mexico and the Arctic where prospective drilling activities or renewable energy projects are permissible.

Around the world, offshore activities are changing, as is reflected in international offshore policy disagreements that are similar to domestic policy disagreements. Economic opportunity and technological advances are driving the global search for energy sources in deeper ocean waters. These activities may clash with national or international environmental policies. Within the framework of the United Nations Convention on the Law of the Sea (UNCLOS), a number of countries are establishing parameters for offshore activities, including preparing claims for extended continental shelf areas. Although the United States has not ratified UNCLOS, U.S. efforts are underway to address extended continental shelf areas in a manner not inconsistent with the UNCLOS process.

The expiration of congressional moratoria is part of a series of changes in domestic and international OCS energy development policy. Moratorium policies have impacted federal-state coordination on economic and environmental concerns. As a result of changes in these policies, federal-state coordination and nation-to-nation coordination may emerge as issues for Congress as it addresses economic and environmental challenges in the OCS.

RECENT DEVELOPMENTS

On March 31, 2010, the Secretary of the Department of the Interior announced the Obama Administration policy with respect to outer continental shelf (OCS) oil and gas development.[1] The Administration proposed a range of actions in OCS areas, including expanded oil and gas production in some areas and protection of certain other offshore places. President Barack Obama issued an executive memorandum on March 31, 2010, pursuant to his authority under Section 12(a) of the Outer Continental Shelf Lands Act (OCSLA), creating a new moratorium on oil and natural gas leasing in the Bristol Bay area of the North Aleutian Basin of Alaska.[2] This withdrawal runs through June 30, 2017.

BACKGROUND

From 1982 until the end of fiscal year 2008, Congress enacted yearly measures that restricted spending of appropriated funds for certain OCS oil and gas leasing and drilling activities. Expiration of the annual congressional moratoria on offshore oil and gas leasing and drilling on September 30, 2008,[3] coupled with other developments in offshore leasing activity, impacts federal policies in the OCS in a number of ways. In the absence of the annual congressional moratoria, policy makers anticipate an increase in efforts to coordinate federal and state actions to address economic and environmental issues related to OCS energy development.[4]

The OCS is a federal offshore area from the edge of state waters, usually starting at 3 nautical miles from shore, seaward to a distance of about 200 nautical miles, and may in special cases in the future extend out to 350 nautical miles.[5] Energy leasing on the OCS takes place in four regions: the Gulf of Mexico region, the Atlantic region, the Pacific region, and the Alaska region.[6]

The expiration of moratoria opens OCS areas where federal oil and gas leasing had not been permitted for many years, allowing these areas to be considered for potential drilling activity. Other developments in offshore leasing activity include a presidential order[7] to lift executive restrictions on certain OCS areas to allow offshore drilling, the emergence of new offshore operations (including renewable energy leasing), and the use of new technologies related to OCS research and development.

This chapter discusses moratorium policy in the context of the broader debate over OCS drilling.[8] The drilling debate includes separate policy conflicts over the size, timing, and location of OCS oil and gas development activities. In the remainder of this section of this chapter, the moratoria and the OCS drilling debate are discussed in the context of (1) the economic feasibility of oil and gas development activities in the OCS; (2) the environmental risk of OCS activities; and (3) new OCS technology. Later sections identify sources of authority for the OCS moratoria and discuss issues of ocean sovereignty.[9]

Economic Feasibility

The potential for federal revenue from OCS development is a central driver of the drilling debate. Disagreement over the economic feasibility of

OCS leasing activity features strongly in this debate, and in moratorium policy as well. At issue is whether the domestic OCS has sufficient potential for oil and gas production to warrant OCS development, and if so, how additional economic factors impact the size, timing, and location of OCS development. The economic feasibility of OCS development depends on oil prices, future projections about oil markets, commercial access to development areas, economic values assigned to competing ocean uses such as renewable energy development, fishing, tourism, and conservation, and other factors.[10]

It is difficult to determine the economic feasibility of oil and gas development options in the absence of clear statutory authority governing prospective ocean areas, and in the absence of predictable regulatory directives that implement federal policies, particularly in new areas with potentially competing development options. Areas such as the Gulf of Mexico and the Arctic, which have substantial proven oil and gas deposits, are particularly unpredictable with respect to the domestic and international authorities that govern oil and gas development. Uncertainty exists regarding boundaries in certain areas, U.S. legislative and regulatory authority, and in some cases sovereign authority.

Federal data to show the potential economic feasibility of developing OCS energy resources are becoming more sophisticated. However, the data have limitations, and concerns arise about their interpretation. The time frame for recent OCS economic analysis spans the end of the George W. Bush Administration and the beginning of the Obama Administration, a time of transition in some federal policies. As a result, underlying economic assumptions made during this time may reflect an ambiguity about federal priorities and future policy direction on OCS oil and gas development. In the absence of clear policy directives, disagreement remains over the economic feasibility of oil and gas development. For example, economic assessments of OCS oil and gas resources vary based on whether or not the projections consider economic data about renewable energy development options. These differing interpretations of what kinds of data to consider can lead to conflicting conclusions about economic feasibility.

Global economic factors play a major role in deliberations about OCS drilling activity. At the end of FY2008, annual moratoria expired amid global economic turmoil and calls for greater stability in the national economy.[11] Congress consistently finds that domestic oil and gas development is vital to the nation, despite disagreements over the economic feasibility of specific oil and gas development projects.[12] Development advocates raise competitiveness arguments, specifically claiming that other coastal countries are allowing greater access to offshore resources and that the United States should not fall behind in the international race to develop offshore resources because of concerns about the marine environment. Those in favor of OCS drilling observe that on a global scale, the use of drilling restrictions is changing, and that continuing an annual congressional moratorium, for example, would be out of step with policies being considered by other countries engaged in OCS development.[13] Concerns about competitiveness influence congressional consideration of OCS development policy in legislative proposals and consideration of international treaties and conventions addressing OCS governance.

Environmental Risk

Given data that suggests that prospective oil and gas reserves exist, another concern raised in the drilling debate generally, and raised about former moratorium areas specifically, is the potential for environmental harm associated with OCS activities. This concern reflects general uncertainty over federal ocean priorities and a potential clash between environmental policy directives and directives for ocean energy development.

Discussions of environmental risk are often accompanied by claims that federal regulators lack sufficiently comprehensive approaches to assess environmental risks in the marine environment.[14] It is widely acknowledged that federal ocean management authorities are fragmented and that both overlapping areas of agency authority and gaps in authority exist in federal ocean administration. How environmental risks are assessed and mitigated is at issue particularly where OCS programs have recently expanded to include new types of development (such as renewable energy programs) and new areas for leasing consideration (due to the expiration of moratoria).

Opinions on the environmental risks associated with OCS development vary widely. Those who oppose drilling cite numerous examples of environmental risks inherent in OCS activity. The list of potential threats to the environment include air and water degradation, oil spills, sea bed disturbances, and numerous harms to marine life. Those who support drilling counter that while certain environmental risks are unavoidable, improvements in offshore oil and gas operations and compliance with laws and regulations sufficiently mitigate environmental risks associated with OCS operations. Federal efforts to prevent oil spills and to improve oil spill response include passage of the Oil Pollution Act of 1990 (P.L. 101-380, OPA90), which established penalties for oil spills and established U.S. Coast Guard prepositioned oil-spill response equipment sites, vessel and facility response plans, and contingency planning. Under OPA90, oil-carrying vessels operating in U.S. waters are to have double hulls by 2015.[15]

Resolving concerns about environmental risk is central to moratorium policy. Some contend that moratoria on oil and gas development are among the only effective ways to address concerns about environmental risk and that measures short of this do not sufficiently mitigate risk. Measures other than moratoria might include oil spill preparedness requirements, coastal compliance measures, use of new technologies, and opportunities for public scrutiny of federal offshore oil and gas activity to address environmental risk.[16]

Policy makers seeking to reach a compromise to resolve environmental concerns have focused on a range of proposals, including proposals to substitute a combination of other measures as a replacement for moratoria. Such efforts have tended to reach an impasse, however, as advocates remain largely divided on what environmental precautions would constitute adequate protection for the marine and coastal environments. Advocates opposed to OCS oil and gas development often associate oil and gas consumption with harmful greenhouse gas emissions and other global climate change concerns. From this perspective, only permanently restricting the offshore development of conventional energy sources would protect against these risks to the domestic and global environment. This perception complicates efforts to reach a compromise involving a combination of possible restrictions designed to tailor OCS development activities. Advocates in support of conventional OCS development view environmental risk on a different scale and largely reject global climate change as a basis for defining the risk. These advocates claim that compliance with current environmental laws and regulations can be an adequate substitute for moratoria, and that new technologies are emerging to manage harmful greenhouse gas emissions and other global climate change concerns. Improvements in offshore technology are broadly viewed by the Obama administration as potential measures to bridge the impasse over environmental risk in shaping OCS policy.[17]

Improvements in Offshore Technology

Technological advancements are emerging that impact OCS operations from pre-leasing activities to platform removal, potentially improving operational performance, environmental protection, and other aspects of OCS activity. Advances in geophysical resource assessment, drilling technology, platform and pipeline design, communications, operational monitoring, and training are helping to minimize environmental impacts and improve economic benefits.

Technology is widely recognized as an important feature of the drilling debate, with relevance to moratorium areas specifically. Congress incorporates information about new technologies and new applications of technology in the development of OCS policy. Considerations of the economic feasibility of OCS leasing activity and of the environmental risks related to OCS development are viewed in association with technology applications intended to safeguard the environment and increase economic resource exploitation.

Technical progress is globally recognized as a factor in the evolution of offshore operations. Changes in technology are impacting OCS policy by creating new options for OCS operations farther and farther from shore, even beyond a country's exclusive economic zone (EEZ).[18] The expiration of OCS moratoria, coupled with applications of new technology, have turned attention to international governance concerns in the OCS drilling debate. Concerns related to possible OCS operations near international waters reflect divergent points of view. Some argue that U.S. involvement and participation in international organizations should increase and should include ratifying the United Nations Convention on Law of the Sea (UNCLOS).[19] On the other hand, those opposing ratification contend that fuller participation in international organizations may diminish U.S. sovereignty in ocean management. These concerns are evident in the debate on UNCLOS accession that is before the U.S. Senate Committee on Foreign Relations. (UNCLOS is discussed in more detail in the section on "United Nations Convention on Law of the Sea (UNCLOS)," below.)

SOURCES OF U.S. MORATORIUM POLICY

Legislative Authority

Congress has authority to set policy for OCS activity and to determine incentives and restrictions for OCS development. Congress enacted OCS moratoria provisions annually between 1982 and 2008 in Department of the

142 Curry L. Haggerty

Interior appropriations. Moratoria provisions were modified from year to year to address specific interests and to cover specific areas. See **Table 1**.

Outside of the annual appropriations process, Congress also considers legislation[20] and treaties[21] that impact leasing, exploring for, developing, or producing oil and gas in OCS areas. For example, Congress designates national marine sanctuaries and enacts other laws that restrict development in certain areas of the OCS. Congress has the authority to provide advice and consent for ratification of treaties that may contain moratoria provisions.

Table 1. Chronology of Annual Congressional Moratoria Enacted in DOI Appropriations

Fiscal Year	Public Law	Alaska Region	Pacific Region	Gulf of Mexico	Atlantic Region
1982	97-100		X		
1983	97-394		X		X
1984	98-146		X	X	X
1985	98-473		X		X
1986	99-190				X
1987	99-591		X		X
1988	100-202				X
1989	100-446	X	X	X	X
1990	101-121	X	X	X	X
1991	101-512	X	X	X	X
1992	102-154	X	X	X	X
1993	102-381	X	X	X	X
1994	103-138	X	X	X	X
1995	103-332	X	X	X	X
1996	104-134	X	X	X	X
1997	104-208	X	X	X	X
1998	105-83	X	X	X	X
1999	105-277	X	X	X	X
2000	106-113	X	X	X	X
2001	106-291	X	X	X	X
2002	107-63	X	X	X	X
2003	108-7	X	X	X	X
2004	108-108	X	X	X	X
2005	108-447	X	X	X	X
2006	109-54	X	X	X	X
2007	110-329	X	X	X	X
2008	110-161	X	X	X	X

Source: CRS. Table represents moratoria provisions established in DOI appropriations by region. The restrictions varied widely by fiscal year in terms of the amount of acreage, the specific location of moratoria, and the specific activities restricted.

Annual Congressional OCS Moratoria

Federal policy for OCS development is intended to span planning horizons of several years.[22] The Department of Interior appropriations legislation between 1982 and 2008 banned agency spending on programs related to OCS drilling, leasing and preleasing activity, and scientific studies one year at a time. This was inconsistent with long-standing OCS policy, which set planning horizons at no less than five years.

One legacy of congressional moratoria is their impact on the timing of possible OCS development. From a developer's point of view, predictability in the pace, timing, and sequence of OCS development projects is key to strategic business decisions. From a regulator's standpoint, agency discretion for OCS development is tied to program planning horizons set by statutory or regulatory timetables. Features of the annual congressional moratoria varied from year to year, and from region to region, as reflected in **Table 1**, and the resultant uncertainty had a disruptive effect on the pace of OCS activity, which was viewed negatively by those in favor of OCS drilling. Among those opposed to OCS drilling, the disruptive effect was considered a positive outcome.[23]

Changes to the specific provisions of annual moratoria measures created tensions due to the unpredictability of the bans on leasing activities, timeframes, and locations.[24] It was not uncommon for developers to engage in litigation against the federal government and to claim damages related to reliance on leases and federal OCS policies that were disrupted by the annual congressional moratoria.[25] Although observers agreed that appropriations measures were out of sync with the timetable used to coordinate federal OCS planning functions, proponents of annual congressional moratoria provisions countered that restrictions were defensible in the absence of more permanent alternatives for similar leasing prohibitions.

Gulf of Mexico Energy Security Act of 2006 (GOMESA)[26]

In addition to the annual appropriations process, Congress also enacts other legislation with moratoria provisions that restrict OCS leasing and drilling. Gulf of Mexico Energy Security Act of 2006 (GOMESA) restricts areas in portions of the Gulf of Mexico until 2022.[27] A moratorium on oil and gas leasing under GOMESA went into effect on December 20, 2006, and is to end on June 30, 2022. GOMESA areas are depicted in **Figure 1**.

Upon enactment of GOMESA, leases within areas designated as moratoria areas became eligible for exchange for a bonus or royalty credit[28] that could be used against other leasing obligations in the Gulf of Mexico.[29] The estimated aggregate value of relinquishing leases in GOMESA moratoria areas is estimated at slightly more than $60 million.

Executive Authority

The President may determine activities on the OCS and has done so under the authority to direct OCS leasing moratoria in the Outer Continental Shelf Lands Act (OCSLA)[30] and in the Antiquities Act.[31] As opposed to annual moratoria in appropriations legislation, presidential directives ordering moratoria usually authorize restrictions for durations that exceed the annual congressional moratoria.

On January 9, 2007, President George W. Bush modified the Executive Directive on OCS leasing withdrawal to reflect congressional modifications to OCS leasing in two areas—the North Aleutian Basin planning area offshore Alaska, and the 181 South Area of the Gulf of Mexico.[32] On July 14, 2008, President George W. Bush issued another executive order lifting executive constrains that remained on offshore leasing activities covered by the annual congressional moratoria.[33]

Agency Authority

Minerals Management Service (MMS)[34]

Generally, federal agencies take OCS leasing moratoria direction from Congress and the President. In some cases however, lack of coordination between federal agency actions and the actions of Congress and the President in terms of OCS leasing moratoria, has created tension and controversy.

For example, MMS has exercised agency authority to constrain leasing activities in areas *not* under moratoria policy set by Congress or the President. Deferring oil and gas development is within agency authority even when it is inconsistent with prevailing moratoria policy. MMS has deferred from offering OCS areas numerous times over the years in response to recommendations from governors, stakeholders, and others.[35]

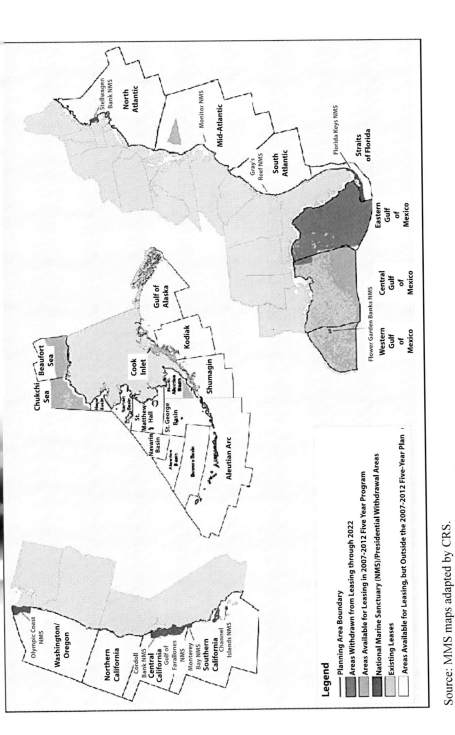

Source: MMS maps adapted by CRS.
Figure 1. OCS Oil and Gas Development Locations

It is rare that areas designated by MMS for potential OCS leasing would include areas designated by Congress as under moratoria constraints. However, in the current Five-Year Plan which took effect on July 1, 2007, MMS proposed a possible lease sale in an area under moratoria offshore the Commonwealth of Virginia.[36] Sale 220 was proposed while the area was under moratoria to prohibit leasing activities. By 2009 however, the area was no longer under moratoria, and became eligible for leasing consideration.

Marine Sanctuaries and Marine Monuments

Federal agencies other than MMS administer moratoria policy on the OCS. National marine sanctuaries and national marine monuments are generally areas under moratoria[37] and are located in protected areas that encompass more than 300,000 square miles of ocean area.[38] National marine sanctuaries and national marine monuments are depicted in **Figure 1**.

Marine sanctuaries can be established and maintained in a variety of ways. Congress and the President can designate national marine sanctuaries and the Secretary of the Department of Commerce is authorized to designate areas of the marine environment as National Marine Sanctuaries.

Under the Antiquities Act, the President has the authority to unilaterally designate national monuments.[39] In 2006 and 2009, President George W. Bush used the Antiquities Act to establish the Northwestern Hawaiian Islands Marine National Monument, making it the largest single conservation area in U.S. history.[40]

BACKGROUND ON OCEAN GOVERNANCE

With few exceptions, nations exercise jurisdiction over marine areas within approximately 200 nautical miles of their coasts and recognize this area as their exclusive economic zone (EEZ) under domestic law,[41] and under the United Nations Convention on Law of the Sea (UNCLOS).[42] The United States has not ratified UNCLOS. The EEZ is a zone where the United States applies sovereign rights and third party nations are generally allowed limited rights in this zone as well. The two most common sources of authority for OCS oil and gas leasing in the EEZ and beyond are the Outer Continental Shelf Lands Act (P.L. 103-426, OCSLA) and UNCLOS. Consideration of both OCSLA and UNCLOS is apparent in the U.S. effort addressing extended continental shelf (ECS) areas.[43] However there is some disagreement over when to consider the OCSLA and when to consider UNCLOS, in the development of OCS policy. This is largely due to issues that arise in the UNCLOS ratification debate. Regardless of UNCLOS ratification, some degree of alignment with UNCLOS principles is a factor in United States OCS leasing policy, particularly in areas that would impact trans-boundary reserves or territorial clams of other nations.

Ocean governance is among the topics that are addressed by a task force formed at the direction of President Obama and led by the Council on Environmental Quality to make recommendations on national ocean policy.[44] In 2009, interim recommendations from the Interagency Ocean Policy Task Force proposed numerous reforms to improve coordination of domestic ocean governance.[45] The Task Force also recommended UNCLOS ratification as an expression of national ocean policy.

Outer Continental Shelf Lands Act (OSCLA)[46]

Among several federal statutes governing OCS activities, the chief statute for drilling and leasing activity is the OSCLA which grants the Secretary of the Interior authority over OCS energy and mineral leasing activities. The OCSLA, in conjunction with other statutes, extends broad powers to the President and federal agencies such as MMS over leasing activities on the OCS. Under the OCSLA, oil and gas lease sales are conducted in conjunction with numerous other federal and state authorities.[47] Renewable energy projects are also conducted in conjunction with numerous other federal and state authorities; however, under OCSLA federal planning does not integrate oil and gas and renewable energy projects. Expiration of moratoria restrictions impacts all programs (conventional and renewable) under the OCSLA because it signals a shift away from annual measures focused on certain controversial leasing areas for oil and gas, and it allows Congress to frame OCS policy with a comprehensive approach to all areas and all types of energy projects.

United Nations Convention on Law of the Sea (UNCLOS)[48]

As moratoria restrictions expire or are lifted, ocean areas that were formerly closed have the potential to open for energy development. U.S. leasing policy alternatives recognize certain areas under moratoria pursuant to bilateral treaty agreements and customary international law. Despite not ratifying UNCLOS, the United States seems to align domestic OCS policy with UNCLOS.[49]

The same themes that prevail in domestic OCS policy debates, seem to prevail in global development scenarios. International policy in favor of expanding ocean energy development offshore is driven by competition for energy resources; policy to stem certain development efforts is largely driven by global climate change concerns. The U.S. and other coastal countries are considering leasing activities farther and farther offshore, and as a result the potential for international ramifications of leasing in international areas is an emerging concern.[50]

Currently, amidst some uncertainty about OCS leasing policy in international areas, leasing opportunities are emerging near international marine boundaries. Issues likely to arise in these areas include jurisdictional issues and issues associated with joint development, particularly in areas where moratoria have expired or is set to expire.[51] UNCLOS is broadly viewed as the international standard by which to govern joint development in OCS areas in the North Atlantic, in the Arctic region, and in the Gulf of Mexico. Development issues in these areas are the subject of diplomatic and national security policy as well as economic and environmental policy.

U.S. MORATORIA IN INTERNATIONAL AREAS

In the Gulf of Mexico and in the Arctic, U.S. offshore activity is determined by a number factors, including conformance to customary international law. U.S. policy with respect to increasing domestic production in areas near international waters reflects general conformance to customary international law and consistency, if not full alignment, with the UNCLOS framework.[52]

In 1978, the United States and Mexico signed a treaty establishing maritime boundaries in the Gulf of Mexico.[53] The governance of deepwater areas was of particular interest in the 1978 draft treaty because two territorial "gaps" existed in areas beyond 200 miles from each nation's respective coastlines.[54] At that time there was no international consensus for nations to claim natural resources in areas beyond the 200-mile EEZ.[55] The Mexican parliament ratified the treaty in 1979. Eighteen years later, the United States Senate ratified a maritime boundary treaty. The period of consideration was largely due to debates about how the treaty impacted governance of deepwater areas.[56]

Treaty provisions between the U.S. and Mexico established a 1.4 nautical mile buffer zone on each side of the marine boundary and both countries agreed to a 10-year moratorium on oil and gas exploitation in the buffer zone.[57] When the Treaty was ratified, it was generally understood that after the 10-year period, each country would potentially determine drilling and exploitation of oil and gas in its respective buffer zone.[58] Under the Treaty, the moratoria area that was established appears to expire in 2010.

ISSUES FOR CONGRESS

Expiration of moratoria has created the potential for oil and gas exploration and production in areas of the OCS along the Atlantic and Pacific Coasts, parts of Alaska, and the Gulf of Mexico that had been restricted since 1982. These areas include some parts of the OCS that are largely unexplored. Although the annual congressional moratorium was not the only restriction to leasing these offshore areas, it was a significant bar on development. In the absence of the annual congressional moratoria, new OCS policy alternatives emerge for Congress and for the states.

Federal Revenue[59]

Moratoria reduces the potential for federal and state revenue. In FY2008 MMS collected approximately $18 billion from OCS leases.[60] Funds from offshore production also support the Land and Water Conservation Fund and the National Historic Preservation Fund. Both of these funds provide money to all 50 states. Where OCS oil and gas leasing is currently underway, and states participate in specific revenue sharing policies, revenue management programs seem to have broad support.[61]

Revenue sharing between the states and the federal government is typically established by statute. Congress has enacted three OCS revenue sharing programs that disburse money to coastal states. These programs are discussed in the following sections.

OCSLA Amendments of 1986 Created the 8(g) Zone

OCSLA amendments of 1986 mandated that the federal government share with affected coastal States 27% of revenues generated from oil and natural gas leases located in the federal 8(g) zone. The 8(g) zone is three miles wide and is located directly adjacent to a state's seaward boundary.[62] The Energy Policy Act of 2005 expanded revenue sharing in the 8(g) zone to include 27% of the revenues generated from renewable energy leases.

The Coastal Impact Assistance Program (CIAP)

CIAP is a grant program established under the Energy Policy Act of 2005. States with an approved CIAP State Plan are eligible to receive a portion of $250 million for each fiscal year 2007 through 2010. This revenue is shared among Alabama, Alaska, California, Louisiana, Mississippi, and Texas.[63]

The Gulf of Mexico Energy Security Act of 2006 (GOMESA)

GOMESA established a revenue sharing program for four coastal producing states in the Gulf of Mexico—Alabama, Louisiana, Mississippi and Texas—and their coastal counties and parishes. There are two phases: (1) starting in FY2007, these four states would receive 37.5% of the oil and gas revenues generated from leases issued in two areas of the Gulf of Mexico where sales were mandated in the Eastern and Central Gulf of Mexico Planning Areas; and (2) beginning in FY2017, the four states will share 37.5% of qualified OCS revenues from Gulf of Mexico leases issued after December 20, 2006. Payments to states are made annually. In March 2009, $25 million of GOMESA qualified revenues from bonuses and first year rental payments from leases issued in FY2008 were disbursed.[64]

International Ocean Policy for Energy Development

UNCLOS and Extended Continental Shelf Claims

Upon the expiration of the annual congressional moratoria, certain international marine boundary areas gained relevance in OCS leasing policy because these areas became open for new leasing consideration. Although U.S. maritime zones conform generally to UNCLOS, the United States has not ratified UNCLOS and is therefore not a party to this Convention.

The U.S. OCS extends beyond the EEZ in certain areas and the U.S. is engaged in efforts to establish its outer boundaries, or its extended continental shelf, to ultimately have the extended boundaries recognized generally by the international community. Similarly, other coastal nations are also engaged in efforts to establish their extended continental shelf boundaries. Among the coastal nations that have ratified UNCLOS, international recognition of their extended continental shelf would be recognized under UNCLOS rules. If the United States does not ratify UNCLOS, the United States likely cannot establish full UNCLOS recognition of its jurisdiction in offshore areas beyond 200 miles. This could result in uncertainty associated with U.S. marine boundaries and may jeopardize U.S. interests in certain activities such as security, navigation or oil and gas development.

The U.S. relies on its general conformance to international law as a substitute for ratifying UNCLOS in its approach to certain international ocean matters.[65] However, the difference between choosing to align with UNCLOS and choosing to ratify UNCLOS is becoming increasingly more pronounced, specifically with respect to the process to establish U.S. extended continental shelf jurisdiction.

Establishing OCS policies that allow for extended marine boundaries and establishing international recognition of U.S. ECS areas are emerging as significant concerns absent UNCLOS ascension. Arguments have been made that UNCLOS ratification is the only way to establish international recognition for extended continental shelf jurisdiction. Others disagree. It is unclear whether there is an available substitute for ratifying UNCLOS for the purpose of establishing UNCLOS recognition for extended continental shelf areas.

Trans-boundary OCS Resources

In the late 1990s, petroleum resources were discovered in progressively deeper water in the Gulf of Mexico. When in 2000, the United States signed and ratified the Delimitation Treaty with Mexico, both countries recognized the possibility that trans-boundary oil and gas reservoirs may exist.[66]

When prospective marine resources appear to straddle marine boundaries, it can be impractical for different national regulations to apply on different sides of an imaginary line in the middle of the ocean. The legal and policy issues associated with trans-boundary reservoirs have not been fully analyzed. Taking this into account, countries potentially consider mutual policy options, including moratoria alternatives, and address trans-boundary resources with a combination of unilateral and bilateral (or multi-lateral in the case of more than two countries) options.

U.S. and Mexico—Gulf of Mexico Moratoria Areas

In the case of the marine boundary between the U.S. and Mexico, which is depicted in **Figure 2**, a moratorium established by bilateral treaty is set to expire in 2010. As the restriction on development nears its expiration, both countries may be considering OCS development in that area. Opportunities exist to allow for oil sharing, joint development, or unitization schemes. If the United States and Mexico's constitutional and legal framework allow, this potentially provides many federal policy options and alternatives.

Marine development activities in the Gulf of Mexico are of interest to the United States, Mexico, and Cuba.[67] Concerns associated with governing transboundary resources such as those in the Gulf of Mexico are becoming increasingly evident. Despite various attempts within each nation to establish governance within their own jurisdictions, there is little to indicate progress between the United States, Mexico, and Cuba in developing coordinated maritime policies.[68]

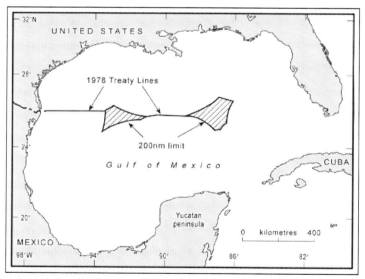

Source: Adapted by CRS from International Boundaries Research Unit (IBRU) Boundary and Security Bulletin Autumn 1997.

Figure 2. Marine Boundary Areas Between the U.S. and Mexico

U.S. and Canada—Georges Bank Moratoria Areas

Georges Bank straddles the U.S.-Canada border off southwest Nova Scotia in the North Atlantic. On the U.S. side, the West Georges Bank Basin had been under moratoria since 1982. With the expiration of the annual congressional moratoria, U.S. areas of the West Georges Bank Basin may be considered for oil and gas leasing.

On the Canadian portion of Georges Bank a general leasing ban has been in effect for many years, which covers the East Georges Bank Basin. BP Canada Energy Company and Chevron Canada Limited hold three large exploration concessions there, indicating potential development interests.

Exploration rights belonging to these companies were suspended during a Canadian moratorium, which was in place through 1999, and extended to December 31, 2012, matching the adjoining U.S. moratorium at that time. It is unclear whether the Canadian moratorium will be maintained after 2012 or whether the Canadian government is considering lifting that moratorium.

CONCLUSION

Expiration of moratoria policy is a significant legislative development and in the absence of this restriction, new policy alternatives emerge for domestic ocean energy development. While in place, the annual congressional moratoria may not have been consistent with executive orders and agency regulations at times, but it set parameters for federal OCS activity that generally satisfied coastal state interests and it provided a generally stable atmosphere for overall management of the OCS. While in place, moratoria policy diminished options to develop OCS areas and obviated the need for certain aspects of federal-state coordination to address economic and environmental concerns discussed in this chapter.

In the absence of legislation that seemed to quell controversy over energy projects in certain ocean and coastal areas, two broad consequences emerge. One likely consequence of lifting the moratoria is that policy makers would focus on coordination between the federal government and coastal states over concerns such as OCS environmental matters and revenue sharing. Another likely consequence of lifting the moratoria is that policy makers would focus on international marine boundaries, including the prospect of U.S. alignment with international governance bodies such as UNCLOS.

154   Curry L. Haggerty

Domestic policy debates about OCS energy development correspond to international policy debates about offshore energy development. In both domestic and international contexts, controversy seems to be widespread over economic and environmental policies. A prevailing view among advocates on both sides of the "drilling debate" is that ambiguity in federal ocean policy can impede achieving both economic and environmental objectives. Clarifying national ocean policy related to OCS development may lead to consistency in legislative and regulatory approaches to OCS development and may allow federal ocean agencies to more effectively reach economic and environmental objectives. Clarifying national policy related to OCS development also would likely facilitate cooperation between federal ocean agencies and state authorities and with international authorities.

OCS energy development options are in a state of change. This state of change is a theme of the Obama Administration Interagency Ocean Policy Task Force[69] and is the basis for the Task Force Interim Report, which raises questions about national priorities for ocean policy and recommends reforms intended to improve federal administration of ocean activities, including ratification of UNCLOS. U.S. ocean policy is attracting the interest of some policy makers in Congress, and it remains unclear what role this Congress will take in addressing these topics.

End Notes

[1] The Department of the Interior strategy for exploring and developing oil and gas resources on the OCS is posted at http://www.doi.gov/news/doinews/2010_03_31_news.cfm.

[2] *Memorandum on the Withdrawal of Certain Areas of the United States Outer Continental Shelf from Leasing Disposition* (March 31, 2010).

[3] The Continuing Appropriations Resolution, 2009 (P.L. 110-329), did not extend the annual congressional moratoria on oil and gas leasing activities. On March 11, 2009, the Omnibus Appropriations Act, 2009 (P.L. 111-8), was enacted without moratorium provisions, thus lifting in FY2009 the oil and gas development moratoria that had been in place since 1982 in the OCS along the Atlantic and Pacific coasts, in parts of Alaska, and in the Gulf of Mexico.

[4] This chapter does not focus on state-to-state or federal-state coordination on OCS policies. See CRS Report RL33404, *Offshore Oil and Gas Development: Legal Framework*, by Adam Vann.

[5] A geographical or nautical mile is equal to 6,080.20 feet, as opposed to the typical statute mile, which is equal to 5,280 feet.

[6] Certain other specific moratoria areas still exist by statute, by regulation, and by international treaty. These areas are not impacted by the expiration of the annual congressional moratoria.

[7] "Memorandum on Modification of the Withdrawal of Certain Areas of the United States Outer Continental Shelf from Leasing Disposition," *Weekly Compilation of Presidential*

Documents, vol. 44 (July 14, 2008), p. 986. It is in the combined effect of presidential directives from 1990 to 2008 that the policy impacts of moratoria are most apparent.

[8] The OCS drilling debate is a combination of several discrete debates about oil and gas leasing activity on the OCS. In the context of the OCS drilling debate Congress addresses multiple OCS activities (research, exploration, drilling, operations, and decommissioning). Also in this context, Congress addresses policy concerns related to the suitability of the size, timing, and location of oil and gas leasing and the adequacy of federal revenue management.

[9] This chapter focuses on the congressional moratorium, a policy option used to restrict OCS activity. Numerous other policy options serve as incentives to oil and gas development. One such incentive is royalty relief. For more information on incentives for OCS oil and gas development, see CRS Report RS22928, *Oil Development on Federal Lands and the Outer Continental Shelf,* by Marc Humphries.

[10] Global demand for oil and gas and global prices impact the economic feasibility of OCS development. Offshore activity depends on sustained capital investment by oil companies and independent producers. Periods of tight credit and uncertain projections for oil and gas demand can affect capital investment.

[11] The moratoria expired during a period of economic crisis in late 2008, when a liquidity shortfall in the U.S. banking system resulted in congressional action to halt what was considered at the time to be a crisis comparable to the Great Depression.

[12] The Outer Continental Shelf Lands Act (43 U.S.C. § 1337) and accompanying Congressional Declaration of Policy state, "The OCS is a vital national resource reserve held by the federal government for the public, which should be made available for expeditious and orderly development." The Energy Policy Act of 2005 (P.L. 109-58) was enacted in part to encourage domestic energy investment in new offshore leasing and development.

[13] The ways other countries with OCS development goals address environmental risk vary widely and are beyond the scope of this chapter. The Department of State is a source for learning about actions by other countries related to addressing environmental risk. See http://www.state.gov/g/oes/env/.

[14] A recent expression of this point of view was published in the Interim Report of the Interagency Ocean Policy Task Force, coordinated by the White House Council on Environmental Quality, available at http://www.whitehouse.gov/administration/eop/ceq/initiatives/oceans/interimreport.

[15] Numerous federal regulations exist to implement pollution control laws. See CRS Report RL34384, *Federal Pollution Control Laws: How Are They Enforced?,* by Robert Esworthy.

[16] Statutes provide for public scrutiny throughout the regulatory process and through litigation. See CRS Report RS20621, *Overview of National Environmental Policy Act (NEPA) Requirements,* by Kristina Alexander; and CRS Report RL33603, *Ocean Commissions: Ocean Policy Review and Outlook,* by Harold F. Upton and Eugene H. Buck.

[17] Obama Administration officials have broadly supported the notion that modern technology allows OCS energy development while protecting the environment.

[18] EEZ areas extend for 200 nautical miles beyond the baselines of the territorial sea, and encompass the territorial sea and its contiguous zone. The United States has jurisdiction over resources within its EEZ, including fishing, mining, and oil exploration, and has jurisdiction with regard to artificial islands and installations, marine scientific research, and marine pollution.

[19] EEZ rights are a matter of customary international law and are generally codified in Articles 55-60 of UNCLOS, entered into force November 16, 1994.

[20] H.R. 1696 and S. 783 would prevent leasing for the exploration, development, or production of oil, natural gas, or any other mineral in areas of the Atlantic.

[21] UNCLOS.

[22] A five-year leasing plan governs federal offshore leasing. For more information on the legal framework of federal leasing, see CRS Report RL33404, *Offshore Oil and Gas Development: Legal Framework,* by Adam Vann.

[23] The ramifications of moratoria for sectors marginally associated with OCS development are not readily apparent. Those opposed to drilling claim the effects are positive for air, water, and habitat quality in coastal areas. Those in favor of drilling claim ramifications are negative for coastal infrastructure, such as shipbuilding and repair facilities. The impact of the moratoria on "jobs" is unclear and is beyond the scope of this chapter.

[24] A sampling of acreage from 1983 to 2005 is as follows: 35 million acres were withdrawn in 1983 in Central and Northern California and the mid-Atlantic, 54 million acres were withdrawn in 1984 in California planning areas, the North Atlantic, and the Eastern Gulf of Mexico, 45 million acres were withdrawn in 1985 in California planning areas and the North Atlantic, 8 million acres in the North Atlantic were withdrawn from 1986 to 1988, 33 million acres were withdrawn in 1989 in Northern California, the North Atlantic, and the Eastern Gulf, and 84 million acres were withdrawn in 1990 in California planning areas, the North and Mid-Atlantic, the Eastern Gulf, and all of the North Aleutian Basin. (Energy Information Administration, Office of Oil and Gas, September 2005 Overview of U.S. Legislation and Regulations Affecting Offshore Natural Gas and Oil Activity).

[25] See DOI testimony before the Subcommittee on Energy and Mineral Resources, August 5, 1999 describing litigation related to OCS moratoria policy, specifically about the relinquishment of certain leases in the North Aleutian Basin, in areas of the Gulf of Mexico, and areas offshore of North Carolina.

[26] P.L. 109–432.

[27] GOMESA restricts leasing for about 15 years in areas of the Eastern Gulf of Mexico within 125 miles of Florida, including areas in the Gulf of Mexico east of the Military Mission Line and certain areas in the central Gulf of Mexico within 100 miles of Florida.

[28] GOMESA provided for the establishment of a process to exchange existing leases in the new moratorium areas for bonus or royalty credits. Regulations for bonus or royalty credits authorized under GOMESA are found in the final rule titled Bonus or Royalty Credits for Relinquishing Certain Leases Offshore, RIN 1010–AD44, published September 12, 2008 (73 FR 52917).

[29] Of a total of 85 leases eligible to apply for the credit, some leases have expired with no credit being issued, some leases have been relinquished for credits, and other leases are not yet responsive. The requests for credit must be received prior to the expiration date of the lease; the last day to apply for a credit is October 14, 2010.

[30] 43 U.S.C. 1341(a).

[31] 16 U.S.C. §§431-433.

[32] In 2003, Congress did not extend the moratoria in the North Aleutian Basin at the request of the Alaska delegation, and when Congress enacted GOMESA in 2006, a new moratorium on leasing activities in most of the new Eastern Gulf Planning Area as well as a portion of the Central Gulf Planning Area within 100 miles of the coastline of Florida was established until June 30, 2022.

[33] On July 14, 2008 a Modification of the Presidential Withdrawal of areas of the United States Outer Continental Shelf from leasing disposition was announced by President Bush in the following statement, "Under the authority vested in me as President of the United States, including section 12(a) of the Outer Continental Shelf Lands Act, 43 U.S.C. 1341(a), I hereby modify the prior memoranda of withdrawals from disposition by leasing of the United States Outer Continental Shelf issued on August 4, 1992."

[34] MMS, a bureau in the U.S. Department of the Interior, is the federal agency that manages the nation's ocean's oil, gas, renewable and other mineral resources on the outer continental shelf (OCS). See Minerals Management Service at http://www.mms.gov/.

[35] In 1997, MMS deferred offering 336 blocks in the Gulf of Mexico during treaty negotiations with Mexico. In 2001, Lease Sale 176 was deferred based upon insufficient time to complete review of an environmental analysis. In 2003, Lease Sale 186 in the Beaufort Sea was modified by deferrals recommended by Alaska governor Frank Murkowski.

Outer Continental Shelf Moratoria on Oil and Gas Development   157

[36] MMS prepares a five-year leasing plan, subject to annual revisions, that governs any offshore leasing that takes place during the period of plan coverage The current MMS Five-Year Oil and Gas Program Plan took effect on July 1, 2007. The Plan is available on MMS's website at http://www.mms.gov/offshore/PDFs/OMMStrategicPlan2007-2012.pdf.

[37] In 1998 President Clinton withdrew indefinitely all national marine sanctuaries at that time: Washington-Oregon (Olympic Coast); Central California (Cordell Bank, gulf of Farallones and Monterey Bay); Southern California (Channel Islands); Western Gulf of Mexico (Flower Garden Banks); Straits of Florida (Florida Keys); South Atlantic (Gray's Reef); Mid-Atlantic (Monitor); and North Atlantic (Stellwagen Bank).

[38] See CRS Report RL32486, *Marine Protected Areas (MPAs): Federal Legal Authority*, by Adam Vann.

[39] By Executive Order 13178, in 2000, President Clinton established the Northwestern Hawaiian Islands Coral Reef Ecosystem Reserve, directing steps to be taken to bring this site into the National Marine Sanctuary System.

[40] The Marine National Monument in the Northwestern Hawaiian Islands includes three new monuments in remote sites around the northernmost Mariana Islands, including the Mariana Trench and associated active underwater volcanoes and hydrothermal vents; Rose Atoll in American Samoa; and seven remote U.S. islands in the Central Pacific – Kingman Reef and Palmyra Atoll, Howland and Baker islands, and Jarvis, Johnston Atoll and Wake Island.

[41] The U.S. declared its EEZ in Proclamation No. 5030, 48 Fed. Reg. 10,605 (March 14, 1983).

[42] EEZ rights are a matter of customary international law and are generally codified in Articles 55-60 of UNCLOS, entered into force November 16, 1994.

[43] ECS areas are rights to the continental shelf beyond the 200-nautical-mile limit up to 350 miles in certain cases. As of mid-2009, 51 claims by 44 countries had been made to extend their continental shelf. Some countries have multiple submissions and joint submissions with other countries. There are numerous benefits to ECS areas including benefits related to military operations, resource development and other benefits.

[44] President Obama directed the Council on Environmental Quality (CEQ) to convene an Interagency Ocean Policy Task Force to address concerns related to national ocean policy.

[45] The Interagency Ocean Policy Task produced an Interim Report available at http://www.whitehouse.gov/ administration/eop/ceq/initiatives/oceans/interimreport.

[46] P.L. 103-426, 43 U.S.C. 1341.

[47] In addition to the OCSLA, several federal environmental and safety statutes apply to OCS leasing activity. OSCLA provides for regulations and procedures for leasing federal OCS areas, and procedures for environmental analysis of affected areas. OCSLA intends the government to receive fair market value for oil and gas production and establishes that rents and royalties are to be collected from OCS leasing activities.

[48] UNCLOS provides a comprehensive international legal framework intended for building consensus on actions related to the world's ocean spaces, uses, and resources. See United Nations Convention on the Law of the Sea, opened for signature December 10, 1982, in force November 16, 1994, 1833 U.N.T.S. 396, reprinted in *United Nations, the Law of the Sea: United Nations Convention on the Law of the Sea* (UN Pub. Sales No. E.83.V.5). For additional information, see CRS Report RS21890, *The U.N. Law of the Sea Convention and the United States: Developments Since October 2003*, by Marjorie Ann Browne.

[49] The governance of OCS areas can be approached a number of ways. The use of bilateral agreements and the exercise of unilateral rights and duties relative to an international framework of recognized ocean jurisdictions are two approaches that are used by the United States.

[50] In recent years there is increased attention to claims to establish extended OCS jurisdiction in areas beyond 200 nautical miles under certain conditions. Such extensions are of particular interest off Alaska and in the Gulf of Mexico.

[51] The marine boundary between the U.S. and Mexico is governed by the treaty noted at footnote 53. The moratorium established in this bilateral treaty is expected to expire in 2010. In the

158   Curry L. Haggerty

case of the marine boundary between the United States and Canada in the North Atlantic, the Canadian moratorium, appears to be in place until 2012.

[52] UNCLOS provides a framework for ocean governance based on customary international law. U.S. actions are generally in conformance with customary international law. With respect to certain UNCLOS proceedings, such as claiming extended continental shelf, there is no parallel in customary international law.

[53] Treaty on Maritime Boundaries between the United Mexican States and the United States of America (Caribbean Sea and Pacific Ocean), May 4, 1978; available at *http://www.un. org/Depts/los/LEGISLATIONANDTREATIES/PDFFILES/TREATIES/* MEX-USA 1978 MB.PDF.

[54] The "gaps" are depicted in the map at Figure 2. One area is located in front of the Mexican coastline of Tamaulipas and the United States coast of Texas. This area is known as the Western Gap, while the other one, the Eastern Gap is in front of the Mexican coast of Yucatan, the coast of New Orleans and the coast of Cuba.

[55] Today an UNCLOS process is established for countries to submit claims to a special UNCLOS commission which reviews the evidence related to ECS recognition. This UNCLOS review and determination is governed by Article 76 of UNCLOS and is the subject of some controversy.

[56] For more information see S.Rept. 105-4, *U.S.–Mexico Treaty on Maritime Boundaries*, October 22, 1997, Committee on Foreign Relations.

[57] Moratorium is the subject of Article 4 of the Treaty which reads, "Due to the possible existence of oil or natural gas reservoirs that may extend across the boundary set forth in Article I (hereinafter referred to as "trans-boundary reservoirs"), the Parties, during a period that will end ten (10) years following the entry into force of this Treaty, shall not authorize or permit oil or natural gas drilling or exploitation of the continental shelf within one and four-tenths (1.4) nautical miles of the boundary set forth in Article I. (This two and eight-tenths (2.8) nautical mile area hereinafter shall be referred to as "the Area" (…)."

[58] U.S. Department of the Interior, Minerals Management Service, Gulf of Mexico OCS Region press release on July 13, 2000 available at http://www.gomr.mms.gov/homepg/whatsnew/ newsreal/2000/000713.html.

[59] Revenue management has been the subject of considerable interest and controversy. See CRS Report RS22764, *Recent Litigation Related to Royalties from Federal Offshore Oil and Gas Production*, by Adam Vann.

[60] MMS statistics available at http://www.mms.gov/ooc/PDFs/MMSFastFactsApr09.pdf.

[61] The way royalty payments work is set forth in the lease instrument itself. The royalty clause is the main provision in OCS leases for the compensation of the federal government. At the time the lease is executed, the federal government typically receives a bonus payment for the grant of the lease and during the primary term of the lease may receive periodic payments of rentals. If production is obtained, the federal government receives royalty, usually stated as a percentage of production or of the proceeds from the sale of production minus the costs associated with producing the oil and or gas.

[62] According to MMS, in FY2008, MMS disbursed $103.6 million in 8(g) oil and gas revenues to seven coastal states. Alabama: $15.0 million; Alaska: $17.8 million; California: $11.0 million; Louisiana: $45.8 million; Texas: $13.3 million; Mississippi: $ 564,068; Florida: $ 83. Disbursements to Mississippi and Florida (compared to Alabama, Alaska, California, Louisiana, and Texas) show a difference in scale. This may be related to adherence to each state's state coastal planning requirements. See http://www.mms.gov/ooc/PDFs/ MMSFastFactsApr09.pdf.

[63] For more information see http://www.mms.gov/offshore/ciapmain.htm.

[64] According to MMS, funds were disbursed to Alabama: $7.7 million; Louisiana: $7.9 million; Mississippi: $6.8 million and Texas: $2.6 million. See http://www.mms.gov/ooc/PDFs/ MMSFastFactsApr09.pdf.

Outer Continental Shelf Moratoria on Oil and Gas Development   159

[65] Mutual adherence to UNCLOS has been instrumental in the diplomatic discussions to set marine boundaries between the United States and Mexico. It is typical that countries attempt to adhere to the same customary definitions when settling marine boundaries, and determining the sovereignty of marine areas. For example, when Mexico and the United States negotiated a marine boundary each country adhered to the position that the continental shelf of each country would extend past the 200 nautical mile boundary, pursuant to Article 76(1) of UNCLOS. This was a fundamental principle of the delimitation of marine areas between Mexico and the United States. It was by each country's adherence to this principle that both countries were able to agree.

[66] A trans-boundary resource is a resource that straddles two national territories.

[67] See U.S. Geological Survey report titled "Assessment of Undiscovered Oil and Gas Resources of the North Cuba Basin 2004," published in February 2005, which estimates a mean of 4.6 billion barrels of undiscovered oil and a mean of 9.8 trillion cubic feet of undiscovered natural gas along Cuba's north coast.

[68] The U.S. negotiated a boundary with Cuba but has not ratified the Cuba boundary treaty. The boundary treaty with Cuba was submitted to the Senate on January 23, 1979. On September 17, 1980, the Senate unanimously returned the boundary treaty with Cuba to the executive calendar. See 126 *Cong. Rec.* S25722–23 (Sept. 17, 1980).

[69] President Obama directed the Council on Environmental Quality (CEQ) to convene an Interagency Ocean Policy Task Force to address concerns related to national ocean policy. The Interagency Ocean Policy Task produced an Interim Report available at *http://www.whitehouse.gov/administration/eop/ceq/initiatives/oceans/interimreport*.

In: Energy Policies and Issues
Editors: Edgar R. Thompson

ISBN: 978-1-61122-685-0
© 2011 Nova Science Publishers, Inc.

Chapter 9

ACCELERATED VEHICLE RETIREMENT FOR FUEL ECONOMY: "CASH FOR CLUNKERS"

Brent D. Yacobucci and Bill Canis

SUMMARY

In an attempt to boost sagging U.S. auto sales and to promote higher vehicle fuel economy, the President signed legislation on June 24, 2009, P.L. 111-32, establishing a program to provide rebates to prospective purchasers toward the purchase of new, fuel-efficient vehicles, provided the trade-in vehicles are scrapped. The program was known as Consumer Assistance to Recycle and Save (CARS), or, informally, as "cash for clunkers." It provided rebates of $3,500 or $4,500, depending on fuel economy and vehicle type of both the new vehicle and the vehicle to be disposed of. Congress appropriated $3 billion for the program in two separate installments. CARS ran for a month, from July 24, 2009, until August 25, 2009.

During this period, nearly 700,000 vehicles were traded. Estimates of new vehicle sales induced by the rebate system range from 125,000 to as many as 440,000. Motor vehicle sales in August 2009 hit 14 million seasonally adjusted units, compared to only 9.5 million being sold on a seasonally adjusted basis in the first six months of 2009. These CARS-assisted summer sales helped propel overall 2009 car sales to 10.4 million units, comparable to annual sales for 2008.

After officially launching on June 24, 2009, when NHTSA regulations were issued, the CARS program was embraced by thousands of consumers and by auto dealers across the country, who advertised it widely. By the end of the first week, the U.S. Department of Transportation (DOT) announced that nearly all of the initial $1 billion in funds appropriated for it were committed, based on rising dealer applications for rebate reimbursements and surveying of dealer backlogs.

Recognizing the stimulative effect of the program, the House of Representatives voted to appropriate an additional $2 billion (H.R. 3435) on July 31, 2009, tapping funds from the economic recovery act (American Recovery and Reinvestment Act, or ARRA, P.L. 111-5). The Senate followed suit on August 6, 2009, and President Obama signed the supplemental CARS funding into law (P.L. 111-47) on August 7, 2009.

By most measures, CARS was successful in stimulating auto sales. Among the benchmarks listed by NHTSA, which oversaw CARS:

- August 2009 sales were 43% higher than in June 2009, the last pre-CARS month;
- The total value of all CARS transactions was $15.2 billion;
- About 60,000 jobs were estimated to have been created in auto parts, assembly, and sales, and an estimated $7.8 billion added to U.S. Gross Domestic Product.

Similar programs have been implemented in various U.S. states, but this was the first federal program. In general those state pilot programs focused on retiring vehicles with older, and in some cases malfunctioning, emissions control systems in order to promote better air quality. CARS focused, instead, on higher fuel economy and promoting U.S. auto sales. Similar vehicle retirement programs have been implemented in other countries, such as Japan, Germany, France, and China, and provided a similar boost in auto sales.

This chapter outlines the key provisions of the CARS program and discusses the impact of the program on the economy. It also summarizes similar programs in other industrial countries.

INTRODUCTION

A severe recession and major decline in auto sales in 2009 motivated lawmakers to consider ways to support the domestic automotive industry. Since December 2008, a new, expanded federal presence in the automotive industry has developed, including new grant and loan programs, support through the Troubled Asset Relief Program (TARP), and partial federal ownership of Chrysler and General Motors. Coupled with the economic concerns about the auto industry have been historically high gasoline prices experienced through the summer of 2008 and the prospect of future price hikes when the global recession ends. In response to high fuel prices and growing concerns over greenhouse gas emissions and climate change, Congress has pursued new policies on fuel economy, including tighter Corporate Average Fuel Economy (CAFE) standards enacted in the Energy Independence and Security Act of 2007 (EISA, P.L. 110-140), as well as even tighter standards on fuel economy and greenhouse gases proposed by the Obama Administration's EPA.[1]

As a way to promote new vehicle sales, higher fuel economy, and lower emissions, an accelerated vehicle retirement (AVR)—also called "cash for clunkers" or fleet modernization—program was enacted in 2009.[2] AVR programs provide financial incentives for a vehicle owner to "retire"—that is, usually shred or crush[3]—an old vehicle and purchase a new vehicle. Previous state-level AVR programs[4] in the United States have generally focused on air quality,[5] since newer tailpipe emissions standards are significantly more stringent than older standards,[6] and many older vehicles no longer meet the less stringent standards for which they were originally certified. However, some recent programs abroad have focused directly on motivating new vehicle sales and propping up the automotive sector.

The 2009 Consumer Assistance to Recycle and Save (CARS) was part of these initiatives to both address the health of the domestic auto industry and to retire older, inefficient vehicles. To boost sagging U.S. auto sales and to promote higher vehicle fuel economy, Congress passed several proposals in 2009:

- On June 9, 2009, the House passed a CARS authorization, H.R. 2751, for a four-year, $4 billion program; the Senate did not act on it.
- On June 18, 2009, the Senate passed the conference report to the Supplemental Appropriations Act of 2009 (H.R. 2346) that the House had passed two days earlier. While focused on supplemental military

appropriations, Title XIII of the bill included a scaled-down version of CARS. Added in conference, the provision is similar to H.R. 2751,[7] but appropriated a billion dollar program instead of the $4 billion in the earlier, House-passed legislation. A bill with more stringent qualification requirements had been introduced in the Senate (S. 247), but was never considered on the Senate floor. The President signed the supplemental bill on June 24, 2009 (P.L. 111-32).

- With the $1 billion funding running out for CARS after only a week, Congress turned again to CARS funding before the summer recess. On June 31, 2009, the House passed H.R. 3435, appropriating an additional $2 billion for CARS, with funding to be taken from the economic stimulus law, the American Recovery and Reinvestment Act of 2009 (P.L. 111-5). The Senate passed the bill on August 6, and President Obama signed the bill into law (P.L. 111-47) on August 7. The CARS program would have ended if additional funds had not been approved.

The CARS program provided consumers with a rebate of up to $4,500 toward the purchase of a new, more fuel-efficient vehicle. The value of the rebate was based on the fuel economy and fuel savings of the new vehicle compared to the old vehicle, as well as the vehicle class of both (i.e., passenger car, light truck, or work truck). To qualify for a rebate, the auto dealer certified that the engine of the old vehicle would be disabled, and that the vehicle was sent to be crushed or shredded.

CARS combined the goal of promoting auto sales with improved fuel economy. The general argument has been that the United States is at a critical juncture and has an opportunity to use any recovery in the auto sector to foster a switch to more fuel efficient vehicles. Therefore, most cash for clunkers proposals in the 111th Congress, including the legislation signed by the President, have tied incentives to the purchase of vehicles with higher fuel economy.

CARS PROGRAM

As enacted, the CARS program provided a rebate toward the purchase of a new, more fuel-efficient vehicle, provided the old vehicle was transferred by the auto dealer to a facility where it was crushed or shredded. Consumers were

Accelerated Vehicle Retirement for Fuel Economy...

not responsible for the actual scrapping of the vehicle. The legislation established many of the elements necessary for the program, including the criteria for obtaining a rebate, as well as requirements for auto dealers to be registered under the program. The National Highway Traffic Safety Administration (NHTSA), within DOT, had responsibility for developing regulations to implement the program. Although some original proposals limited CARS rebates to vehicles manufactured in the United States or North America, these limitations were removed over concerns that the CARS program be compliant with World Trade Organization (WTO) rules, and so buyers were eligible for a rebate regardless of where the vehicle was made.

Program Regulations

NHTSA was given one month to develop regulations implementing the program, and it did so, issuing them and officially launching the CARS program on July 24, 2009.[8] Those regulations include

- procedures for dealers to register for the program;
- procedures for dealer reimbursement for the value of the rebate within 10 days of submitting required information;
- a prohibition on dealers using the rebate to offset other rebates or discounts;
- a requirement that dealers disclose the estimated scrappage value of the trade-in and to retain up to $50 of the actual scrappage value for administrative costs;
- requirements and procedures for the disposal of trade-in vehicles; and
- enforcement of penalties (up to $15,000 per violation of the above requirements and prohibitions).

P.L. 111-32 includes a clause "[n]otwithstanding the requirements of section 553 of title 5, United States Code, the Secretary shall promulgate final regulations to implement the Program not later than 30 days after the date of the enactment of this Act." Despite various statutory requirements that could have precluded promulgation of regulations within 30 days—most notably the Administrative Procedure Act, which generally requires sufficient time for public notice and opportunity for comment on proposed regulations[9]—the regulations were issued on time.

Value of a Rebate

Under the CARS program, NHTSA issued rebates directly to auto dealers when they sold an eligible vehicle after July 1, 2009, and until funding ran out at the end of August. The value of the rebate was deducted from the price of the vehicle and the dealer was in turn reimbursed by NHTSA. Only one rebate was allowed per person, and only one rebate was issued per vehicle (regardless of the number of joint owners). NHTSA issued rebates only up to the total value of its appropriation (initially $1 billion for the CARS program, increased by an additional $2 billion on August 7).

The value of the rebate was based on the type of new vehicle purchased, the type of trade-in vehicle, and the fuel economy of both. Four classes of vehicles were eligible: (1) passenger automobiles (cars); (2) category 1 trucks[10] (sport utility vehicles and smaller vans and pickup trucks); (3) category 2 trucks (larger light-duty pickup trucks and vans); and (4) category 3 trucks (medium-duty pickup trucks and cargo trucks and vans).

Eligible Trade-in Vehicle

To qualify for the rebate, the trade-in vehicle had to be in drivable condition; had to be continuously insured by the same owner for at least one year;[11] and had to have been manufactured less than 25 years before the date of trade-in (i.e. since 1984). For all vehicles except category 3 trucks, the trade-in vehicle had to have a combined estimated new Environmental Protection Agency (EPA)-rated fuel economy (as defined on the fueleconomy.gov website) of no more than 18 miles per gallon (mpg). Category 3 trucks had to be from model year 2001 or newer.

Eligible New Vehicle

To qualify for the rebate, the manufacturer's suggested retail price (MSRP) had to be less than $45,000 for the new vehicle. For cars and category 1 and 2 trucks, the vehicle had to comply with EPA's Tier 2 emissions standards, and for category 3 trucks the vehicle had to comply with new heavy-duty engine standards. Except for category 3 trucks, new vehicles had to meet the following mileage standards: 22 mpg for a passenger car; 18 mpg for a category 1 truck; and 15 mpg for a category 2 truck.

Rebate Value

Rebates were worth either $3,500 or $4,500, depending on different parameters, as shown in **Table 1**.

Impact of the Program: Expectations and Reality

Impact on Auto Industry/Sales

Originally, the impact of the CARS program on the auto industry was expected to be limited by the narrow scope of the program. First, the program was limited to vehicles purchased over a month-long period in the summer of 2009. Second, the number of rebates was limited to the available appropriation—only about 222,000 to 286,000 rebates were expected to be issued under the initial $1 billion appropriation,[12] and about 750,000 under the total $3 billion program.[13] Therefore, it was thought that this program would more likely provide a "shot in the arm" to U.S. auto sales rather than provoking a systemic change in the auto industry, the new vehicle fleet, or fleet-wide fuel economy.

Table 1. Criteria for Determining CARS Rebate Value

Rebate Value	New Vehicle Category			
	Passenger Automobile	Category 1 Truck	Category 2 Truck	Category 3 Truck
$4,500	At least 10 mpg higher fuel economy than trade-in 22mpg minimum	At least 5 mpg higher than trade-in 18 mpg minimum	At least 2 mpg higher than trade-in 15 mpg minimum	None
$3,500	At least 4 mpg higher than trade-in 22mpg minimum	At least 2 mpg higher than trade-in 18 mpg minimum	At least 1 mpg higher than trade-in OR trade-in is a MY2001 or newer category 3 truck 15 mpg minimum	Trade-in is a MY2001 or newer category 3 truck Trade-in is of similar size or larger than new truck

Source: CRS Analysis of H.R. 2346.

Note: Category 1 includes sport utility vehicles and smaller vans and pickup trucks. Category 2 includes larger pickup trucks and vans. Category 3 includes medium-duty pickup trucks, cargo trucks, and cargo vans.

168 Brent D. Yacobucci and Bill Canis

After the CARS program ended, it became clear that it had, in fact, provided a positive stimulus for auto sales, by drawing back many would-be consumers to auto showrooms. As the program was wrapping up, Transportation Secretary Ray LaHood said,

American consumers and workers were the clear winners thanks to the cash for clunkers program. Manufacturing plants have added shifts and recalled workers. Moribund showrooms were brought back to life and consumers bought fuel efficient cars that will save them money and improve the environment.[14]

Estimates of the number of car sales prompted by the program vary. The Council of Economic Advisers (CEA) reviewed the CARS program, noting that "our baseline analysis below will assume 50,000 postponed June sales, which yields an estimate of 440,000 net CARS-induced sales over the June-July-August time frame."[15] The CEA estimated that CARS raised economic growth in the third quarter 2009 by between 0.1% and 0.4%, at an annual rate, due to increased retail sales of motor vehicles in July and August, 2009. The CEA report adds this caveat:

To put it another way, the estimates imply that the $3 billion program will increase output in the automobile sector in the second half of the year by between about $2.5 billion and $6 billion—a substantial direct effect. It is important to note, however, that the boost to the level of GDP is temporary, and is followed by a drop that slightly more than reverses the increase, reflecting the slightly lower level of sales in the "payback" period.[16]

Edmunds.com, an online source for auto research and information, painted a very different picture. It estimated that only 125,000 of the 690,000 sales were prompted by the federal rebates and that rising auto sales were prompted by a rebounding auto market. Edmunds issued a press release in October 2009 saying that the rest of the sales would have taken place without "cash for clunkers" and stating that "taxpayers paid $24,000 per vehicle sold."[17] Edmunds developed this estimate by dividing the $3 billion federal program by the 125,000 vehicle sales it says were spurred.[18]

A third estimate of sales induced by "cash for clunkers" was developed by the Center for Automotive Research (CAR) in Ann Arbor, Michigan, which estimated that 303,000 vehicles sold in July and August 2009 were induced by the rebates. CAR looked beyond the summer duration of the clunkers program and further estimated that there was a net positive effect on sales after the clunkers program ended, thereby concluding that 395,000 new vehicles were spurred by the rebates.[19]

CEA also suggested that the fourth quarter 2009 GDP would benefit as automakers increased production after CARS to replace depleted inventories: Ford, GM, and Honda announced third and fourth quarter production increases at U.S. facilities. CEA estimated that 60,000 jobs had been saved or created as a result of CARS.

U.S. sales of cars and light trucks, at a seasonally adjusted annual rate, hit 14 million units in August 2009, far ahead of the 9.5 million units sold in the first six months of the year.[20] While sales in September then fell to about 8 million units, reflecting sales moved forward by "cash for clunkers," sales in the rest of 2009 were stronger, finishing out with an especially strong December and overall, seasonally adjusted sales for all of 2009 reached 10.4 million units.

Petroleum and Emissions Savings

In its report to Congress, NHTSA estimates that the CARS program will save roughly 820 million gallons of fuel and 9.5 million metric tons of carbon dioxide over the next 25 years. These savings are relatively small compared to projected fuel consumption and transportation emissions. For example, compared to the Energy Information Administration's (EIA) estimates for motor gasoline consumption and carbon dioxide emissions from petroleum consumption in 2020 in the transportation sector, the estimated annual savings from the CARS program represent roughly 0.02% of both consumption and emissions.[21] The CARS program has been criticized by environmentalists because its scope was too small to affect significant change in the auto sector, and the required increases in fuel economy were not stringent enough.[22]

However, regardless of the size of the program, the costs of the program may balance the benefits in at least one sense. In its report, NHTSA estimates that the fuel saved from the program will lead to cumulative savings of between $1.3 billion and $2.7 billion over the next 25 years.[23] Assuming a social cost of carbon dioxide of $20 (the mid-range of NHTSA's scenarios),[24] the social benefit of the reduced carbon dioxide emissions from both fuel savings and new vehicle production is between $0.2 billion and $0.3 billion.[25] Thus total cumulative social benefits from reduced gasoline consumption and emissions range between $1.5 billion and $3.0 billion. The upper end of this range is roughly in line with the total federal appropriation for the program. That said, while the net costs and benefits to society may be equal, those who received rebates from the program will benefit (both through reduced vehicle purchase price and reduced fuel costs) more than those who did not receive rebates.

**Table 2. CARS Program by the Numbers
(Highlights of the Motor Vehicle Rebate Program)**

Benchmark	Result
Number of motor vehicle dealers that participated	18,908
States that participated[a]	50
Number of voucher applications submitted to NHTSA	690,114
Number of voucher applications paid	677,842
Number of voucher applications cancelled by dealers	12,272
Average voucher	$4,209
Total federal funds paid out in vouchers	$2.85 billion
Trade-ins that were passenger cars	14%
New vehicles that were passenger cars	59%
Trade-ins that were SUVs or trucks	85%
New vehicles that were SUVs or trucks	41%
Average age of vehicles traded in	14 years
Average odometer reading of trade-ins	160,170 miles
Average combined EPA fuel economy rating of tradeins	15.7 mpg
Average combined EPA fuel economy rating of new vehicles	24.9 mpg
Estimated number of jobs saved or created	60,000
Percent of new vehicles manufactured domestically	49%
Estimated reduction in carbon dioxide emissions and related greenhouse gases over 25 years	9 million metric tons
Resulting fuel consumption reduction over 25 years	824 million gallons (33 million gallons per year)

Source: National Highway Traffic Safety Administration (NHTSA), "Consumer Assistance to Recycle and Save Act of 2009: Report to Congress," December 2009.

Notes: Category 3 trucks, used mainly for commercial purposes, were also eligible for CARS and constituted one percent or less of the trade-ins and new vehicles.

a. In addition to the 50 states, dealers in Puerto Rico, Guam and the U.S. Virgin Islands also participated.

CARS Program Results

About 690,114 CARS vouchers were submitted in July and August 2009 and NHTSA had reviewed 99% of them by late September. Eligible CARS sales reported on the NHTSA hotline grew from about 4,000 on the first day to six times that a few days later. This surge in sales and reporting is one reason that many dealers had difficulty in reaching NHTSA to register and report their eligible sales. According to a survey by *Automotive News*, 90% of dealers were dissatisfied with the time it took to be reimbursed by the government.[26]

This large surge in transactions in a short period of time overwhelmed the initial DOT system and, eventually, 7,000 people were assigned to review the transactions, many of them contract employees.[27]

According to the December 2009 report to Congress on the CARS program by NHTSA, and shown in **Table 2**, most of the vehicle trade-ins were SUVs and light trucks, whereas most newly-purchased vehicles were cars. The NHTSA report noted that "The total new vehicles sold or leased under the CARS program included 401,274 passenger cars, 274,602 light trucks (Category 1 and 2) and 1,966 heavy trucks (Category 3). The top ten models sold under the program were:

1. Toyota Corolla
2. Honda Civic
3. Toyota Camry
4. Ford Focus FWD
5. Hyundai Elantra
6. Nissan Versa
7. Toyota Prius
8. Honda Accord
9. Honda Fit
10. Ford Escape FWD

The model breakdown of the 677,842 new vehicles purchased through CARS is shown in **Table 3**. It is notable that Chrysler's three brands—Jeep, Dodge and Chrysler—sold less than 7% of CARS vehicles because the company shut down all its plants in the spring as part of its bankruptcy and restructuring. The timing of the CARS program caught Chrysler with not enough inventory on hand, and so it ran out of vehicles to sell during the CARS program.

Table 3. New Motor Vehicles Purchased Under CARS
(by Make of Vehicle)

Make Of New Vehicle	Number of Transactions	Share of New Vehicles (%)
Toyota	120,507	17.78
Ford	90,135	13.30
Honda	87,585	12.92
Chevrolet	86,354	12.74
Nissan	58,700	8.66
Hyundai	48,780	7.20
Kia	28,974	4.27
Dodge	24,119	3.56
Subaru	16,816	2.48
Pontiac	16,644	2.46
Mazda	16,144	2.38
VW	12,418	1.83
Jeep	11,211	1.65
GMC	9,704	1.43
Chrysler	9,033	1.33
Scion	7,851	1.16
Mercury	6,626	0.98
Saturn	5,334	0.79
Suzuki	3,707	0.55
Lexus	3,663	0.54
Other	13,537	2.00
Total	677,842	100.00

Source: National Highway Traffic Safety, Report to Congress on CARS Program, December 2009, p. 24

Of all the motor vehicles sold during CARS, just under half were made in the United States, according to NHTSA. The largest number of non-U.S. cars sold was imported from Japan, as shown in **Table 4**.

One of the concerns about a vehicle retirement program, expressed prior to the CARS enactment, was that it would pull forward sales that would normally have been made in the following months and years. The experience with CARS shows that this is a valid issue, but it has had a limited impact thus far on the recovery of the U.S. retail motor vehicle market.

Accelerated Vehicle Retirement for Fuel Economy...   173

Table 4. Country of Origin of CARS Vehicles

Country	New Vehicles	Trade-Ins
United States	329,173	499,365
Japan	115,526	54,958
Mexico	81,655	11,307
South Korea	73,119	3,738
Canada	65,177	90,420
Germany	10,056	11,199

Source: NHTSA Report to Congress on CARS Program, December 2009.

The major evidence that CARS had pulled sales forward occurred in September 2009, when U.S. motor vehicle sales fell 40% from the CARS-supported levels of August 2009. Nearly all major brands saw a fall-off in sales when "cash for clunkers" ended. Overall U.S. motor vehicles sales came in at a seasonally adjusted annual rate (SAAR) of 9.5% that month, similar to the lackluster performance in the first half the year and well below the SAAR of 14 million in August 2009.

The change was more modest, however, when compared to year-over-year sales: September 2009 sales were 23% lower than the same month in 2008. Compared to the same month in 2008, Ford's sales in September 2009 fell by 5%, GM's by 45%, Chrysler's by 42%, Toyota's by 13% and Honda's by 20%. Only Hyundai saw a spike, with sales rising by 27%.[28]

Fourth quarter U.S. auto sales—October through December—took on a more robust complexion, however, indicating that the pull-forward effects of CARS seemed fairly limited. October sales ran at 10.4 million SAAR, November's at 10.9 million and December's at 11.9 million.[29] Despite these gains during the year, 2009 was the worst year for U.S. car sales since 1982 and the lowest on a per capita basis since 1950.[30]

COMPARISON TO PROGRAMS IN OTHER MAJOR INDUSTRIAL COUNTRIES

AVR[31] programs have been popular in other countries around the world, from Japan, Korea and China in Asia to many European countries and Russia. (See **Table 5**.)

In Europe, at least 13 countries enacted AVR rebates and tax incentives in 2009.[32] In addition to the European countries shown in **Table 5**, these countries also offered programs: The Netherlands, Portugal, Romania, Luxembourg, Cyprus, Slovakia, and Greece. Some European programs (such as the one in France) required that the new vehicle have tighter emissions standards, but others did not have such a requirement (such as the UK's).

One of the most-discussed programs has been Germany's, which provided vouchers for 2,500 Euro (roughly $3,500)[33] toward the purchase of a new vehicle for scrapping a vehicle at least nine years old. It is credited with boosting auto sales during its one year duration by over 25%. These rebate programs had less dramatic impacts elsewhere, increasing auto sales in France by 4.2% and Austria by over 6%, for example. (In the European Union, auto sales in 2009 were 13.7 million units, down from 15.3 million vehicles sold in 2008 and lower than the 16-16.5 million vehicles sold each year earlier in the decade.)

The success of some European scrappage programs was evident soon after they were enacted in 2009. According to *BusinessWeek*, the German "cash for clunkers" program "caused auto sales to spike 21.5% in February [2009] and created the best sales quarter for GM's Opel brand in a decade."[34] In June 2009, European auto sales rose by 2.4%, "their first year-on-year rise in 14 months, thanks almost entirely to scrappage schemes in a dozen countries."[35] Some analysts say these programs may eventually lead to a "severe slump in car sales after the expiration of the incentives, which they say will artificially pull forward demand for new cars. 'We're definitely setting up problems for the future,'" said an auto industry analyst at UBS in London.[36] When the French offered a similar program in the 1990s, sales fell by 20% when it ended.[37]

Similarly, Japan is offering a 250,000 Yen (about $2,600) subsidy for turning in a car at least 13 years old.[38] The Japanese government plans to extend the program from its March 2010 deadline until September 2010.

The initial Japanese clunkers program did not permit U.S.-made vehicles to participate, but the extension will permit some low-emission U.S. cars to be eligible. Under Japanese car import rules, all vehicles are subject to an expensive testing procedure, the Type Approval System. For about 30 years, the Japanese government has offered an alternative, less costly certification system for automakers who sell only a limited number of models a year there. Known as the Preferential Handling Procedure, or PHP, it relies, in the case of U.S. automobiles, on EPA and other U.S. standards. The original Japanese clunkers program specifically excluded all PHP vehicles, which the government argued did generally not meet their AVR standards of low emissions and high fuel economy. In January 2010, the government decided to modify the program to permit certain PHP vehicles to qualify for purchase under the rebate program.

China's auto market, assisted by several purchased incentive programs, grew by 45% to over 13.6 million vehicles sales in 2009, boosting it for the first time to the largest automobile market in the world, replacing the United States in that category.[39] China's auto sales are expected to rise by 10% or more in 2010 according to some observers.

Table 5. Recent Foreign Fleet Modernization Programs in Major Industrial Countries

Country	Production and Sales Incentives
Canada	The Canadian government approved C$92 million to support a limited scrappage program for vehicles produced before 1996 when more stringent pollution laws were enacted. The "Retire Your Ride" program offers consumers C$300 to scrap their older vehicle, a program administered by a nonprofit foundation. Although auto dealers and manufacturers called on the federal government to commit $350 million to a scrappage program that would offer consumer a $3,500 voucher to trade in cars that are at least 10 years old, the federal government did not enact the larger program.[a] As much as 75% of Canadian vehicles are made elsewhere, and it was thought that clunkers program would do little to stimulate the Canadian economy.
Europe	
France	A fleet modernization plan was in effect for a year and provided motorists with a €1,000 ($1,400) subsidy and a staggered tax rebate of up to €5,000 if they replaced and scrapped vehicles more than 10 years old for more fuel efficient vehicles. Eligible-purchase vehicles had to emit reduced carbon dioxide. The French government set aside €380 million for this program,[b] which ended in December 2009; French sales rose nearly 11% in 2009. Proposed extensions of the program of up to a year—until the end of 2010—may be considered by the government.
Germany	Germany had one of the most successful fleet modernization programs, where consumers scrapping at least a nine-year-old vehicle received a €2,500 subsidy ($3,500). Trade-ins had to have been certified as scrapped, with certain parts recycled. The government provided €5 billion to fund it.[c] Eligible vehicles had

Table 5. (Continued)

Country	Production and Sales Incentives
	to be more than 9 years old and meet older, Euro 4 emission standards. (The European Union's Euro 4 emissions were set in 2005; requirements for reduced nitrogen oxides and particulates are lower than for comparable U.S. and Japanese vehicles at that time.) A further tax rebate was available for those who purchased Euro 5/6 compliant vehicles. (Euro 5 standards took effect in 2009, raising the nitrogen oxide and non-methane hydrocarbon standard levels; Euro 6 standards will take effect for all vehicles in 2014.)The German scrappage program ran for 7 months, ended in September 2009, and is credited with boosting sales by over 23%.
Italy	Italy's 11-month scrappage program was based on a €2 billion stimulus package for auto and domestic goods industries, including an incentive of €1,500-5,000 to buy a new, less-polluting motor vehicle.[d] Cars had to be more than 9 years old and exceed Euro 4 emissions guidelines. The basic €1,500 subsidy could be combined with other incentives (up to €5,000) for cars running on compressed natural gas, liquefied petroleum gas, electricity or hydrogen. New cars sales in 2009 were essentially flat.
Spain	Spain's scrappage program provided a €2,000 ($2,800) subsidy and interest free loans for the purchase of a new car with low carbon dioxide emissions. Under the program, which ran for 11 months until October 1, 2009, cars had to be at least 10 years old to be eligible for trade and then had to be scrapped. The program also applies to used cars no more than five years old and requires that a scrapped car is at least 15 years old.[f] Despite the scrappage incentive, new car sales in Spain fell by nearly 18%, a fact some attribute to the complexity of the Spanish program.
United Kingdom	With a total of £400 million budget, the UK program provided a "scrappage grant" that was available from May 2009 until February 2010 to car owners who turned in a car or van that was at least 10 years old. Owners received a £2,000 ($3,300) subsidy, the cost of which is split evenly between automakers and the UK government.[g] New car sales in the UK fell by over 6% in 2009.
	Asia
Japan	A fleet modernization program is under way in Japan, with consumers eligible for a ¥250,000 ($2,600) subsidy if they turn in their car (at least 13 years old). New cars must be used for at least a year.[e] The government extended the program until Septe-mber 2010, modifying it to allow some low-emission US-made vehicles for the first time to be eligible for the clunkers program.

Table 5. (Continued)

Country	Production and Sales Incentives
China	Under China's stimulus program, sales taxes were cut in half for small cars (under 1.6 liters). Consumers are encouraged to trade in older vehicles with poor emissions, for which there are rebates of $450 to $900. Rural areas were also targeted, with special incentives for farmers to buy cars, trucks and motorcycles. The government hopes to remove about 2.9 million vehicles under its year-long incentive program that ends in May 2010.
South Korea	The government implemented a temporary tax incentive program in May 2009, reducing taxes to retire an automobile made before 1999, up to a subsidy of 2.5 million Won ($2,041). The program ran from May 1, 2009, until the end of the year. New car registrations rose by 3.4% for the year.[h]

Sources: Peterson Institute for International Economics, *Money for the Auto Industry: Consistent with WTO Rules?*, February 2009; *Does the Auto Bailout Undermine Global Trade Rules*, interview with Gary Hufbauer, February 26, 2009; Automotive Trade Policy Council, *Foreign Government Actions to Support Their Auto Industries*; also see notes below; European Automobile Manufacturers Association (ACEA), website viewed January 22, 2010. Information on Euro 4, 5, and 6 emissions standards from http://www.carmall.eu/emission_standards.html.

Note: This table highlights activities in some major industrial countries, but programs have also been enacted in Austria, Greece, Malaysia, The Netherlands, Portugal, Romania, Slovakia, Turkey, and Taiwan. Source: Automotive Trade Policy Council.

a. CBC.ca, "Support car sales with $350M 'scrappage' program, auto industry pleads," August 4, 2009.

b. *The Wall Street Journal*, "In France, Oui to Bailout, Non to Layoffs," March 19, 2009.

c. *The Wall Street Journal*, "Merkel Pledges Backing for Opel," April 1, 2009.

d. *The Wall Street Journal*, "Italy Passes Stimulus Package," February 7, 2009.

e. *Reuters*, "Update1-New Japanese Good For Car Sales-Nissan COO," April 10, 2009.

f. *Automotive News Europe*, "Subsidies Lead to a Mixed May Sales Result in Europe," June 2, 2009.

g. Deloitte Touche Tohmatsu, *Deloitte Says More Needed to Revitalize Ailing Automotive Industry*, March 23, 2009.

h. Korea Automotive Manufacturers Association, "Reports & Statistics."

End Notes

[1] For more information on CAFE standards and the Administration proposal, see CRS Report R40166, *Automobile and Light Truck Fuel Economy: The CAFE Standards*, by Brent D. Yacobucci and Robert Bamberger.

[2] The official name of the legislation establishing the program was Consumer Assistance to Recycle and Save (CARS).

[3] In most cases, the state or the dealer is responsible for scrapping the old vehicle. In the case of the federal AVR program (CARS) the dealer, not the consumer, was responsible for transferring the old vehicle to a facility for scrappage.

[4] For more information on these programs, see CRS Report 96-766, *A Clean Air Option: Cash for Clunkers*, by David M. Bearden.

[5] Specifically to remove the most polluting vehicles from the road to help the states comply with National Ambient Air Quality Standards (NAAQS) for ozone and particulate matter.

[6] For example, federal standards for hydrocarbon emissions from new cars are 94% lower then they were 30 years ago (1970). Nitrogen oxide (NOx) standards are 97% lower. J.G. Calvert, J.B. Heywood, and R.F. Sawyer, et al., "Achieving Acceptable Air Quality: Some Reflections on Controlling Vehicle Emissions," *Science*, vol. 261 (July 2, 1993), p. 37; Frank M. Black, "Control of Motor Vehicle Emissions—The U.S. Experience," *Critical Reviews in Environmental Control*, vol. 21 (1991), p. 376; National Research Council, *State and Federal Standards for Mobile Source Emissions*, 2006, pp. 92-93; CRS Report RS20247, *EPA's Tier 2 Emission Standards for New Motor Vehicles: A Fact Sheet*, by David M. Bearden.

[7] The key difference is while H.R. 2751 authorized $4 billion for a one-year program, with the actual funding subject to appropriation, the Supplemental *appropriated* $1 billion for a four-month program, through October 2009.

[8] Although not officially under way until July 24, 2009, a number of auto manufacturers encouraged their dealers to begin trading under the system as early as the first week in July, promising that they would guarantee the transactions, as long as they followed the law. This created a backlog of transactions that were filed with NHTSA starting on July 24, 2009.

[9] For more information on the Administrative Procedure Act, see CRS Report RL32240, *The Federal Rulemaking Process: An Overview*, by Curtis W. Copeland.

[10] These category definitions are different from the weight-based definitions used to classify trucks (e.g., classes 1 through 8) generally.

[11] Because two states, New Hampshire and Wisconsin, do not require auto insurance under state law, NHTSA updated its regulations to exempt vehicles in those two states from the insurance requirement. National Highway Traffic Safety Administration, *Requirements and Procedures for the Consumer Assistance to Recycle and Save Program*, Docket No. NHTSA-2009-0120, Washington, DC, August 2009, http://www.cars.gov/files/amendment.pdf.

[12] Assuming $1 billion, and assuming all rebates are worth $4,500, NHTSA could issue 222,222 rebates. Assuming all rebates are worth $3,500, NHTSA could issue 285,714 rebates.

[13] Council of Economic Advisers, "Economic Analysis of the Car Allowance Rebate System," September 10, 2009, p. 2.

[14] Statement of DOT Secretary LaHood, issued by DOT, August 26, 2009.

[15] Council of Economic Advisers, "Economic Analysis of the Car Allowance Rebate System," September 10, 2009, p. 4.

[16] Ibid., p. 12. The "payback" period is a reference to the likely pull forward effect of CARS, bringing forward sales in summer 2009 that would have otherwise taken place later in 2009 or in later years.

[17] Edmunds.com, "Cash for Clunkers Results Finally In: Taxpayers Paid $24,000 per vehicle sold, Report Edmunds.com," October 28, 2009.

[18] The Obama Administration rebutted the Edmunds.com estimate and said, "The Edmunds' analysis rests on the assumption that the market for cars that didn't qualify for Cash for Clunkers was completely unaffected by this program. In other words, all the other cars were being sold on Mars, while the rest of the country was caught up in the excitement of the Cash for Clunkers program. This analysis ignores not only the price impacts that a program like Cash for Clunkers has on the rest of the vehicle market, but the reports from across the country that people were drawn into dealerships by the Cash for Clunkers program and ended up buying cars even though their old car was not eligible for the program... Edmunds also ignores the beneficial impact that the program will have on 4th Quarter GDP because automakers have ramped up their production to rebuild their depleted inventories." Source: National Public Radio: "Edmunds.com Cash for Clunkers Analysis Riles Obama Team," October 29, 1009.

[19] Center for Automotive Research, "The Economic and Fiscal Contributions of the 'Cash for Clunkers' Program—National and State Effects," January 14, 2010.

[20] *BusinessWeek*, "After the Clunkers Party, an Auto Sales Hangover," September 1, 2009.

[21] The CARS program will save roughly 33 million gallons of gasoline per year and 380,000 metric tons of carbon dioxide. In its preliminary Annual Energy Outlook for 2010, EIA estimates that 141 billion gallons of motor gasoline will be consumed, and roughly 1.9 billion metric tons of carbon dioxide will be emitted from petroleum combustion in the transportation sector. U.S. Energy Information Administration, *Annual Energy Outlook 2010 Early Release Overview*, DOE/EIA-0383(2009), Washington, DC, December 14, 2009, Tables A11 and A18, http://www.eia.doe.gov/oiaf/aeo/index.html.

[22] American Council for an Energy-Efficient Economy, *Vehicle Scrappage Program Needs Repair*, Washington, DC, May 6, 2009, http://www.aceee.org/press/0905scrappage.htm.

[23] The range depends on the discount rate for future savings. If future savings are not discounted, then the present value of those savings is higher. If the future is discounted, the present value of the savings is lower. U.S. Department of Transportation, National Highway Traffic Safety Administration, *Consumer Assistance to Recycle and Save Act of 2009*, Washington, DC, December 2009, p. 46.

[24] It should be noted that estimates for the social cost of carbon vary widely, from zero for those who believe that the effects of greenhouse gas emissions are negligible, to hundreds of dollars for those who believe that the effects of climate change could be drastic.

[25] Again, this range depends on the discount rate (between 0% and 7%). Ibid., p. 49.

[26] *Automotive News* survey reported on August 3, 2009.

[27] The initial delays in processing CARS applications were eventually remedied. According to NHTSA's December 2009 report to Congress: "NHTSA did not anticipate the volume of the initial demand on the CARS system or a tripling of the demand on that system just twelve days after it began as a result of additional appropriations. Nor did the agency anticipate that the statute's many requirements and those added by NHTSA's rule in order to help deter fraud would prove so difficult for many dealers to meet without repeated submissions. More than half of all the submissions had to be submitted and reviewed more than once, and tens of thousands of them took several iterations before approval was possible. Moreover, to ensure the integrity of the process, any transaction had to be reviewed by two different people in order to be approved for payment. In all, NHTSA conducted approximately two million transaction reviews in order to eventually approve 677,000 requests for payment. Nevertheless, despite the many obstacles it faced and the unprecedented nature of this program, NHTSA managed to achieve an overall mean processing time of 16.9 days from the final submission (i.e., when all necessary documentation was included and errors corrected) of a transaction to the date of payment."

[28] September 2009 data on auto sales is from *CNNMoney.com*, "Auto Sales Fall as Clunkers Rush Ends," October 1, 2009.

[29] *ABCnews.go.com*, "Ford Surges as U.S. Auto Sales End Year on Uptick," January 5, 2010 and *Automotive News*, "Ford, Hyundai and Toyota Lead Industry to 15% Gain," January 5, 2010.

[30] *Automotive News*, "Analysts See Signs of Life After Miserable Year," January 11, 2010.

[31] AVR is accelerated vehicle recovery.

[32] Data in this section on European scrappage programs is sourced from the European Automobile Manufacturers Association (ACEA). Website viewed January 22, 2010.

[33] All currency conversions are from Washingtonpost.com, *World Currencies—Current Values and Conversion Tool*, June 22, 2009, http://financial.washingtonpost.com/custom/wpost/html-currencies.asp. 1 Euro = $1.38. 1 Japanese Yen = $0.0103. 1 Canadian dollar = $0.882. 1 British pound = $1.643.

[34] *BusinessWeek*, "Cash-for-Clunkers Proposals Gain Popular Traction," April 1, 2009.

[35] *Financial Times*, "US Drives Its Claws into Scrappage Deals," July 31, 2009.

[36] Ibid.

[37] *The Globe and Mail*, "The Ugly Economics Behind Europe's Car Scrappage Bonanza," May 16, 2009.

[38] Japan has recently agreed to extend its ATV program until September 2010.

[39] By comparison, in 2009, there were 10.4 million vehicles sold in the United States.

In: Energy Policies and Issues
Editors: Edgar R. Thompson

ISBN: 978-1-61122-685-0
© 2011 Nova Science Publishers, Inc.

Chapter 10

CRS ISSUE STATEMENT ON AGRICULTURE-BASED BIOFUELS

Randy Schnepf

Since the 1970s, federal incentives have played a major role in encouraging agriculture-based renewable energy production. Policy goals include the stimulation of alternative uses of domestic grain and oilseeds, the promotion of national security through greater energy independence, and the encouragement of rural economic development. Federal incentives, notably tax credits, a minimum renewable fuel use requirement, and research and development funding, have helped biofuels output (ethanol and biodiesel) to surge in recent years, growing from 1.4 billion gallons in 1998 to over 11 billion in 2009. Nearly all of the growth has been in corn-starch ethanol.

A key issue facing Congress is the appropriate level and type of federal intervention in renewable energy markets in general, and the biofuels sector in particular. While the expansion of agriculture-based biofuels (particularly corn-based ethanol) has arguably achieved some success in increasing grain and oilseed demand, stimulating rural economies, and raising farm incomes, there has also been considerable spillover effect in other markets—most notably in land, energy, livestock, and farm input markets. This policy debate routinely confronts Congress because every year several of the federal policy provisions that support the U.S. biofuels industry, for example, certain tax credits or the import tariff, are set to expire pending congressional action to extend them.

Three important bills have been enacted in recent years with major impacts on the biofuels industry. First, the Energy Policy Act of 2005 (EPAct, P.L. 109-58) established a renewable fuel standard (RFS) that mandated minimum-use volumes of biofuels in the national transportation fuel supply. Second, the Energy Independence and Security Act of 2007 (EISA, P.L. 110-140) greatly expanded the RFS. In particular, under EISA the biofuels blending mandate, or RFS, expands from 9 billion gallons in 2008 to 36 billion gallons in 2022, with special carve-outs for advanced biofuels (i.e., non-corn-starch ethanol), cellulosic biofuels, and biodiesel. Finally, the Food, Conservation, and Energy Act of 2008 (the farm bill, P.L. 110-246) extended and expanded incentives for ethanol production, extended tariffs on imported ethanol, and promoted use of biobased products.

On February 3, 2010, the Environmental Protection Agency (EPA), the federal agency in charge of administering the RFS program, announced final rules for implementing the RFS. In addition to the specific volume mandates, the new rules include mandatory reductions in life-cycle greenhouse gas (GHG) emissions for each biofuels category, and restrictions on the type and nature of feedstocks used to produce RFS-qualifying biofuels.

Congress will likely be confronted with the ability (or inability) of the U.S. biofuels sector to expand production capacity to meet the ever-increasing RFS mandate. Through 2009, U.S. biofuels production has easily exceeded the RFS since its inception in 2005. However, under EISA the cellulosic biofuels mandate grows quickly from 100 million gallons per year (mgpy) in 2010 to 16 billion gallons by 2022. As a result, after 2015, most of the increase in the overall RFS is intended to come from cellulosic biofuels (rather than corn-starch ethanol). However, the speed of cellulosic biofuels development remains a major uncertainty.

Congress might face issues relating to cellulosic biofuels production such as the effectiveness of incentives to spur commercial viability. In early 2010, cellulosic biofuels were being produced in the United States on a very small, non-commercial, scale, thus making the 100 mgpy mandate for 2010 a daunting target. As a result, the EPA announced (February 3, 2010) a reduction in the 2010 cellulosic biofuels RFS to 6.5 million gallons. Waivers are built into EISA to accommodate shortfalls if the U.S. biofuels industry (with imports) fails to meet the RFS. If shortfalls are expected to continue to occur, Congress might debate legislative remedies such as changing eligibility requirements or reducing RFS volumes to accommodate potential long-term shortfalls.

As the RFS mandate for biofuels steadily increases and becomes binding, it will have important consequences for food and energy markets. The short-lived commodity price spikes of mid-2008 hinted at the potential conflict associated with conversion of domestic food crops to biofuels. In an attempt to shift biofuels policy distortions away from livestock feed and other markets, both EISA and the 2008 farm bill redirect biofuels research and development emphasis to cellulosic biofuels, since they can potentially be produced from non-food feedstocks such as crop residues, dedicated energy crops, and woody biomass. As a result, any shortcomings in the development of cellulosic biofuels production could compound the potential unintended consequences of U.S. biofuels policy.

Another contentious biofuels issue confronting Congress is whether the ethanol-to-gasoline blending rate should be expanded from 10% to 15%. In the absence of such an expansion, many in the ethanol industry fear that producers will confront a "blending wall" that will limit the ability of the U.S. fuel market to absorb further production increases in ethanol. The resulting surplus, if it were to occur, would likely depress biofuels prices and investment. The EPA is presently reviewing this issue and is expected to make a recommendation in mid-2010.

From an international perspective, Brazil and the United States are leading biofuels producers and the European Union is a major consumer and importer. Numerous biofuels trade issues are potential areas of debate for Congress during the 111th Congress. A leading trade issue is the $0.54 per gallon tariff that the United States applies to ethanol imported from most countries. Although the tariff was implemented to offset benefits intended for U.S.-produced biofuels, it raises the price of ethanol and reduces potential supply, a key issue in light of the RFS. Furthermore, the domestic tax credit for ethanol has been reduced gradually over time from $0.54 per gallon to $0.45 per gallon today. As a result, the tariff not only offsets the domestic benefit, but imposes a punitive charge of $0.09 per gallon on qualifying imported ethanol.

Another trade-related biofuels issue is whether tax credits for U.S. biodiesel production should apply if the fuel is exported rather than sold in the United States. Some maintain the credit should only apply to fuel that contributes to U.S. energy independence, not fuel that is exported for consumption in other countries.

ISSUE TEAM MEMBERS

Randy Schnepf, Coordinator
Specialist in Agricultural Policy
rschnepf@crs.loc.gov, 7-4277

Ross W. Gorte
Specialist in Natural Resources Policy
rgorte@crs.loc.gov, 7-7266

Anthony Andrews
Specialist in Energy and Energy Infrastructure
Policy
aandrews@crs.loc.gov, 7-6843

Peter J. Meyer
Analyst in Latin American Affairs
pmeyer@crs.loc.gov, 7-5474

Kelsi Bracmort
Analyst in Agricultural Conservation and Natural
Resources Policy
kbracmort@crs.loc.gov, 7-7283

Fred Sissine
Specialist in Energy Policy
fsissine@crs.loc.gov, 7-7039

Cynthia Brougher
Legislative Attorney
cbrougher@crs.loc.gov, 7-9121

Megan Stubbs
Analyst in Agricultural Conservation and Natural Resources Policy
mstubbs@crs.loc.gov, 7-8707

Carol Canada
Information Research Specialist
ccanada@crs.loc.gov, 7-7619

Adam Vann
Legislative Attorney
avann@crs.loc.gov, 7-6978

Lynn J. Cunningham
Information Research Specialist
lcunningham@crs.loc.gov, 7-8971

Brent D. Yacobucci
Specialist in Energy and Environmental Policy
byacobucci@crs.loc.gov, 7-9662

For detailed information select from the following topical links.

Agriculture-Based Biofuels

Cellulosic Biofuels: Analysis of Policy Issues for Congress
Meeting the Renewable Fuel Standard (RFS) Mandate for Cellulosic Biofuels: Questions and Answers
Intermediate-Level Blends of Ethanol in Gasoline, and the Ethanol "Blend Wall"
Biofuels Incentives: A Summary of Federal Programs
Biofuels Provisions in the 2007 Energy Bill and the 2008 Farm Bill: A Side-by-Side Comparison
Renewable Energy Programs in the 2008 Farm Bill
Selected Issues Related to an Expansion of the Renewable Fuel Standard (RFS)
Calculation of Lifecycle Greenhouse Gas Emissions for the Renewable Fuel Standard (RFS)
Waiver Authority Under the Renewable Fuel Standard (RFS)
Biochar: Examination of an Emerging Concept to Mitigate Climate Change
Biomass: Comparison of Definitions in Legislation

CHAPTER SOURCES

The following chapters have been previously published:

Chapter 1 – This is an edited, excerpted and augmented edition of a United States Congressional Research Service publication, Report Order Code RL34130, dated March 22, 2010.

Chapter 2 – This is an edited, excerpted and augmented edition of a United States Congressional Research Service publication, Report Order Code RL34705, dated April 16, 2010.

Chapter 3 – This is an edited, excerpted and augmented edition of a United States Congressional Research Service publication, Report Order Code R40186, dated May 24, 2010.

Chapter 4 – This is an edited, excerpted and augmented edition of a United States Congressional Research Service publication, Report Order Code RL34560, dated May 24, 2010.

Chapter 5 – This is an edited, excerpted and augmented edition of a United States Congressional Research Service publication, Report Order Code R40667, dated May 4, 2010.

Chapter 6 – This is an edited, excerpted and augmented edition of a United States Congressional Research Service publication, Report Order Code RS22990, dated May 25, 2010.

Chapter 7 – This is an edited, excerpted and augmented edition of a United States Congressional Research Service publication, Report Order Code RL33404, dated April 6, 2010.

Chapter 8 – This is an edited, excerpted and augmented edition of a United States Congressional Research Service publication, Report Order Code R41132, dated April 7, 2010.

Chapter 9 – This is an edited, excerpted and augmented edition of a United States Congressional Research Service publication, Report Order Code R40654, dated March 3, 2010.

Chapter 10 – This is an edited, excerpted and augmented edition of a United States Congressional Research Service publication, Report Order Code IS40524, dated March 3, 2010.

INDEX

A

abatement, 32, 35, 38, 72, 86
accounting, 54, 73
advantages, 42, 46, 120
Africa, 65
agencies, 5, 14, 24, 34, 35, 63, 144, 146, 147, 154
agricultural sector, 38, 47, 86
agriculture, ix, 1, 2, 3, 4, 27, 30, 31, 32, 36, 38, 42, 45, 47, 65, 86, 94, 181
air quality, 46, 162, 163
Alaska, viii, 75, 76, 97, 99, 100, 101, 105, 106, 108, 113, 114, 115, 116, 117, 126, 133, 136, 137, 142, 144, 149, 150, 154, 156, 157, 158
alcohols, 14, 24
American Recovery and Reinvestment Act, 95, 162, 164
anaerobic bacteria, 82
anaerobic digesters, 81, 96
annual rate, 168, 169, 173
antitrust, 117
appropriations, ix, 2, 11, 12, 13, 16, 19, 20, 49, 98, 108, 112, 113, 135, 142, 143, 144, 164, 179
Arctic National Wildlife Refuge, 100
Asia, 65, 77, 173, 176
assessment, 11, 49, 73, 100, 105, 106, 131, 141
Austria, 174, 177
authorities, 108, 119, 138, 139, 147, 154
auto dealers, 162, 165, 166, 175

auto sales, ix, 161, 162, 163, 164, 167, 168, 173, 174, 175, 179
auto sector, 164, 169
Automobile, 167, 177, 178, 180
automobiles, 166, 174
automotive sector, 163
avoidance, 25, 26, 47, 55, 94

B

bankruptcy, 171
barriers, 32, 79, 91
base year, 59
Beaufort Sea, 115, 156
benchmarks, 162
biodiesel, ix, 3, 4, 5, 14, 16, 65, 181, 182, 183
bioenergy, vii, 1, 13, 15, 19, 43, 49
biofuel, 4, 5, 15, 20, 29, 31, 36
biomass, 1, 2, 6, 11, 13, 14, 15, 16, 17, 18, 19, 24, 29, 36, 45, 46, 48, 49, 50, 51, 52, 53, 66, 67, 90, 93, 183
biomass materials, 6
bonds, 118
boreal forest, 66, 68
Brazil, 183
breakdown, 43, 171
Brooks Range, 100
Bush, President George W., 112, 144, 146, 156
butyl ether, 21

C

carbon dioxide, viii, 27, 45, 47, 53, 54, 59, 80, 86, 87, 88, 89, 90, 94, 95, 98, 169, 170, 175, 176, 179

carbon emissions, 47, 48, 54, 59, 64

carbon monoxide, 51, 88

cargo trucks, 166, 167

cargo vans, 167

Caribbean, 158

category d, 178

cattle, 12, 24, 87, 88

cellulose, 5

cement, 54, 104

certification, 5, 63, 68, 72, 174

CFI, 62

China, 57, 65, 98, 162, 173, 175, 177

Clean Air Act, 95

clean development mechanism (CDM), 50

clean energy, viii, 79, 80, 81, 92

climate, vii, viii, 26, 30, 35, 41, 42, 47, 49, 50, 55, 56, 59, 61, 69, 86, 88, 92, 93, 94, 140, 148, 163, 179

climate change, vii, viii, 26, 41, 42, 47, 49, 50, 55, 56, 59, 61, 69, 86, 88, 92, 93, 94, 140, 148, 163, 179

clunkers, ix, 161, 163, 164, 168, 169, 173, 174, 175, 176

CO2, viii, 27, 31, 35, 36, 39, 40, 45, 47, 53, 54, 55, 56, 59, 60, 61, 64, 69, 74, 86, 89, 94, 95, 98

coal, 27, 29, 34, 98, 105

Coast Guard, 140

combined effect, 155

combustion, 94, 95, 179

commodity, 1, 3, 24, 183

community, 17, 18, 19, 30, 46, 47, 92, 94, 151

compensation, 69, 158

competition, 20, 32, 67, 111, 114, 117, 148

competitiveness, 138

complement, 39

complexity, 27, 91, 176

compliance, vii, 25, 27, 28, 30, 31, 34, 35, 38, 39, 54, 56, 57, 61, 63, 64, 69, 70, 117, 120, 132, 139, 140

complications, 27

conference, 163

conflict, 111, 183

consensus, 148, 157

consent, 117, 142

conservation, 18, 19, 24, 30, 31, 42, 51, 58, 64, 68, 92, 96, 107, 126, 138, 146

Constitution, 130

consumption, vii, viii, 3, 19, 95, 97, 100, 140, 169, 170, 183

coordination, 13, 17, 136, 144, 147, 153, 154

cost, vii, viii, 11, 14, 15, 16, 17, 18, 25, 26, 28, 30, 32, 35, 37, 38, 46, 49, 53, 54, 58, 68, 83, 90, 91, 92, 96, 105, 169, 176, 179

costs of compliance, 132

Court of Appeals, 121, 122, 124, 125

crop production, 2, 31

crops, 6, 13, 18, 183

crystalline, 105

Cuba, 152, 158, 159

currency, 55, 180

Cyprus, 174

D

damages, iv, 120, 132, 143

decomposition, 66, 67

deforestation, 54, 55, 58, 59, 62, 64, 65, 69, 70, 71, 72, 73

degradation, 58, 59, 62, 64, 139

delegation, 156

Denmark, 59

Department of Agriculture, 2, 4, 39, 44, 49, 50, 64, 81, 94

Department of Commerce, 146

Department of Energy, 2, 11, 63, 81, 98, 99, 105

Department of State, 128, 155

Department of the Interior, ix, 99, 105, 112, 115, 116, 125, 133, 135, 136, 142, 154, 156, 158

deposits, 103, 105, 120, 138

Index

191

developed countries, 50, 56
developing countries, 46, 50, 57, 58, 69
developing nations, 35, 54, 69
development policy, 136, 139
deviation, 117
diesel fuel, 24
digestion, vii, viii, 79, 80, 90, 91, 92, 93, 94, 95, 96
directives, 138, 139, 144, 155
disposition, 112, 113, 156
District of Columbia, 75
domestic policy, 136
draft, 42, 48, 52, 124, 148

E

East Asia, 77
economic activity, 72
economic assessment, 138
economic crisis, 155
economic development, ix, 3, 181
economic growth, 49, 168
economic incentives, 30
economy, ix, 11, 36, 54, 60, 95, 135, 138, 161, 162, 163, 164, 166, 167, 169, 170, 175
Efficiency, 2, 5, 7, 12, 16, 22, 48
electricity, viii, 14, 36, 79, 80, 81, 88, 90, 91, 92, 93, 95, 176
emission, vii, 5, 25, 26, 27, 28, 29, 30, 31, 32, 34, 35, 36, 37, 38, 39, 45, 57, 58, 59, 60, 61, 62, 69, 72, 73, 80, 81, 92, 93, 94, 174, 176, 177
emitters, 47, 62, 88
encouragement, ix, 181
energy consumption, 19
energy efficiency, 5, 16, 49
Energy Independence and Security Act, vii, 1, 3, 163, 182
energy markets, 181, 183
Energy Policy Act of 2005, 4, 98, 104, 108, 150, 155, 182
energy supply, 126
energy technology, 16
enforcement, 71, 165
engineering, 91, 92, 119

environmental factors, 71
environmental harm, 139
environmental impact, 4, 20, 55, 114, 118, 119, 122, 125, 131, 132, 141
environmental issues, 3, 94, 137
environmental policy, 139, 148
environmental protection, 120, 141
Environmental Protection Agency, 5, 24, 28, 48, 52, 66, 76, 77, 81, 83, 86, 87, 94, 95, 96, 166, 182
environmental risks, 139, 141
environmental standards, 107, 113
EPA, 5, 11, 19, 20, 28, 30, 31, 32, 33, 38, 39, 40, 48, 52, 66, 76, 82, 83, 85, 86, 87, 94, 95, 96, 125, 163, 166, 170, 174, 178, 182, 183
equipment, 50, 88, 91, 96, 97, 102, 120, 140
erosion, 45
ethanol, ix, 1, 2, 3, 4, 5, 6, 11, 13, 18, 20, 21, 24, 65, 80, 181, 182, 183
ethyl alcohol, 21
EU, 52, 59, 75
European Union, 59, 75, 174, 176, 183
exclusion, 131
Executive Order, 15, 110, 157
executive orders, 153
exercise, 109, 132, 146, 157
exploitation, 141, 149, 158
exploration, 46, 105, 107, 108, 113, 114, 115, 118, 119, 120, 121, 125, 127, 128, 129, 130, 131, 149, 153, 155
extraction, 126, 127

F

family farms, 26, 38
Farm Bill, v, 1, 4, 5, 7, 12, 13, 14, 15, 16, 17, 18, 19, 20, 21, 22, 24, 49, 76, 94, 185
farm income, 181
farmers, 16, 30, 38, 177
farms, 26, 31, 38, 64
federal courts, 121, 122
federal funds, 170
federal law, ix, 107, 110, 111, 116, 118, 121
federal programs, 4
federal statute, 147

fermentation, 45, 86, 94
fertility, 43, 45, 49
fishing, 128, 138, 155
flatulence, 94
flexibility, 28, 56
food prices, 11, 24
Ford, 169, 171, 172, 173, 180
forest management, 53, 58, 62, 67, 68, 70, 72
France, 162, 174, 175, 177
fuel costs, 170
fuel economy, ix, 95, 161, 162, 163, 164, 166, 167, 169, 170, 175
funding, ix, 2, 5, 6, 10, 11, 12, 13, 14, 15, 16, 17, 19, 24, 37, 90, 95, 162, 164, 166, 178, 181

G

gasoline consumption, 3, 169
General Motors, 163
geology, 105, 109
Georges Bank, 153
Georgia, 50
Germany, 76, 162, 173, 174, 175
global climate change, 42, 54, 55, 56, 59, 140, 148
governance, 139, 141, 147, 148, 152, 153, 157, 158
grazing, 45, 94
Great Depression, 155
Greece, 174, 177
greed, 124
greenhouse gas emissions, viii, 41, 42, 45, 47, 50, 64, 79, 80, 81, 90, 94, 140, 163, 179
greenhouse gases, 45, 52, 55, 74, 86, 87, 94, 163, 170
groundwater, 45
growth rate, 67
guidance, 49, 122
guidelines, 62, 63, 64, 176

H

habitat quality, 156

habitats, 68
half-life, 86
harvesting, 53, 54, 65, 66, 67, 68
Hawaii, 13, 60, 127
hazards, 42, 106
hemicellulose, 5
heterogeneity, 39
high density polyethylene, 84
host, 71, 100, 101, 102
HTS, 21
human activity, 54, 73
hybrid, 6
hydrogen, 17, 51, 88, 89, 176
Hyundai, 171, 172, 173, 180

I

immigration, 109
impacts, 1, 4, 11, 20, 54, 55, 82, 89, 114, 118, 119, 125, 137, 141, 147, 155, 174, 179, 182
imports, 2, 6, 11, 21, 98, 182
income support, 24
increased competition, 20
independence, ix, 181, 183
Independence, vii, 1, 3, 163, 182
India, 57, 65, 98
indigenous peoples, 69
Indonesia, 58, 77
infancy, 41, 50
inflation, 1, 3, 33
infrastructure, 2, 4, 19, 105
integration, 13
interdependence, viii, 79
international law, 110, 148, 151, 155, 157, 158
intervention, 181
isolation, 29
Italy, 176, 177

J

Japan, 98, 106, 162, 172, 173, 174, 176, 180
judicial review, 121, 122
jurisdiction, 108, 109, 110, 111, 121, 129, 146, 151, 155, 157

Index

justification, 120

K

Korea, 98, 173, 177

L

landfills, 32, 34, 36, 40
landscape, 62
Latin America, 184
Law of the Sea Convention, 157
leakage, 54, 69, 70, 72
learning, 155
legislation, ix, 27, 30, 36, 48, 49, 52, 55, 60, 80, 90, 92, 93, 108, 112, 113, 143, 144, 153, 161, 164, 165, 178
legislative proposals, 31, 32, 34, 35, 60, 108, 139
lifetime, 86, 89
light trucks, 169, 171
lignin, 5
Limitations, 21
liquidity, 155
liquids, 81
litigation, 108, 122, 143, 155, 156
livestock, viii, 3, 79, 80, 81, 82, 83, 86, 87, 88, 90, 91, 92, 93, 94, 95, 96, 181, 183
local government, 16, 19, 116
logging, 6, 66, 72
logistics, 60, 83
Louisiana, 76, 124, 127, 129, 130, 150, 158
low temperatures, 98
lying, 110, 117, 133

M

machinery, 119
Maine, 75
majority, 72
Malaysia, 177
management, 12, 33, 45, 49, 53, 58, 62, 67, 68, 70, 72, 82, 86, 91, 94, 95, 96, 111, 118, 139, 141, 149, 153, 155, 158
manufacturing, 19
manure, vii, viii, 20, 41, 42, 43, 45, 46, 49, 79, 80, 82, 83, 84, 86, 88, 93, 94

marine environment, 109, 139, 146
Marine Mammal Protection Act, 121
market penetration, 26, 37
methodology, 122
migration, 101
military, 157, 163
mineral resources, ix, 107, 108, 111, 127, 156
mining, 155
missions, 52, 59, 75, 86, 94, 169, 170, 176
modeling, 30, 31, 32, 37, 39, 100
modernization, 163, 175, 176
modification, 117
moisture, 45, 51, 89, 94
molecules, 98
monitoring, 34, 38, 54, 68, 71, 73, 81, 141
Montana, 75
moratorium, 112, 113, 115, 136, 137, 138, 139, 140, 141, 143, 149, 152, 153, 154, 155, 156, 157

N

National Ambient Air Quality Standards, 178
National Environmental Policy Act (NEPA), 114, 131, 155
national policy, 154
National Public Radio, 179
National Research Council, 178
national security, ix, 120, 148, 181
natural gas, viii, 32, 51, 88, 95, 97, 98, 99, 100, 104, 105, 108, 113, 115, 136, 150, 155, 158, 159, 176
natural resources, 109, 110, 148
navigable waters, 110
Netherlands, 174, 177
New Zealand, 78
nitrogen, 88, 176
nitrous oxide, 45, 52, 74, 94
North America, 65, 165
Nuevo León, 75
nutrients, 45, 67, 90, 93

O

Obama Administration, 98, 104, 115, 136, 138, 154, 155, 163, 179
Obama, President, 2, 115, 147. 157, 159, 162, 164
Obama, President Barack, 113, 136
obstacles, 179
oceans, 155, 157, 159
Oil Pollution Act of 1990, 139
oil production, 103
oil spill, 131, 132, 139, 140
oilseed, 181
Omnibus Appropriations Act,, 104, 154
opportunities, viii, 26, 27, 30, 34, 35, 36, 38, 53, 54, 55, 60, 65, 69, 140, 148
Opportunities, 96, 152
organic matter, 24, 43, 94
Outer Continental Shelf Lands Act, 107, 111, 121, 123, 136, 144, 146, 147, 155, 156
ownership, ix, 47, 107, 108, 110, 163

P

Pacific, 13, 115, 137, 142, 149. 154, 157, 158
payback period, 93
penalties, 28, 140, 165
performance, 34, 36, 88, 91, 92, 96, 118, 141. 173
permit, 118, 120, 121, 123, 126, 158, 174
personal communication, 104
physical properties, 51
pickup trucks, 166, 167
pipelines, 97, 102, 105, 131
plants, 5, 15, 27, 56, 59, 60, 67, 168, 171
platform, 103, 140
policy choice, 28, 34
policy makers, 137, 153, 154
policy options, 36, 151, 152, 155
pollution, 82, 95, 155, 175
poor performance, 91
porosity, 105
portfolio, 36, 38, 58

Portugal, 174, 177
positive stimulus, 168
poultry, 47, 83
power plants, 27, 56, 59, 60
predictability, 143
preparedness, 140
prescribed burning, 67
present value, 179
President Clinton, 157
price changes, 37
private investment, 50
private sector investment, 105
probability, 100, 131
procurement, 5, 14
producers, 3, 16, 18, 27, 42, 47, 48, 80, 81, 89, 91, 92, 93, 155, 183
production capacity, 182
production costs, 95, 96
production technology, 47, 48, 50
profit, 80, 91, 117
project, 14, 16, 18, 32, 34, 35, 38. 39, 48, 54, 55, 56, 57, 58, 60, 67, 69, 70, 71, 72, 73, 74, 76, 95, 119, 131
protected areas, 146
public safety, 46
Puerto Rico, 170
pyrolysis, 43, 45, 50

R

Radiation, 28, 77
reality, 30, 71, 72
rebate system, 161
recession, 57, 60, 163
recognition, 63, 64, 151, 158
recommendations, iv, 75, 76, 116. 122, 144, 147
recreation, 31, 128
refinery capacity, 5
reforms, 147, 154
Registry, 62, 63, 95
regulatory requirements, 49
rejection, 114
relevance, 110, 141, 150
reliability, 47, 79, 81, 88, 92
removals, 73

Index

renewable energy, vii, ix, 1, 2, 3, 4, 11, 12, 14, 15, 16, 18, 19, 20, 42, 80, 88, 92, 93, 94, 95, 135, 136, 137, 138, 139, 147, 150, 181
renewable fuel, ix, 3, 181, 182
repair, 156
replacement, 51, 140
research and development, vii, ix, 1, 17, 19, 41, 42, 48, 49, 97, 98, 102, 104, 137, 181, 183
reserves, viii, 97, 99, 105, 139, 147
residues, vii, 6, 41, 42, 43, 46, 183
resources, ix, 2, 16, 30, 31, 32, 36, 83, 95, 99, 100, 101, 103, 105, 106, 107, 108, 109, 110, 111, 126, 127, 128, 138, 139, 148, 151, 152, 154, 155, 156, 157
restructuring, 171
retail, 61, 62, 92, 166, 168, 172
retirement, 162, 163, 172
retrofitting, 5, 14
revenue, 42, 48, 49, 93, 137, 149, 150, 153, 155
rights, iv, 68, 109, 117, 120, 127, 129, 146, 153, 155, 157
Romania, 174, 177
royalty, 107, 117, 122, 123, 124, 132, 143, 155, 156, 158

S

Samoa, 157
sampling error, 71
sanctuaries, 113, 127, 142, 146, 157
saturation, 35
savings, vii, 25, 164, 169, 179
Secretary of Commerce, 118
sediments, 97, 102, 103, 104, 105, 106
seedlings, 65
Senate, 4, 14, 141, 148, 159, 162, 163, 164
sensing, 71
sensitivity, 39
shape, 26, 27, 34, 74
shipbuilding, 156
shores, 108
signals, ix, 135, 147
simulation, 106

siphon, 103
site use, 88
Slovakia, 174, 177
small businesses, 16
social acceptance, 26, 38
social benefits, 169
soil erosion, 45
solid phase, 103
South Dakota, 75, 76
South Korea, 173, 177
sovereignty, 109, 136, 137, 141, 159
species, 35, 65, 66, 68, 73, 74
sport utility vehicles, 166, 167
stakeholders, 54, 144
starch, ix, 3, 4, 13, 24, 181, 182
state control, 110
state laws, ix, 107, 111
statistics, 158
statutes, 110, 121, 147, 157
steel, 54, 73, 84, 103
stimulus, 164, 168, 176, 177
storage, 2, 5, 45, 62, 65, 67, 68, 71, 73, 80, 83, 88
Strategic Petroleum Reserve, 126
subjectivity, 35, 70
subsidy, 174, 175, 176, 177
substitutes, 29, 54
Supreme Court, 110, 121, 124
surplus, 10, 18, 183
survey, 171, 179
systemic change, 167

T

Taiwan, 177
tariff, 1, 2, 11, 21, 181, 183
TARP, 163
tax incentive, 2, 3, 37, 174, 177
technical assistance, 16
technology transfer, 48, 49
temperature, 43, 84, 88, 100, 103, 104
territory, 98, 109, 127
testing, 14, 100, 174
thermal properties, 103
time frame, 35, 123, 138, 168
time periods, 30, 45

Title I, 2, 4, 10, 12, 13, 17, 22
Title V, 1, 4, 12, 22, 52
total energy, 90
tourism, 138
Toyota, 52, 171, 172, 173, 180
transaction costs, 35, 38
transactions, 59, 64, 162, 171, 178
transport, 5, 19, 83
transportation, 18, 19, 36, 49, 82, 120, 130, 169, 179, 182
transshipment, 131
treaties, 139, 142
tropical forests, 66
Troubled Asset Relief Program, 163
trucks, 166, 167, 169, 170, 171, 177, 178
Turkey, 177

U

U.S. Geological Survey, viii, 97, 99, 104, 159
U.S. history, 146
U.S. policy, 148
United Kingdom, 176
United Nations, 50, 56, 75, 109, 129, 136, 141, 146, 147, 157
United States, 187, 188
universe, 34
universities, 5, 13

USDA, 2, 4, 5, 6, 10, 11, 13, 14, 15, 16, 17, 18, 19, 20, 24, 32, 39, 44, 50, 51, 52, 64, 76, 81, 87, 92, 94, 95, 96

V

vegetation, 65, 67
vehicle sales, 161, 163, 168, 173
vehicles, ix, 60, 61, 90, 161, 162, 163, 164, 165, 166, 167, 168, 170, 171, 172, 173, 174, 175, 176, 177, 178, 180
vessels, 131, 140
volatility, 105, 135
vouchers, 170, 171, 174

W

Wake Island, 157
waste, vii, 6, 12, 13, 24, 41, 46, 67, 70, 80, 86, 90, 93, 96
waste management, 86
water quality, 65, 68
wells, 102, 103, 119, 123
withdrawal, 113, 136, 144
wood, 6, 19, 53, 62, 65, 66, 67, 68, 72, 73
wood products, 53, 62, 65, 66, 67, 68, 72, 73
World Bank, 57, 59, 61, 76
World Trade Organization, 165
WTO, 165, 177